TRAPPED WITH MS. ARIAS

Part 1 of 3 From Getting the File to Being Ready for Trial

L. KIRK NURMI

Lead Counsel For Ms. Arias

Foreword by Caroline Aeed

Copyright

DEDICATION

So many people have played a part in helping me get to this point in my life. So many people played a role in getting me to the point in time that I was able to become a death penalty qualified defense attorney who was capable of handling the responsibilities that came with serving as lead counsel for Ms. Arias. The friends who encouraged me to apply to law school, my wife who put up with me in law school, during my entire legal career including the two infamous trials that I did not want to be a part of. The dozens of mentors I had both during law school and during my legal career. I'm in debt to you all. Having said this, I'm sure that you will all understand that this dedication belongs to my grandparents, who not only provided me with the means to get to law school but somehow were able to raise me in a way that also instilled in me the sort of values and temperament that allowed me to somehow survive this monumental challenge. I hope that I did you both proud and that I will continue to do so because little is more important to me than making you both proud.

ACKNOWLEDGEMENTS

My first book was a 39 page diet book entitled "Trimmer More There." Putting that book together certainly involved more work than I expected. So when I finally decided to write this book, a much more complex and lengthy endeavor, I knew that even more work would be required of me and that I would also need a great deal of help from others. I got that help from many wonderfully talented people whom I wanted to thank directly. To my friend Caroline, you are like a sister to me and I thank you for taking the time to write such a wonderful Foreword. To my friend and co-worker Paula, thank you so much not only for editing the book but also your unwavering support. To the young and brilliant Nikkole who also edited this book, I thank you for your work and being such a trustworthy ally. I suspect your future will include far greater things than editing books for infamous lawyers as you yourself are destined to be a brilliant lawyer. Finally, to the woman who not only served as an editor to this book but who listened to me talk endlessly about all aspects of its creation and publishing. I thank you for listening and giving me your thoughts. You prove to me every day that the smartest thing I ever did or ever will do was marry you.

TABLE OF CONTENTS

Foreword

By Caroline Aeed

In August of 1997, 85 students embarked on the path to earning their law degree at The University of Wyoming College of Law, we would be the class of 2000 and the first lawyers of the new millennium. Students came to The University of Wyoming College of Law located in Laramie, Wyoming at 7,200 feet above sea level for many reasons. Some because they were multi-generation Wyoming lawyers, others because the school was touted to be the "best bargain" for a law degree and others loved the outdoor recreation opportunities. At the time I thought everyone went to law school because they wanted to make a difference in the world, to help people, and defend the poor. In reality, that lawyer was the minority.

In your first year of law school and in every law school in the country, every 1L takes the standard schedule, contracts, property, civil procedure, torts and you are taught to write like a lawyer not an author. We would have to suffer through all the basics before learning about the practice of law we were passionate about. Out of the 85 1L's starting that year there were only a handful that shared the same ideals as myself, one of those 1L's was Kirk Nurmi.

I remember Kirk Nurmi sat in the back of the class where he could plug in his laptop. I sat in the back of the class because I didn't like being called on and I sometimes read a magazine. I was passionate but not terribly serious about my studies. Kirk was passionate and very serious about his studies. It was through this seating arrangement chosen for different reasons that I got to know Kirk better. We had similar goals and both wanted to participate in the school's criminal defense clinic. He was funny and had a great high pitched laugh that invoked a laugh right back. Little did we know Laramie would become embroiled in a firestorm of controversy in one of the biggest criminal cases of the decade.

In 1998, our second year of law school Matthew Sheppard was killed in Laramie. The case garnered national attention for many reasons and many Americans had strong opinions about the case. However, for us 2L's it was thrilling to those of us that wanted to practice criminal defense to be right in the middle of a notorious criminal case. Laramie's single room courthouse could not accommodate the masses and many of the pre-trial hearings were held at our law school. During class breaks we would bump into the defendants shackled in the hallway and got our first glimpses of "real criminals". Kirk became a clerk for the defense team and we all quickly learned the perils of media attention.

One of the first lessons learned is do not talk to the media about your case or your client. Dianne Courselle the clinic's director was in charge of teaching the few of us that applied to the criminal defense clinic. In most law schools the clinics had waiting lists and often students weren't able to participate. Not at Wyoming, the few of us that year wanting to defend were able to enroll in the clinic without any wait. Kirk was selected to be our fearless student leader and boss in the quest to "fight the man" for the little guy. We were in charge of filing post-conviction relief appeals for sentenced defendants. It was a thrilling assignment because the appeals were heard by the Wyoming Supreme Court and the students argued them. By the time Kirk left law school he had already argued in front of the Supreme Court of Wyoming several times, something many practicing attorneys never accomplish.

Once graduation rolled around I had applied to the Maricopa County Public Defender's Office for a position in my hometown of Phoenix. The position started out as a law clerk then advanced to attorney position once you passed the bar. Kirk thought a sunny and warm Phoenix sounded like a good place to start after many long cold winters, so he applied as well. At the time there were four law clerk positions available at the downtown office which was one of the largest public defender's office in the nation. Kirk and I were selected for two of those positions, settled in and began studying for the bar exam.

Although it sounded exciting, we did very little but sit in our offices all day and wait for an attorney to ask us to research something. The Public Defender's Office was housed in a decrepit although charming Luhrs Building which offered a great view of Patriot's Park and the homeless population. At the time we did not have the internet in our offices, we only had basic research tools and listened to the radio. We were assigned to court once a month but only to hand the defendant a piece of paper with their next court date on it. It was a demotion to us to have once argued in front of the Supreme Court of Wyoming and then reduced to a court date clerk. It was frustrating to not be able to participate in any case or see the inside of a court room for any real purpose. Only passing the bar exam would free us from our prison of boredom so we could finally take cases. It was very clear that Phoenix had plenty of criminals that would need fantastic up and coming attorneys like Kirk and myself.

Kirk and I both failed the bar exam. He failed it by only a few points and I failed it by many points. Given the bar exam was only administered twice a year, we would have to wait until May 2001 for our results. Thus began a year of figuring out ways to entertain ourselves. We listened to Dr. Laura on the radio daily and laughed often at her style in dealing with people. She was rude and shut people up with her advice. Looking back we were seriously bored and lacking in the type of social media outlets available today at one's fingertips. Fortunately we had plenty of time to study again for the bar exam, which thankfully we both passed the second time around.

We began training class and embarked on learning how to be a trial attorney. Russ Born was in charge of teaching us this skill. He was energetic, funny, and was a fast talking former capital attorney from Chicago, a place with more criminals than Phoenix. Russ had a secret weapon in the courtroom, sweet-tarts. He carried these around throughout training and touted this as the best way to keep from having dry mouth when speaking. Although we didn't need motivation, Russ was the kind of lawyer that I had envisioned when I started law school, a passionate fighter for the little guy. After training we were assigned to the Regional Court Center where we handled cases for early dispositions. Once one mastered client control, preliminary hearings, change of pleas, and sentencings we were able to move to trial group.

Trial lawyers at last, Kirk was assigned to group D and later moved out to Mesa where he was assigned to group C. It was there that he earned a fierce reputation for himself. He took on clients that no one wanted, child molesters, rapists, and eventually moved to capital defense work. The path to capital defense work is a long one, as it should be. It takes a certain type of lawyer that can defend not only a homicide case but one so heinous it is alleged as a death penalty case. Kirk is this type of lawyer, balanced, serious, and a methodical organized trial lawyer. His most important character trait is that he can stay in "lawyer mode" with his client and not get personally involved. If the government wants to kill your client, you have to fight like hell to stop them and not let your own emotions get in the way. Kirk was cut out for this type of client and caseload.

Unlike Kirk, I was not cut out for death penalty defense work and I left the Public Defender's Office in 2004. I started my own practice following in the shoes of my famous uncle Fred and began doing DUI defense. To me, alcohol related crimes were easy to defend as it was common for people to make mistakes with alcohol. I could easily defend this type of case and not worry about my client getting the death penalty.

Although we no longer worked together, Kirk and I remained good friends over the years. In 2011 my private practice was busy and I had work that I was referring out to other attorneys. I suggested to Kirk that he leave the Public Defender's Office, try something new and make more money. Ultimately he quit his job and moved into my office building. Together again after all these years, I embarked on trying to teach Kirk the passion a lawyer can have over misdemeanor offenses. No one was going to prison, no one was going to get the death penalty, and a mean fight over a few days in jail was exhilarating right?

When Kirk got the news that he was ordered to remain as Jodi Arias' lawyer even though he didn't work as a public defender anymore our plans to practice together were put on hold for Jodi Arias. In fact for Kirk, every plan he had was put on hold for Jodi Arias. Saving Jodi Arias' life took precedence over everything. How long could it take, really to resolve her case right? That was the understatement of the century.

INTRODUCTION

Several years ago, long before I met Jodi Arias I was a fan of Deepak Chopra. I had read a few of his books and I found many of his teachings to be thought provoking. To that end, back in the days before cell phones had calendars built in, I had a daily desk calendar that was based around his teachings or philosophies. Each date of the year had a page and each page contained a short passage or thought for the day. One thought stood out to me so much that, rather than toss it into the garbage like I did on most days after I had read the thought of the day, I placed it in a place where I could see it every day when I came into work. Even now, several years later this portion of this historic relic known as a paper calendar has been placed where I can see it every day. In my mind, the thought was both simple and yet profound. The thought is this; "The best thing that could happen to you is happening right now." Best as I can discern this thought stood out to me because, in my mind, it serves as a great reminder that things happen for a reason and somewhere down the road you will discover that reason. It may mean something else to you but this was my take away and for years I have glanced at these words periodically as a reminder to myself that what I was now seeing as an obstacle might compel me in a greater direction. I never really questioned this philosophy until I became involved in "The State of Arizona v. Jodi Arias." Once I became involved in this case I began to question this philosophy in that I began to wonder how being ordered to be Ms. Arias' attorney was the best thing for me. I would look at these words often during the several years that I served as Ms. Arias' lead counsel and I remember thinking that time has always proven these words to be correct as it related to my life so maybe someday I will know why being her attorney was the best thing for me. In this regard, to me writing this book served as an exercise that I hope will get me closer to the answer of why.

As I write this book, I still don't know the answer to the question of why serving as Ms. Arias' attorney was the best thing for me and perhaps I never will. I realize that some of you out there would think that being Ms. Arias' attorney was best for me because I made a ton of money off her case and will make even more money now when I sell this book. To that I say, I did not make as much money off the trial as the media would lead you to believe and secondly, while it is true I will make money off this book assuming somebody buys it, this book is not about the money. Though like all of us, I like to get paid for my work. This book is about more than that because the real goals of this book do not relate to money. I have already shared the first goal with you, my desire to learn why I was placed in this position. However, this book is more about satisfying my own curiosities, it is also about aiding others.

One goal I had in mind when I decided to write this book is to help others by doing what I can to prevent tragedies like the one that occurred on June 4, 2008 from happening in the future. In my mind, one way to do that is to talk about the dynamics between these two young lovers in honest terms so that we can all learn something from their story. Likewise, in my mind preventing such tragedies in the future requires that I honestly examine the mental health issues that also played a role in this sad tale. To me, that means telling the truth about the circumstances that surrounded the case that you are not yet aware. This book then serves as my attempt to interject a reality based lesson into what has otherwise been a sensationalized reality television experience. That does not mean that I will avoid the sensational aspects of this case but rather I am choosing to share all these facts with you with the hope that some readers might learn something from the truth of what occurred between Ms. Arias and Mr. Alexander. To that end, the decision to write this book turned on the idea that there are lessons to be learned from the truth that surrounded this unhealthy relationship and that I wanted to share these lessons and/or realities with others in hopes if they find themselves in such a situation, they will get out of the relationship before they harm themselves or others.

A direct consequence of articulating the truth is that I could not write this book seeking acceptance by any one group of "trial watchers" or media talking heads. Instead, in seeking to teach the lessons that can be learned from this case I think I will anger many a reader. Not typically what an author tries to do, but in order to be true to myself, true to the story, true to the lesson that must be taught and obtain the answers we are all seeking, I think I must be objective and honest. In writing this book and the books that will follow, I realize that I could endear myself to Mr. Alexander's supporters and the public at large if I wrote a book in which I feed into the narrative that Ms. Arias is the most evil person to ever walk the earth. I would likely sell thousands upon thousands of books taking such a tactic. I could also write a book that professes that Ms. Arias was wrongly convicted and sell a few books to her misguided supporters. Certainly, both these tactics might endear me to one "side" or the other, but I don't see the case in such terms. First of all, I don't understand why there are "sides" in this case. In my mind the only sane way to view this case is that it was a tragedy for many reasons. Primary amongst those reasons is that a beloved young man is dead and the woman he loved is now spending her life in prison and it didn't have to be this way. This tragedy could have been prevented and in this book I discuss how I think this tragedy could have been prevented. Sadly, a discussion of this nature got lost in all the hoopla that surrounded this case.

That is not to say I do not have one more self-serving reason for writing this book that I have not mentioned yet. One important reason I had for writing this book, beyond using it as a therapeutic tool, is redemption. Yes, redemption. In my role as Ms. Arias' attorney I took a lot of flak from supporters of Mr. Alexander simply because I was asserting Ms. Arias' defense. Conversely, at the same time I was taking flak from those who support Ms. Arias because I was not doing enough to show how she was truly innocent (their thoughts not mine). Additionally, I took flak from the media, many of whom asserted or implied that I was a poor lawyer without having any clue of the strategy that I was employing. A truly no win situation for me and to make matters worse all these attacks were taking place at a time that I could not really offer a response.

Now I can respond and respond I will. In this book I talk about how I knew exactly what I was doing. I led the team that saved the life of a woman who, in my mind, at the time was one of the most hated people in the entire United States and perhaps one of the most hated people in the entire world for that matter. In my mind, you have to have a pretty good idea of what you are doing to accomplish such a feat. In this book I will discuss my background, what my life and career entailed before Ms. Arias became my client. I will then continue on describing how I was assigned the case and the course of the case all the way to the point that opening statements were delivered on January 2, 2013. Describing these things may not redeem me in the eyes of some, but that is okay with me, my true redemption comes from being judged on the truth of who I am and the course I took.

Several times during this introduction I referenced the truth. As I write this I can almost hear the cynics claiming that I am lying or that what I will be offering you is my version of the "truth." Not at all, when I speak of the truth it will be in objective verifiable realities. Granted these realities may not fit with what you believe or want to believe about the case or the people involved in it, but it will be the truth. You see for those of you who are not aware our second President John Adams before he was President, was a lawyer. As a lawyer Mr. Adams was tasked with representing a British soldier who was accused of murder. This incident is famously known as the "Boston Massacre." I suspect many historians have done a fantastic job of outlining the entire situation so I would refer you to their work if you have an interest in learning more, but for my purposes it is sufficient that you know that Mr. Adams was representing a very unpopular individual accused of murder. During the trial it is said that he advised the jury that "facts are stubborn things" and he was right. What he seemingly meant by this is that when you put all emotion aside and when you put what you want to believe up against what is actually true what you want to believe may not be the truth. You will see me articulate this point on several occasions during my writing when I feel it necessary to remind you "facts are stubborn things." I will repeat this mantra when I suspect that what you want to believe faces challenge by my words and you may be feeling angry. In that regard, if you want to hang onto what you want to believe regardless of what "side" you are on this probably is not the book for you. Furthermore, it would not be the type of book I want to write as it would not lead to any level of self-awareness or redemption for me nor would it offer you any lesson.

Having said all of this and running the risk of authoring an introduction that is too long, before you delve into the book, I thought you might be wondering; why is this book entitled "Trapped with Ms. Arias?" You might also be wondering; why do gold handcuffs take "center stage" on the cover. The first word of the title relates to the fact that once I had a sense of where this case was going I was willing to give up a job that I liked simply to get away from Ms. Arias and when I did not get away I realized that I was truly trapped on her case, which also meant I was trapped with her. Now you might be wondering; why do I describe to whom I was trapped with as "Ms. Arias" instead of "Jodi" or "Jodi Arias" or any other name? The reason is simple. More than being called "P458434" her jail booking number, or being called "281129," her Arizona Department of Corrections Booking number, Jodi Ann Arias, hates being referred to as Ms. Arias. I know this because once she started complaining about me to the courts and others I took the high road and tried to be as professional as possible by calling her Ms. Arias. In response, she would scream at me for calling her by her formal name. Behind these screams was the threat that I discuss in this book, her threat that she would ruin my career if I did not follow her commands. I might also point out, so as to prevent any confusion; I do not call Mr. Alexander, Mr. Alexander as an expression of disdain, but instead out of respect because I feel that it would be disrespectful of me to simply call him Travis.

All of this serves as backdrop to my explanation as to why the handcuffs were golden. For those of you who are not familiar, the term "golden hand-cuffs" relates to a situation you do not wish to be in but the money is good. Yes, I got paid to represent Ms. Arias but it was always against my will and it was not truly worth it. Representing Ms. Arias took up the bulk of my time, it prevented me from truly starting my practice, heck it may even prevent me from ever having a real practice. It is for these reasons that the money was not worth it, that the handcuffs may have been golden but they were still handcuffs. Handcuffs, that I could not get out of, no matter how hard I tried.

Given that I was never able to make it out of these handcuffs, what follows is the story of what it was like for me to wear these handcuffs for so many years. What follows is Part 1 of a three part explanation, in the clearest manner I can offer it to you of what it was truly like to be "Trapped with Ms. Arias."

SECTION 1

BEFORE GETTING THE FILE

M ost of you who followed The State of Arizona v. Jodi Arias had no idea who I was until January 2, 2013. If you were one of those people who followed the trial before opening statements you may have heard of me before that exact day, but I think you would be in the minority; and an even smaller amount of you actually knew me before I was assigned to be Ms. Arias' attorney. What that means is that the great majority of you have no idea who I am, no idea where I come from and no idea of the things that are important to me. What the majority of you know is what you saw on television. Certainly in other sections of this book we will talk about my thoughts on the case but in an effort to give you a full flavor of the case, I wanted to give you a true sense of who I am. I do this in Chapter 1, "Who is Nurmi?" In an effort to describe for you what the role and/or job of lead counsel in any capital case truly involves I offer you Chapter 2, "The Ultimate Job of a Capital Defense Attorney." In Chapter 3, I describe the people who help that attorney do their job "The Defense Team." Finally as one of my goals in writing this book is to help prevent others from walking this same path, the path of hurting or killing someone they love. I wanted to offer my insight, the insight I have gained through being a capital defense attorney for many years, as to how these tragedies can be prevented. Thus before I get involved in telling the tale of the relationship that Ms. Arias and Mr. Alexander shared, before I anger you with something I say, I wanted to put forth a simple thought that

I will convey in Chapter 4 "Here is to Wishing that I Never got the File." Think about it, how wonderful would that be for everyone who was affected by the case, especially Travis Alexander and his family if the events of June 4, 2008 that gave rise to this case, never happened.

CHAPTER 1

WHO IS NURMI?

Most of the world had no idea who I was until January of 2013, when the trial began and frankly I was happy in my anonymity, though I must admit I probably did not value it as much as I should have at the time. I guess few of us really value the things we think that we will never lose. It never occurred to me that I would ever lose my anonymity. Certainly, during my career I had never shied away from the big case, but at the same time I was never the type to seek fame from my work. It was never my dream to become a "high profile attorney" what some indigent clients call a "TV Lawyer," that just was not the type of person I was. In fact, I was very happy working as a lawyer helping people and enjoying a life-style that most might consider mundane. However, the trial of Jodi Arias thrust infamy upon me.

Given my obligation to my client, Ms. Arias, I had no choice but to do my job and accept the reality that the anonymity I had enjoyed in the past might be gone forever. What was even worse about this reality is that my infamy and the associated media and/or social media driven hatred directed towards me had nothing to do with who I was as a person, instead the sole focus of this hatred was the fact that I was Jodi Arias' lawyer so I must be a terrible person. No thought was given to who I was, the things I valued and what I had accomplished as a professional. Of course, all of this was being done at a time when responses to such attacks would have been ill advised or a waste of time, but times have changed. So given the fact that I was born many years before 2013, given that I had a life before I came to be "Trapped with Ms. Arias" and given my desire to have a life free from Ms. Arias, now that my involuntary servitude is over it might be of interest to you and therapeutic to me for you to learn who I am as a human being.

I was born in the south and my father was in the Navy. He and my mother moved to Seattle shortly after I was born. I assume that they did this to be close to my mother's parents Stella and Leo so that my biological parents could have Stella and Leo's assistance raising me while they both worked and went to school. Ultimately, the way things worked out my grandparents, Stella and Leo, became my parents in the sense that I lived with them on a day to day basis and they were the ones who drove me to soccer practice and all those type of things. I don't refer to Stella and Leo as my parents to slight my mother and father. In fact, while Stella and Leo served as my parents they were always Grandma and Grandpa to me. While I might have had some angst about this situation in my younger years, as an adult I now understand that my parents were confronted with a tough situation. They were young parents with an adorable baby boy (even my "haters" might agree with that). Neither of them had completed college. I assumed that they were keenly aware that completing those degrees was imperative to their future as well as the future of this adorable baby. Thus, looking back I can see that they were confronted with a situation that many young people today may find themselves in, they had a baby and little prospects for careers that would help them raise the baby to be a viable adult unless they completed their educations. Fortunately, for myself and my parents we all had Stella and Leo.

Leo came to the United States from Finland. He served our country in World War II. He married Stella when she was a single mother at a time when single motherhood was supposedly something to be ashamed of. This fact alone speaks to his character. He was the sort of man that made his own choices. He didn't let others choose the paths in life that he would take. He made those decisions for himself. Furthermore, he did not seem to care about what others might think of his choices. This is not to say that he had a belligerent attitude, in fact, far from it. He simply had a "live and let live" attitude that was fueled by a desire for harmony and peace. When I was younger, of course, I didn't realize all of these things. Instead, I just enjoyed the time we spent fishing, washing the car and watching sports. Even today when I watch a sporting event on TV and they actually televise the singing of the national anthem, something I believe should happen during every broadcast, I reflect back on how I always wanted us both to stand during the anthem because I had such pride in our country, he always complied.

Stella was a mom, not because she had given birth to my mother but because she was highly maternal. She had worked in her life but her real desire was to nurture and she was good at it. For frame of reference, I grew up in the 1970's. The 1970's may seem like ancient history to many. Others may only know of the 70's based upon what they saw while watching "That 70's Show." Certainly, like the characters on that show I spent a great deal of time hanging out in the basements of my friend's house and driving huge station wagons, heck I even had to parallel park one of those monstrous things in order to get my driver's license. However, on a more serious note the 1970's were a time when society was beginning to change. One income households were starting to become a thing of the past as more women entered the work force. Housewives (not the "real" kind you see on television but actual housewives) were a dying breed. However, in the Nurmi household that bit of the past was still alive. Grandma worked at home raising me and caring for my Grandfather, she was a bit of a throwback I guess. She ironed my grandfather's shirts herself and made me a snack every afternoon when I got home from school and whatever that snack was, it always tasted great. My fondest memories of my grandmother are those afternoons after school hanging out with her watching Gilligan's Island reruns while she ironed shirts. Back then I was a happy guy. I loved playing soccer. I loved watching all types of sports on TV and I loved dogs and all animals for that matter. I remember loving animals so much that in order to rescue a bunny from the school snake, the kind of snake most school science labs have residing in them, I brought home a bunny. And to my grandfather's credit he did not traumatize me by making me take it back. He did just the opposite he made a very nice cage for that bunny, he was truly a kind man.

I even loved school as a youngster. Math was my favorite subject. I was way ahead of the curve in math and I attended a summer camp for kids who were gifted in mathematics. However, fate did not determine that I should be a mathematician. Instead my fate was to be a lawyer. How this was determined might be a bit metaphysical and perhaps even I, the person who lived it, can only speculate as to why, but speculate I will. I can think of two things that occurred in my life that might have led me to the path of being a criminal defense attorney. Sometime when I was in grade school I came across a book in the school library. I believe it was called "She wants to be a Lawyer" but an internet search doesn't uncover the existence of such a book so I could be wrong about the title. Regardless of the title, it was the substance that mattered to me at the time. As you might guess, now, decades later, I remember very little about the specific content of the book. However, as best I can recall it was a simple story about a woman who wanted to be a lawyer and she became a lawyer. For whatever reason, I was fascinated with this book and I read it several times. I also recall another incident when I was a child that in retrospect, I can see how it might have fueled my desire to become a lawyer. I can't recall my exact age when this incident happened, but this experience has stuck with me to this day. One of the things the children in my neighborhood would do periodically is go up to the grocery store on "the corner" to buy candy. On this occasion, I went up to the store with my lifelong friend and his older sister. As children tend to do, we went up and down the candy aisle trying to get the most bang for the buck and dreaming of all the candy we wished we could buy. Anyway after making our purchases we were stopped outside by a security guard and/or store manager who accused us of stealing candy. We had our receipt and we didn't have any candy that we didn't pay for so the experience ended there. However, I remember being so upset by being falsely accused of doing something that I didn't do. I couldn't believe that someone would accuse us of stealing without having any evidence to support their claim. Someone just assumed we were stealing. I'm not sure that this experience cemented my path to becoming a lawyer.

As best I can recall I was no more than ten years old at the time, but I guess it couldn't have hurt as it still sickens me to think of people being accused of something they did not do.

Throughout high school I lived with my parents in a suburb of Seattle. My ride back then was a 1968 Buick LaSabre, a huge pea green gas guzzling machine, but it ran pretty well for a car that was purchased for about $500. I kept gas in this beast by working at a grocery store bagging groceries. I graduated high school a year early at the age of 17. My plan at that age might surprise most people. My plan was to become a police officer. I enrolled at a local community college that had a criminal justice program and I kept my job at the grocery store. Most of my friends went off to 4 year universities and joined fraternities while I worked and went to school at a community college. Clearly, they were having more fun than I was. However, given my envy of my friend's lifestyles and given that one couldn't become a cop in Washington until they turned 21, I was able to convince myself that since an Associate's Degree only took two years, I had two "extra" years to have fun. Looking back, undoubtedly this was a very immature decision to say the least, but at the time, I rationalized that I had ample time to complete my education before I turned 21, so I stopped going to school for a fair amount of time. Sparing you the gory details let me just say that while I was not busy going to school I certainly had fun during this time of my life. As you might guess this was also a time during which I did not take my future seriously. School was something that I would get to later, bouncing in and out of school was seemingly the most energy I was willing to put towards my education, however, as those of you who have attended community college know, you bounce around enough and you eventually get your degree.

When I turned 21, I tested for a few police departments in California but for whatever reason that never seemed to work out. So I continued to drift around a bit having more fun, thinking about being a lawyer but wondering if I really wanted to give up my good paying job to go back to school. You see at that time, I was still working in the grocery business and the grocery business paid pretty well. I was making a good wage as a union member and store managers were making well over 6 figures. Despite these internal conflicts, on some level I must have realized that the grocery business was not for me and I needed to grow up. However, as I was also determined to not give up this good paying job, I decided to go back to school and keep my job. Thus, for me "college life" meant working the all-night shift and going to school. In practical terms this meant that most nights of the week, I would start putting groceries on the shelf at 10pm and I would end around 6 am. School was then something I did either directly before or after work. Sleep was something I did far too little of but I was young and I drank a ton of Tab (the predecessor to Diet Coke).

When I finally graduated with my Bachelor's Degree in Criminal Justice I applied to several law schools. I didn't get in to any of them. I now see this as a blessing but at the time it was a huge bummer, a huge defeat. I had worked insanely hard to get through school. Earn my bachelor's degree in the manner that I did it was not fun. To make matters worse, the only real purpose I had in getting this degree was because I needed to have one to get into law school. Apart from a requirement to get into law school, the degree itself meant very little to me at the time. So as you might guess not getting accepted was devastating to me. Not getting into law school created quite the personal dilemma, the question that kept eating at me was "What the heck was I going to do now?" The good news was that at least I had kept my job, so I had that to fall back on and at times I did contemplate the idea that it might be time for me to forget about law school and seek management opportunities in the grocery business.

However, after some time I realized that, even years later, trying to make myself into a grocery store manager was like trying to fit a square peg into a round whole. It was not the right fit. Once I realized that "Store Manager" was not my destiny I also realized that I had to take action to change the course of my life. I knew that I wasn't going to get anywhere in my life if I didn't take action. I knew that I needed to break out of my comfort zone, that good paying job at the grocery store that I had been clinging to for so many years. So after careful contemplation I decided to take a leap of faith. I decided to quit my job and go to graduate school. The idea was that if I could earn my Master's Degree and get good grades while doing so that I could boost my academic resume to such a degree that I would have a better chance of getting into law school.

For reasons I still do not fully comprehend, I decided to seek out a Master's Degree in History at Central Washington University in Ellensburg. I guess at the time, I thought it might be an interesting course of study to partake in until I was able to pursue the field I really wanted to study, law. Once I got on campus, to take the prerequisite course I would need to be accepted into the master's program, I soon realized a Master's in History wasn't for me. I discovered quickly that there was a huge difference between my personal interest in the subject and actually earning a Master's Degree in History. Upon realizing this and having somewhat limited options, I decided to get a second Bachelor's Degree, this time in psychology. As it turned out, this change of course was the best thing I could have done, not because I became Sigmund Freud, but because this change in my academic course is how I met my wife. I have been married to her since 1993 and trust me that is much more valuable to me than any Master's Degree. Not only that, but after getting married I eventually got that Master's Degree, a Master's of Arts in Criminal Justice from Washington State University, aka "Wazzu". I have the diploma on my office wall and everything. Finally, since I am self-published, I can say what I want to in my own book so I am going to end this paragraph and this talk about Wazzu with two important words – Go Cougs!

After I graduated from Washington State University, I tried to get a job that didn't involve working retail and I got one. I was a counselor at a residential group home for delinquent youth. I was pretty good at it and I liked it. However, after a year or so the home got shut down because the actual house wasn't up to code. So it was back to retail for me until I finally decided to apply to law school yet again. This, for those of you who do not know, really takes some effort you do not just fill out a three page application. In those days, along with a ton of other materials, all applications had to include your "LSAT" score. The "LSAT" was a standardized test that was designed to assess your ability to succeed in law school. As much issue as I might take with the concept that a standardized test can truly measure success in any field, if I did not score well on this test, regardless of my qualms about the test itself and its use as a measure, I had no legitimate chance of getting into law school. Fortunately for me, I did fairly well on this test and then I applied to about five schools. Then all I could do was to live my life while waiting impatiently for these schools to respond. Though Tom Petty might be right, the waiting might be the hardest part, however, in reflecting back I do not remember the worrying, instead I remember the day I got my first acceptance letter. We had been at a friend's house for dinner. The mail came while we were gone and when we returned home late that evening we retrieved the mail and I learned I had been accepted into Gonzaga School of Law. It was too late to call my grandparents, but it was not too late to celebrate a dream several years in the making. Thus, the cheap champagne flowed freely that night because no matter what the other schools had to say I was going to law school regardless because one school had let me in and that was all I needed.

Believe it or not I was actually accepted by more than one law school, which was thrilling because I actually got to have some say in where I went to law school. Ultimately, I decided to attend the University of Wyoming. I chose Wyoming in large part so that my wife could complete her degree in Education without having to spend a fortune on private school tuition only to earn the small salary that we pay our teachers in this country. The cost of this school was also a benefit to me because I assumed I would work in a Public Defender's Office of some sort when I graduated. For those of you who are not familiar with the University of Wyoming the university is located in the small town of Laramie, Wyoming. Most of Laramie's population consists of students when school is in and when school is out the streets of Laramie are empty. But the real "joy" of living in Laramie has nothing to do with the size of the city; heck who could move to Wyoming and expect big city life? The real "joy" of living in Laramie is that it is so cold it has to be experienced to be believed. It is not unheard of for it to snow in June. The winters are unreal. Temperatures in the single digits and strong winds made it hard to get up out of bed, leave my warm house and go to class. However, as difficult of a journey as it was for me to get into law school in general I was not going to let any amount of chill get in my way, I was determined to succeed. Unfortunately for me I was never the sort of guy who was smart enough to skate by with sheer brain power. Sadly, hard work was the only way I knew how to succeed and work hard I did. In fact in between my second and third year of law school I got my first touch of the death penalty process doing research for attorneys who were working on a capital case. At this same time, I also began working as the "Student Director" of the Defender Aid Clinic, a clinic run by the school in which students get real life experience by writing appeals for defendants who were convicted of crimes in Wyoming. Both experiences were awesome and I must say that the education I received at the University of Wyoming was extraordinary. I even had the opportunity to argue with Gerry Spence and I'm pretty sure I held my own. I certainly didn't give up (as you might have noticed during the Arias trial, I never give up).

After graduating I took a job as a law clerk at the Maricopa County Public Defender's Office. I had one other job offer in another state. Had I taken that offer, you wouldn't know who I am. I would have been just another anonymous spectator of the trial not a participant. Had I taken another course some other attorney would have received the wrath of so many angry trial watchers. However, as I chose the path that led me to Maricopa County, as the saying goes "it is what it is" and you know who I am and I am the target of many a trial watcher's wrath, choices have consequences.

After I was licensed to practice law in Arizona, I became an attorney with this same office. I soon learned that my clients didn't think I was a real attorney because I worked as a Public Defender but that didn't stop me. I went forward and acted as a "real attorney" whether my clients noticed my efforts or not, a habit that would serve me well in the future. Within 6 months I tried my first case in front of a jury. Unfortunately for me my first trial was a major felony and if I didn't win my client was going to prison. Most new attorneys are fortunate enough to begin their careers as a trial attorney on minor offenses where regardless of the outcome their clients will walk out the courthouse door. As you might guess my client was nervous. He hadn't had any criminal convictions before and he was very scared about the fact that he could be going to prison for a few years for a crime he didn't commit. I never told him it was my first trial. If I had, the heart attack he would have had would have precluded the need for a trial. Winning that trial was invigorating in that I was so happy for my client, not to mention myself as I had won my first case. You see to me it has always been about the client because I knew at the end of any trial I would get to go home, some of my clients would not have that same opportunity. Anyway, after walking out of the courtroom with my client who was a free man, he and I stood out on the courthouse steps and he was so exhausted from worry that he could barely stand. To date, I have not seen him in person, since that day. However, I got the greatest thank you of all when a few years later I was watching the local news and my former client was being interviewed for his part in aiding a child in distress. Something he could not have done had he been in prison for a crime he didn't commit.

As time progressed my cases got more and more complex. The next major trial I recall was a sex case. My client had been accused of molesting two of his three step daughters. There was no physical evidence. The only evidence against my client was the testimony of these two young girls, both of whom were under eight years of age and a so called child abuse expert saying that these incidents occurred. It was my first sex crimes trial and I learned first-hand how much vitriol a juror can have against a person because of an allegation alone. Eleven of the twelve jurors wanted to convict my client of all charges and one did not. This was made evident by the jury questions which asked why old men were allowed to be on a jury and if the other jurors could kick him off the jury. That jury hung and with my client being steadfast in his innocence the only way to resolve the case was to try the case again in front of a new jury. The second jury convicted him of all the crimes he was charged with even after the girls claimed that they made the story of being molested up so they could get my client out of the house. Why did they do this? Because they thought he was "mean." Undoubtedly, it might very well be the case that my former client did molest his step-daughters, or perhaps he was completely innocent, it was the kind of case where you could never be certain and where vitriol can take the place of actual evidence. The vitriol was made most evident to me when a few members of the first jury showed up to watch gleefully when my client received his sentence of over 200 years in prison.

Fortunately, for my other clients accused of sex crimes that they may not have or did not commit, not all were found guilty at trial. In fact, many were found not guilty of offenses that could have landed them in prison for the rest of their lives. I remember years ago I was on a bit of a roll and after successfully defending an Afghan War Veteran who came home with Post Traumatic Stress Disorder against charges that he had sexually assaulted his girlfriend (they were involved in a sadomasochistic relationship, an interesting story for another day). When we were outside the courtroom this veteran's father said to me that he doubted I would be working as a public defender much longer because in his estimation I was too good of an attorney for such a job. I certainly was contemplating leaving my job, not because I was too good for the job but because I thought it would be awesome to be my own boss and run my own firm. However, at the same time, I still loved being a Public Defender. I took great satisfaction in providing people who couldn't afford a top-flight attorney with high-quality legal representation. I guess it was this satisfaction that led to my decision to stay working as a public defender. However, at the same time, I wanted a new challenge. Looking back on it I can't help but wonder what life would be like if I had followed my inclinations to go into private practice back then. Who knows how things would have turned out but I am almost certain that I would not have been lead counsel for Ms. Arias had I left my job at that time. Choices have consequences.

My desire to confront a new challenge while still working for indigent defendants combined with my opposition to the death penalty led me to joining the Maricopa County Office of the Public Defender's Capital Unit. From my first day as a death penalty attorney I was acutely aware that this sort of legal practice was above and beyond anything I had done before. Even trying cases where defendants were facing literally hundreds of years did not compare to the responsibility that comes with trying to prevent the government from killing your client. In this regard I still recall that during my first week as a capital attorney I had to tell a father that his son, who had no prior criminal history, was likely going to be facing the death penalty. Granted, I am sure this man knew that the crime of murder was a serious charge but I could see that this news devastated him and understandably so, this was serious business to him and to me. I was beginning to see firsthand that my new path would not be a smooth one.

In my two plus years as a capital attorney with the Public Defender's Office I served as counsel in two death penalty trials. One client received life, one client received death. Being present in a courtroom when your client is sentenced to death is a difficult experience to say the least. The jurors cried, the defendant's family cried out in pain. All I could do was to simply stand there and absorb it all, helpless to do anything about it. Having lived through this experience once, I knew it was an experience I never wanted to have again in my career. I vowed to myself then that I would always do what it takes, within the bounds of my ethical duties, to avoid such an experience in the future.

Beyond this historical data, in July of 2009, one month before I was assigned as lead counsel for Ms. Arias, I was a 40 something year old capital defense attorney with a good reputation amongst my peers (if I do say so myself). I had been married for about 15 years, I loved playing tennis, I struggled with my weight and putting the scorching summers aside, I loved living in the "Valley of the Sun." The love I had for dogs as a child was still a huge part of my life, even if the dog that chose to take over my household was a 4 pound Chihuahua. Though far from perfect, I tried to live my life by the Golden Rule. I had recently lost my grandfather who exemplified that rule and my grandmother was suffering and slowly dying from Parkinson's disease.

So who is Nurmi? Well, if you have been paying attention to what you read in the last few pages you now have, at the very least, a partial answer to that question. You now know a bit more about me as a person, not simply the person you saw on television working as Ms. Arias' attorney. You can now see the choices I made in my life, not all of them of course, but a fair amount of them that relate to how I became a public defender in Maricopa County. You know a bit about some of the choices I made in my career. You know why I made these choices and you now know about how these choices led me to being a capital defense attorney. All of these steps of course put me in a position where I was chosen to serve as Ms. Arias' lead counsel.

So, having said all of this, whether you like it or not, I have gained a little of the redemption I spoke of in the introduction. Because after reading this chapter whether you love me or hate me at least you are basing your feelings on who I am not who you think I might be simply because in August of 2009, I was assigned by the Public Defender's Office to work as lead counsel in CR 2008-031021-001.

CHAPTER 2

THE ULTIMATE JOB OF A CAPITAL DEFENSE ATTORNEY

Killing a human being is a horrible act. Murder is a horrible crime. Most of us who work as defense Counsel for capital defendants do so because we believe that the killing of a human being is just as wrong when it is done by a citizen than when it is done by the government whose job it is to serve and protect all its citizens. Capital defense attorneys serve on the front lines of the fight against the death penalty. Like any battle the front lines of the battle against the death penalty is not a fun place to be. We put up with clients who are oftentimes ungrateful or down right angry about the work we do on their behalf. Based on some of the hate mail I received over the course of the Arias trial, the public seems to be under the perception that someone who serves as the lawyer for a capital defendant supports what their client did. I don't know why the public feels this way, it truly puzzles me. I assume it relates to the fact that we appear to be advocating for our clients when we are really advocating for the constitutional rights of our clients. There is a huge difference between the two that I will try to explain. I know of no capital attorney who supports their client's choice to murder a human being. Conversely, I know of no capital attorney who believes the death penalty should be administered without firm resistance from a defense attorney who zealously asserts the defendant's constitutional rights whenever he or she can do so. There is a saying in the criminal defense community to the effect of "we don't defend the crime, only the constitution and what the client may have done is relatively insignificant to the battle at hand." That is not to say that we are not conscious of the pain and anguish our client caused but we must push our feelings about that to the side because our job of defending the constitution demands that we do so.

Some of you reading this may be of the opinion that those who kill another human being shouldn't have any rights at all. To those people I would say that, while I understand your anger, the legal system that America has functioned under since its birth dictates that every person accused of a crime has rights. In fact, it is a key American principle that the government, if it wants to take a citizen's liberty, must have proof beyond a reasonable doubt that the citizen committed the crime. It is my belief and the belief of many who serve as defense attorneys that if that proof is not challenged at every turn, this restriction on government power becomes meaningless. Furthermore, it is my belief that we will cease to be the great nation that we are if there are not those who are willing to stand up for the rights of each and every citizen no matter the context.

Of course, when the government wants to kill one of its citizens the stakes are even higher and thus the defense must be even stronger. Why? Because, in addition to the principles I just spoke of, the United States Constitution, as interpreted by the United States Supreme Court, demands that every effort must be made to save a person's life when the power of the government is seeking to take their life from them. Think about it, if capital defense attorneys did not make every effort, within the bounds of their ethical duties, to fight for their client's life the government could kill at will or with relative ease. If capital defense attorneys do not fight for their client's lives with vigor, the desire to kill goes unchallenged. Let's face it, the government always has the moral high ground in a criminal case and the cards are always stacked against the defense attorney but for the wall of liberty that protects us all to mean anything the capital defense attorney must do all they can do to accomplish their ultimate job, to save their client's life.

Saving the client's life is job number one for a capital attorney. In fact it is really the entire job, in that ethically doing this job is more important than defending the person against the charge of First Degree Murder. That means that how you attack the State's case, how you present your defense, how you choose your jurors is all geared towards the idea of saving your client's life. Seeking a verdict of "not guilty" really does not come into the picture. As I say this keep in mind that the logistics of a capital case are such that the jury you select to hear the guilt phase of the case is also the same jury that chooses the sentence your client receives and they are told that they are to consider everything they hear from the first day of the trial until the last day of the trial. Furthermore, for several reasons that are not important here, when you have a death penalty qualified jury you have to assume that you are not going to hear "not guilty" at the end of the first phase simply because of the type of person who is chosen to serve. You also have to understand that if you vigorously pursue that "not guilty" verdict it might very well mean a death sentence for your client. A capital defense attorney wins when their client receives a life sentence. A life sentence is the ultimate goal from the first day a capital attorney is assigned a case and it remains the ultimate goal until the client is executed. By this I mean that while the capital attorney is attempting to save the client's life at the trial level, he or she should also be trying to lay the foundation so that the client's life can be saved down the road because that is the ultimate job of a capital defense attorney.

Thus, as lead counsel for Ms. Arias my job and really my only job from day 1, the day I was assigned to the case, was to save Ms. Arias' life either at trial or by making the right record so as to preclude execution of Ms. Arias down the road. I make no apologies to anyone about doing everything it took to save Ms. Arias' life because it was what was required of me not only because of my duty to Ms. Arias but because it was what the United States Constitution demands.

This is not to say that I do not have sympathy for Mr. Alexander's family and all those who cared about him. In fact, just the opposite is true. Often times during this case I thought about how horrible it must be for them having to deal not only with the murder itself but the trial as well. That being said, had I let the sympathy I have for these people diminish my zeal I would not have been doing the job demanded of me and had I failed to do so, there is a good chance that whatever was going to happen at trial would be overturned.

Finally, let me say that if anyone out there thinks that I somehow support what Ms. Arias did on June 4, 2008, they are wrong. I did my job. I accomplished the ultimate job of a capital defense attorney. I saved my client's life. You might not be happy about it because you wanted her to be executed and Ms. Arias may not be happy about receiving a life sentence, but I did my job and if I do say so myself, I did it quite well.

CHAPTER 3

THE DEFENSE TEAM

N ow that you know what job number 1 of a capital defense attorney is I think it is important that you understand how such a person goes about their job. The first thing you should know is that pursuant to the laws of Arizona, lead counsel on a capital case never works alone and that even if they wanted to work alone they could not do so. Why? Because Arizona law dictates that each person whom the State seeks to execute must have two attorneys. The law goes on to dictate that one attorney is designated as lead-counsel for the case, the other as Co-counsel. Lead Counsel is ultimately responsible for everything. Lead Counsel ultimately decides what matters will be investigated, what experts will be used, the strategy that will be implemented at trial and what witnesses, if any the defense will call. Certainly the job entails many more decisions than these but the list I just articulated should give you a pretty good idea of what I mean when I say that they are responsible for everything. Given that lead counsel has this awesome responsibility, you might guess that the law mandates that this attorney had better know what they are doing and you would be right. The law dictates that before someone can be lead counsel in a capital case they must have 5 years of experience and have tried numerous felony cases. Additionally, they must have served as a second chair to lead counsel in a capital case that actually went to trial. The law also requires that this person keep up on the death penalty issues by mandating that they take a certain number of legal education courses related to the death penalty each year. Thus, as you can see it takes a lot of work and dedication to even step up to the plate and accept such a position.

Regardless of whom the client is, on a day to day basis it is the job of lead counsel to make sure that everyone is doing what they are supposed to be doing. It is their job to make sure the client is informed about what is happening with their case and to make sure that all legal angles are covered. Trust me it is a lot of work on a normal case, and as I will explain as this book goes on (and in my other books) a monumental task when Ms. Arias is your client.

The "Second chair" works at the direction of lead counsel. They must fulfill many of the same requirements required of lead counsel but they need not have been involved in a capital case prior to serving as second chair. The great part if you will about working in this capacity is that you ultimately bear no responsibility for the case itself. The downside is you have to accept the decisions of lead counsel even when you believe that they are wrong.

As you might guess the dynamics between the two attorneys can sometimes be difficult in that a second chair may believe that the lead counsel is wrong or that they are not listening to their opinion. At first read you might think that these dynamics aren't that big of a deal. However, I ask you to consider the reality that when egos are involved these dynamics can be a very big deal and that interpersonal dynamics can become an even bigger deal when you have a client who is looking to manipulate his or her defense team. You will definitely hear more about this dynamic moving forward.

A capital defense team in Arizona also contains a person with the title of "Mitigation Specialist." The law dictates that a person who serves in this role must have insight into the mental health field or a similar field so they can help the attorney present any relevant mental health issue(s) to the jury should lead counsel choose to do so. Typically a Mitigation Specialist has a Master's Degree in one of the social sciences. The role that the Mitigation Specialist serves on the team is, at least in theory, at the discretion of lead counsel. The Mitigation Specialist's job often entails interviewing family members, putting a client's school and/or medical records together for the lead attorney to review. It is not atypical for a Mitigation Specialist to spend more time talking to the client than any other member of the team. Why is this the case? By in large it is because the Mitigation Specialist needs to earn the client's trust so that the client will feel comfortable telling them intimate and/or embarrassing details about their life. Having the client's trust also makes it much more likely that the client's family will also be forthcoming in providing crucial information.

Undoubtedly, some of you might be thinking; who cares about the accused killer's childhood or mental health problems? You might wonder why any of this matters at all. Well, the short answer is that it matters because the United States Supreme Court says it matters. In essence, it is the law of the land that before a person can be sentenced to death the jury must give individualized consideration to the person who is being sentenced. The reasons behind this are discussed in various Supreme Court opinions but, in sum, what the court requires is that each person against whom a death sentence is sought must be given individualized consideration by his or her jury before a sentence can be rendered. We will certainly talk more about this idea moving forward, but as it relates to a capital defense team this means that it is the job of lead counsel, with the help of his entire team but in particular his or her Mitigation Specialist, to investigate and obtain as much information as possible about their client's life from conception to the day they are being sentenced. This evidence is often referred to as mitigation.

The final legally mandated member of a capital defense team is an "Investigator." As the title implies, this person, at the direction of lead counsel, investigates what they can of the crime. Their job is to seek out information that might not be in the police reports and/or re-examine the conclusions the police made about the evidence they collected. Depending on the particular case the work of the Investigator can be minimal or extensive. In most cases quite a large amount of work must be done by the Investigator because as is the case with "mitigation" the lead counsel is required to obtain any and all information he or she can related to the offense itself, both to challenge the client's guilt but also to help the jury understand the circumstances of the offense so that an appropriate sentence can be rendered.

Before I received the Arias case I had a great team. We had worked on several cases together and by in large we all got along. But perhaps more importantly we respected each other and thus we were able to avoid the problems that a manipulative client might present. However, as I will explain later at a certain point I lost that team and things happened.

CHAPTER 4

HERE IS TO WISHING THAT I NEVER GOT THE FILE

When I talk about wishing I never got the file, that might be obvious to you but not for the reasons that might immediately come to mind. When I say that I wish I never got the file I do not mean that I wish that the Arias file was placed on the desk of one of my former colleagues instead of mine, certainly that would have been nice for me personally, however, that is not the wish I am making in this Chapter. Instead of wishing away my personal aguish about being assigned to this case, my wish is that there was never a file to begin with. My wish would be that the events of June 4, 2008, never took place, that Jodi Arias never killed Travis Alexander and that both were alive and well today. That might seem obvious or you may disregard it as wishful thinking, but in this chapter I want to speak to some of my thoughts on how this tragedy and other similar tragedies can be avoided.

I had planned to talk about this lesson in my final book on this case and I still may address it in that book as well. However, because of a theme I see frequently in social media posts that I find upsetting and because I currently have your attention, I decided to address the issue now so as to ensure that it is not ignored. The theme I am talking about are the tweets and/or other social media posts that celebrate either the fact that Ms. Arias is spending the rest of her life in prison and/or how she is miserable in her cell. Seeing social media posts of this nature upsets me. To be clear, these posts do not upset me because I believe that Ms. Arias does not deserve to spend the rest of her life in prison. Sadly, for all involved, she made choices that led to such a state of affairs being justified and whatever misery she is currently experiencing is self-imposed, thus I offer her no sympathy in that regard. Instead, what upsets me when I see these posts is that when anyone is celebrating Ms. Arias' incarceration the people celebrating seem to be forgetting the reason she is in prison. Ms. Arias is in prison for the rest of her life because she killed Travis Alexander. Would it not be much better not to celebrate her life sentence at all because the entire situation was a tragedy and that the world might be a much better place if the tragic events of June 4, 2008, never took place? I certainly think so. Thus, for what it is worth, I write to share my thoughts on how this tragedy could have been prevented and how other similar tragedies can be avoided in the future with the hope that one person who reads this might be aided by my words or pass them along to someone else who may need to hear them.

The first issue is one of mental health. In my mind untreated mental health issues are a serious problem in this country. If anyone takes issue with this I would direct their attention to the recent rash of mass shootings we have experienced in this country. The shooters had mental health issues that were either not being treated or whatever treatment they did receive was inadequate. Of course, I am a lawyer, I am not a psychologist so I am not in a position to talk about diagnosing mentally ill people or suggesting treatment options for the mentally ill. The perspective I offer is not designed to help you diagnose anyone or treat anyone. However, as a criminal defense attorney I have seen many a defendant whom was clearly displaying signs of mental illness that were being ignored by friends and family, signs that were only noticed or taken seriously after it was too late, after they had acted out against another person and were charged with a crime. My hope is that reading this chapter will encourage you to take note of the signs of mental illness and/or a troubled person and if you do make note of these signs that you at least try to do something about it before it is too late. In saying this I realize that you cannot simply kidnap people and force them into a psychiatrist's office based on your hunches that they are mentally ill. However, you would not ignore a friend with a broken arm would you? No, you would take that person to the hospital, you would do something. In this regard I believe that when you notice signs of mental illness in a friend or loved one you can certainly do something. To demonstrate my point I will use the situation between Ms. Arias and Mr. Alexander. I use this example because if you are reading this book, it is a situation that I suspect is at least somewhat familiar to you.

In Ms. Arias' life there were many signs of mental illness that went ignored. Think about it, the records that were presented in this case indicated that she was abusing animals at a young age. Keep in mind such reports came from Ms. Arias' own family members. Other family members noted that the young Ms. Arias would often act strangely and keep to herself around this same time-period. Now regardless of whether or not my theory that Ms. Arias was a victim of sexual abuse as a child is correct or not it would seem that in terms of Ms. Arias' mental health, it was clear that something was not right with her, yet nothing was done to determine what was wrong with Ms. Arias as a child. Nothing! Perhaps having the benefit of hindsight makes my condemnation of Ms. Arias' parents less powerful as hindsight is always 20/20; but, as I sit here today, I stand amazed that nobody took any steps to address these issues. Nobody, not one family member! Young Ms. Arias was never examined by a mental health professional so that she could be diagnosed or assessed in anyway. Think about that; how hard would it have been to take the young Ms. Arias to a child-psychologist? I think it is safe to say that it would not be that difficult. Instead, nothing happened, seemingly these clear signs of mental illness were ignored.

It also seems that Bill and Sandy Arias also ignored further signs of mental illness when Ms. Arias was caught growing marijuana on the roof of the family home. Why would she do this at 14? Did her desire to use marijuana at such a young age mean that she was having trouble dealing with the trauma of having a stranger hold a knife to her throat at age 12? Perhaps so, perhaps not, but if I was the parent I would certainly want an answer to this question especially given her earlier history of strange behavior. However, there is no indication that Bill or Sandy ever sought out professional help to answer this question. Think about it, this was at a time when Ms. Arias' parents had complete control of what she did. She was a minor and they ignored the signs of mental health problems. As a teenager Ms. Arias leaves home at 17 to live with her boyfriend Bobby. She also drops out of high school around this same time. If Ms. Arias is being truthful, her then boyfriend Bobby abused her physically. There is some evidence that this occurred because if you recall, Ms. Arias' brother confronted Bobby and Bobby responded by waving a sword at him. After this supposed abusive incident Ms. Arias moved in with her grandparents and at no time was her living at their home dependent on her seeking out counseling or any treatment whatsoever. If Ms. Arias' claims of being an abuse victim were true, one might consider the possibility that some counseling would be in order. Conversely, if her claims about Bobby were not true, some counseling would also be in order as well. Instead, it appears that her family continued to employ the same policy that was in place when Ms. Arias was a child, to just simply ignore the issue(s).

There were signs that Ms. Arias was mentally ill as an adult as well. If you recall, Ms. Arias, at the age of 27, came back to live with her grandparents in April of 2008. Think about it, it was around this same time that Ms. Arias' former boyfriend Matt told Sandy Arias that he was concerned about Ms. Arias. Matt expressed to Sandy that he thought Ms. Arias was bi-polar. Certainly, like me, Matt is not a trained psychologist and Ms. Arias may not actually be bi polar but that does not mean that it was proper to ignore his concerns. Despite the fact that Matt was not a trained psychologist he was certainly aware enough to realize that Ms. Arias' mental health needed to be examined. However, it seems that once Matt did the appropriate things and expressed his concerns to Sandy that, as the saying goes, the concerns he expressed to Sandy went in one ear and out the other. I might also suggest that if Matt's concerns were taken seriously by Sandy Arias maybe the events of June 4, 2008, would never have taken place.

Certainly, all of this begs the question; what should Sandy and Bill Arias have done? What should other members of Ms. Arias' family have done? To start with, they should have taken the signs of their daughter's mental health seriously when she was a child. By all accounts, they had several signs that something was wrong but they just ignored them. Why? Perhaps they did not want to acknowledge that something might be wrong. Maybe they worried it would reflect badly on them or maybe they thought Ms. Arias would grow out of it. I can only speculate as to the reasons but clearly nothing was done. Instead of taking their young daughter to get evaluated they did nothing. Think about what could have happened if they had her evaluated. Perhaps, I am right and she was a victim of sexual abuse. Perhaps she had a personality disorder. Whatever the problem actually turned out to be it could have been addressed years ago through medication or counseling. Perhaps if it had, Mr. Alexander would still be alive and Ms. Arias would be off somewhere taking pictures.

The same can be said for the warnings Sandy Arias received from Matt. What if after hearing of Matt's concerns that Sandy Arias asked her mother to impose conditions upon Ms. Arias living in her home. Just one would have done the trick. If Ms. Arias' grandmother made seeing a counselor a condition of Ms. Arias living in her home, that seemingly small act could have forced the sort of intervention that quite possibly could have prevented the tragic events that took place on June 4, 2008.

As it relates to all of this; do I blame Bill and Sandy Arias or any other members of Ms. Arias' family? Not really in the sense that too many of us ignore the signs of mental illness. Our society is replete with examples of people who are mentally ill, whose family and loved ones just did not believe it was that big of a deal. As a society we need to react to mental illness, as if it is a big deal and we should react in the same way we react to other physical ailments. Think about it, as I alluded to earlier, how many parents would rush their child to urgent care for a rash and yet ignore mood swings? Would any parent ignore their child's broken arm or hope that it will somehow heal itself? Few, if any I would assume. In contrast, how many parents who notice their child's mental health issues would sit and hope that their child grows out of it? The answer is clear, far too many.

In my mind, the lesson that parents can garner from the spectacle that was Arizona v. Jodi Arias is that you not ignore signs of mental illness in your child. Do something! At the very least, take them to a mental health professional. If it turns out everything is fine then what harm could come to your child? Conversely, if you do nothing your child could find themselves sentenced to spend the rest of their lives in prison and some other person's child could wind up dead.

Do I place all the blame on Ms. Arias' parents or parents in general? No. As hard as it is to "blame" the mentally ill person, I must admit I do to some extent. To be clear, I am not talking about the severely mentally ill who cannot function in society and/or who lack complete self-awareness. Instead, I am talking about those that are self-aware, those mentally ill people that are functioning in our society. I am talking about those mentally ill people that have jobs, maybe families and know that something is not right in their head but ignore it, perhaps hoping it will go away. Using Ms. Arias as an example, she had a job, she paid her bills, she was functioning in society but when her former boyfriend Darryl talked to her about getting some psychological help, she chose not to do anything. When yet another boyfriend expressed similar concerns, she also chose to do nothing. Ms. Arias even chose to do nothing when she moved back to Yreka in 2008. Based on her journal writings, she knew she was depressed and she did nothing. Ms. Arias knew there was something wrong with her mentally, yet she did nothing. Perhaps she thought she could handle things on her own, but regardless of the reason(s) she did not seek help. Just think how different her life and the life of Travis Alexander would have been had she gone to see a professional like people had recommended.

Certainly, a key question that arises when we discuss untreated mental illness is; why are both the functionally mentally ill and families of the mentally ill ignoring these issues? In my mind it is because there is a stigma concerning mental illness that makes those who suffer from it or those who are close to someone that they believe might be suffering tend to ignore the problem. This stigma hurts the mentally ill because they do not get the help they need and it might result in others getting hurt by those who are mentally ill. Why such a stigma exists, makes no sense to me. Would society as a whole chastise someone who was born without arms? No, that would not happen amongst the sane. Why then do we chastise a person whose brain is constructed differently? Why then do we chastise a person who has some other psychological ailment? Think about it in terms of Ms. Arias, would not every one of you reading this have preferred that she get the help she needed before she did what she did on June 4, 2008?

Putting Ms. Arias' mental health issues aside, I also believe that women who do not suffer from mental illness can also learn a valuable lesson from Ms. Arias' experiences in this relationship. Certainly, while the lesson I am about to impart is not complex, it might not be easy to hear because women tend to make this mistake over and over again. Here it comes ladies… If a man cannot give you what you want out of a relationship, it does not matter why he cannot give you those things, just get out of the relationship. While I am on my soapbox, ladies you cannot change him. If you want a religious guy who is committed to marriage and having a family, do not start dating an atheist who does not want to get married and have children. He is not going to provide you with what you are seeking. Furthermore, if you are attracted to such an individual it is probably for unhealthy reasons. Okay I will step down now, but as I do so please consider the fact that if Ms. Arias wanted marriage and family why did she remain involved in a relationship with Mr. Alexander? Not to cast aspersions on Mr. Alexander but his conduct clearly demonstrated that getting married and having a family were not his priorities. Had she ended the relationship when she realized this, it seems highly doubtful that she would be spending the rest of her life in a prison cell and Travis Alexander would still be alive.

Certainly, when we talk about the story of the relationship that Mr. Alexander and Ms. Arias shared would not have existed without Mr. Alexander's participation. To be clear, I am not saying that Mr. Alexander is to blame for his own murder or that he deserved to die in such a brutal fashion or at all for that matter. What I am saying is that Mr. Alexander should have taken steps long before the events of June 4, 2008, to rid himself of Ms. Arias. Can anyone take issue with that? I hope that we can all agree on this point. His friends, Chris and Sky Hughes told him to get away from Ms. Arias. Obviously, he did not listen. Leading one to ask the obvious question of; why did he choose to ignore the warnings that the Hughes' were giving him? Did he not take them seriously? I guess we will never know for sure but the fact that he invited Ms.

Arias into his home to have sex in June of 2008 leads one to believe that he did not take these warnings seriously. I guess the lesson is if your friends are warning you about someone you are dating, heed those warnings do not simply dismiss them.

I might also add that in my mind another key lesson to this entire case from the perspective of Mr. Alexander's role in the relationship is that if someone is driving you so crazy that your response to them is to act out of character in a negative way or engage in self-destructive behavior, end the relationship. Why do I say this? Think about it, the testimony of other women Mr. Alexander dated was that he treated them like a gentlemen should, that he did not call them names. In contrast, we know Mr. Alexander called Ms. Arias names like "whore," "slut" and "three whole wonder." Based on the testimony of the aforementioned women, if their testimony was true, this was out of character for him. Other evidence suggests that Ms. Arias was driving Mr. Alexander crazy, adding tension or drama to his life. Yet he was still having a sexual relationship with her when instead of so doing, he should have ended his relationship with her. If he had he might still be alive today.

Before you get all upset thinking that I am blaming Mr. Alexander for his own death, please pause for a minute and ponder this situation. If you were sitting with Mr. Alexander in early 2008 and he was telling you how Ms. Arias was driving him crazy, how she was making him so mad that he would call her terrible names, yet he could not end things with her because he loved having sex with her, wouldn't you advise him to distance himself from her, to stay away from her at all costs because she is not good for him? I have no doubts that you would.

Still think I am blaming Mr. Alexander for his own death? Pause again and take another breath. From what I have heard about Mr. Alexander from people that knew him, was that he was the type of person who wanted to help others. I have no reason to doubt this and it is for this reason that I have no reason to doubt that Mr. Alexander would take no issue with me warning people who are reading this who are in unhealthy relationships to simply walk away no matter how good the sex might be, no matter how hard it might otherwise be to do, simply walk away. Walk away from these unhealthy relationships before the unhealthy becomes the tragic. From what I have heard about Mr. Alexander he would want people to learn from this tragedy. I know that I certainly hope that somebody somewhere will learn this lesson.

SECTION 2

MY NEW CASE

When I worked at the Capital Unit of the Office of the Public Defender each defense team had two or three capital cases. That may not sound like a lot to you but due to the demands of a capital case two or three cases created plenty of work to keep a team busy. As fate would have it in August of 2009, my team was down to one case, which meant it was likely going to be my team's turn to get the next case. That case was "The State of Arizona v. Jodi Ann Arias." In this section I discuss being assigned this case and my initial assessment of the entire case from a legal perspective. Specifically, in Chapter 5, I discuss the day I received the file and how I thought little of it, not realizing that the day I received this file was "The Day My Life Changed Forever." In Chapter 6, "Preparing to meet Ms. Arias" I discuss the things that I did to prepare myself to meet my new client. In Chapter 7 "Meeting Ms. Arias for the First Time" I share what it was like for me to meet my new client for the first time. The rest of the Chapters in this section are dedicated to providing you with insight into my initial thoughts on the various pieces of evidence I reviewed after the life-altering day that I received the file. The Crime Scene is discussed in Chapter 8. In Chapter 9, I discuss the evidence as it relates to Ms. Arias. In Chapter 10, I discuss my initial thoughts on that iconic booking photo that was taken on the day Ms. Arias was arrested. In Chapter 11, I discuss my initial assessment of Mr. Alexander. In Chapter 12, I detail my initial thoughts on the relationship that Mr. Alexander and Ms.

Arias shared. In the last chapter of this section, Chapter 13, I discuss my initial assessment of Juan Martinez.

However, before I delve into this section I want to add a disclaimer of sorts. In this section I will discuss all of these things from a legal perspective. As you read this section, I ask you to bear in mind that I am an attorney tasked to do a job and in that regard I have to look at the situation in a more clinical manner. As I relay my thoughts to you in an equally clinical manner, please do not take this as a sign of disrespect to Mr. Alexander or his family. Please do not think that as I relay these thoughts to you that I am not conscious of the fact that this case and my client's actions caused a great deal of pain to many.

CHAPTER 5

THE DAY MY LIFE CHANGED FOREVER

Life is funny in that when you wake up on a given morning you don't often think that this particular day could change your whole life. If you
think about it it's true of everyday of our lives, but for whatever reason
it seems that most of us never give much thought to this reality. What is
even funnier, in an ironic sense, is that oftentimes a day's happenings can
change your whole life and you don't even realize it at the time. I certainly didn't recognize how my life was about to change on one particular
day in August of 2009. Illustrative of this irony is that to be honest, I do
not even recall the exact date I was assigned to serve as lead counsel in CR
2008-031021-001. You would think that I would, but it was one of those
things that at the time simply did not seem like a big deal to me. From
looking back at the minute entries I know that the exact date lies somewhere between August 10, 2009, when the Office of the Legal Defender
was allowed to withdraw and August 18, 2009, when Judge Steinle issued
his order appointing me to the case.

Though the exact date eludes me, for whatever reason, the happenings of
that day, as it relates to being assigned "my new case" are relatively fresh in
my mind. I was working in the Capital Unit of the Maricopa County Office
of the Public Defender. I was sitting in my office working on another capital
case in what was, by all accounts, an ordinary day. Given that it was August
and we were in Phoenix, it should come as a shock to no one that my capital

unit partner was on vacation on this particular day. Because she was on vacation I was then ultimately the person left to make all the decisions that would affect our team. At the time she and I only had one case which meant another case would be arriving soon as each team with the capital unit typically carried two or three cases. One other defense team was in the same situation but it came as no surprise to me that my then supervisor came to my door with a file in his hand. I immediately knew what he was up to as I had seen that look in his eyes before. I knew that the file in his hand was one that he wanted to place in my hand.

To provide you with a little context of my situation, at that time in Maricopa County most of the death penalty cases dealt with one human smuggler killing another. Those that fell outside of this category typically involved one drug dealer killing another or some other sort of gang related killing. Furthermore, many of the clients were from Mexico which made the job of a capital defense attorney all the more difficult because Maricopa County would not authorize travel to Mexico and because the politics in Arizona at the time were such that it was very tough to get a life verdict for a Mexican client. So at that point in time, if I had to take another case, I was certainly more open to something different. Looking back in this regard, I guess I should have been more mindful of that old saying, "be careful what you wish for." As a caveat, when I say "wish for," let me be clear all the cases one gets when assigned the capital unit are terrible and all of us who do this kind of work would gladly look for new careers should people stop killing each other and should the government stop making the decision to assert the immorality of killing by seeking to kill those who kill. However, as neither of these things seems to be happening, a capital defense attorney in Arizona can become quite busy with the mundane, "typical case" and might find themselves wishing for something of interest, or a case where one has a fighting chance. That is where my mindset was in August of 2009.

So as my supervisor began his attempt to put this new file in my hand he must have sensed my feelings, or perhaps he realized that every attorney in the capital unit was equally worn down from attempting to save the "typical client." Regardless, he began his "sales pitch" by telling me what a unique case this new case was. He advised me that the client was a female, who had no criminal history, which I will admit was definitely unique in the world of capital litigation. He also advised that this girl had been on a CBS program called "48 Hours" and that she was accused of killing her boyfriend. The only other thing I knew was that the case had been in the system for a while and that the Public Defender's Office was getting the case because the Office of the Legal Defender had some sort of ethical conflict that necessitated their need to withdraw from the case. Thus, when the case was presented to me, I hadn't met Ms. Arias nor did I know anything else about her or the facts of the case, I only knew the few facts my supervisor relayed to me, the sparse facts I just relayed to you.

Should you have any doubt about it, when an attorney is being asked to take a case at the Public Defender's Office, while the attorney is technically being asked, "No" is not really an acceptable answer. Typically "Yes" is the only acceptable answer. That is unless one wants to be in the proverbial doghouse with the boss. However, even if saying "No" to a particular case does not put you into the doghouse, you have to be mindful of the fact that the next case, the case you have no choice but to take may be much worse. You see, you have to understand, in capital defense work there are no "good" cases. All the options before you are awful. Sometimes it is just a matter of degree as to which case appears on the surface to be worse. So I hope that you now can understand that saying "No" to the known and awaiting the unknown to arrive is not often a wise move, especially when the known is a woman with no criminal history who killed her boyfriend and the unknown might be a person with a long criminal history who shook a baby to death because it would not stop crying. So rather than going with the unknown I went with what I thought was the lesser of two evils (silly me I know). When I took the case, I remember telling my boss that whatever happens, she won't get the death penalty. I was certainly right about that, but had I known that the resolution of this case would not come until some five years later and at such a personal toll, I would have gone for the unknown.

CHAPTER 6

PREPARING TO MEET MS. ARIAS

As I mentioned in Chapter 5, when I was assigned this case, I did not know very much about the case nor did I know much about Ms. Arias' situation. I knew that my client was named Jodi Arias. I knew that Ms. Arias, who had no criminal history, was accused of killing her boyfriend and/or former boyfriend Travis Alexander. On the day I was assigned to serve as lead counsel on the case, I didn't even have a file yet. The file itself needed to be transferred over to our office from the Office of the Legal Defender. Not only that but once we received the file, my paralegal needed to inventory everything we received before I could start reviewing the actual evidence. Such a state of affairs is not uncommon when a capital case is being transferred between offices. As you might guess, this process takes a few days. Thus, what typically occurs in situations such as this is that the newly assigned capital attorney and his or her team, if they are available, will go out to meet their client before they even know anything about the case just so the client knows who their new attorney is and so that attorney can start building rapport with the client and their family.

Of course, "The State of Arizona v. Jodi Ann Arias" was far from your typical case and rather than knowing next to nothing about the case before I met my client I had the opportunity to learn a few things about the case by watching my client and other involved parties speak about the case. If you recall when I was "sold" on the case one of the things I was told was that Ms. Arias had given an interview to a CBS program called "48 Hours Mystery." Her exact show was called "Picture Perfect" (it may still be online if you are interested). As the show was only about an hour long, I thought that before I rushed out to meet my client it would be best to watch this show. I also asked the Mitigation Specialist that was working on the case to watch the program as well so she too could get a sense of our new client and the case.

So, before I went to visit Ms. Arias, I spent close to an hour watching this show. Those of you who have seen this show know that it contains footage and pictures of Mr. Alexander himself and that Mr. Alexander's life is further illustrated by interviews with his friends and family. His death was illustrated by several crime scene photos and an interview with Esteban Flores, the man whom the Mesa Police Department assigned to serve as the lead detective in the case. Additionally, I also saw the interview that Ms. Arias gave to the CBS correspondent, Maureen Maher, during which she described her relationship with Mr. Alexander and the circumstances of his death. Her description of the circumstances of his death would later become known as the "ninja story." I also noticed that no other person spoke in support of Ms. Arias. After watching this video all the way through, I re-watched a few portions of it in an attempt to wrap my head around the entire situation.

First, I considered the location of the interview. Perhaps you might think that this is a strange thing to consider but please bear with me. From watching Ms. Arias' interview, I could tell that this interview took place in what the Maricopa County Sheriff's Office calls the Estrella Jail. The fact that this interview took place at this facility was very important to me because I knew it occurred after she was extradited to Arizona. Thus, I knew that this interview occurred after she was assigned death penalty qualified counsel. Furthermore, knowing that Ms. Arias' former attorney is well versed in capital litigation, I knew that she undoubtedly had advised Ms. Arias against doing this interview and that Ms. Arias did it anyway. Thus, before I even met Ms. Arias I strongly suspected that I had a client who would not follow the advice I gave her unless she happened to agree with it. I had every reason to believe that Ms. Arias was going to do as she pleased and that in this regard, she was going to be a difficult client. I also knew that for some unknown reason telling this "ninja story" on national television was more important to her than following the advice of her attorney. This was of course perplexing in and of itself because it was readily apparent to me that Ms. Arias was not being truthful when she told this story. She was lying. All this being said it is not as if most people guilty of a crime don't try to lie their way out of trouble, so on some level it made sense that she would lie. However, it made no sense to me why she would tell such a clearly unbelievable story on national television. I was further confounded by why she was so intent on convincing the world that this "ninja story" was true when all that really mattered at that point was that she was able to convince twelve jurors that this story was true. I began to ask myself; why would she grant this interview and say these things on tape? One possible reason that I could discern was her image, as even during this interview Ms. Arias seemed very concerned about what people thought of her. Perhaps she thought by telling this story that the world would see her as a victim not a murderer, thereby enhancing her image. I could not be sure of course I was just speculating. The other possibility was that Ms. Arias actually believed that she could convince the world that this story was the truth. However, regardless of the reasons why Ms. Arias was offering up this story, I had a good sense of the fact that when I met my new client she would likely attempt to convince me that the "ninja story" was a truthful account of the events surrounding Mr. Alexander's death.

I also knew from watching her interview that when I met Ms. Arias that I would be meeting a fairly smart and articulate person. I knew that she would be different than most criminal defendants I had encountered in the past and very different than most capital defendants in that she had no criminal history and clearly had the ability to navigate polite society. By this I mean that unlike most capital defendants, she had an actual job, she paid taxes, made car payments, bought a house, things of that nature. This may sound normal to you but it is abnormal in the world of capital defendants. The reality of capital defendants is that many of these people have done stints in prison, they earn their money in let's just say interesting ways, the kind of ways that do not get one approved for a mortgage. These are not people who tend to navigate polite society, instead they are the sort of people who tend to live and thrive in places that most of us will never find ourselves.

What all of this meant to me was that even before I met Ms. Arias, I knew enough to realize that this case would be far from the mundane. The next step was to meet my client.

CHAPTER 7

MEETING MS. ARIAS FOR THE FIRST TIME

You might think that there is no way I could forget anything about the day I met the infamous Ms. Arias for the first time. In hindsight, I probably should have made more of a note as to the exact date of this meeting and what occurred during my first meeting with Ms. Arias, but I would remind you that back then this case was not the media sensation that it became once trial began. Thus, until this case became the media sensation that it became, there was nothing truly noteworthy about anything I was doing on the case. Meeting a new client was merely part of the job, a regular occurrence. In this regard I would ask you to understand that at this time, in my mind at least, Ms. Arias was simply another client. Don't forget that in August of 2009, Ms. Arias had not yet become the infamous woman that she is now. Instead, in August of 2009, this was a capital case that had gotten some attention, but not a lot. It was also a time in which I never would have guessed that I would be writing a book about my experiences representing Ms. Arias several years later. So I guess this is my way of apologizing for not having all the exact details in my memory, but fortunately, I do have some memories.

Before I discuss my recollections of meeting Ms. Arias for the first time, I think it is important to remind you of what I articulated in Chapter 2. If you recall in that chapter, I advised you that the ultimate goal of a capital defense attorney is to save the client's life. I hope that from reading this chapter that you also came away with the understanding that as lead counsel in a capital case, saving the client's life is more important than trying to "win" the underlying criminal case. I hope that you further understand that as a capital defense attorney you accept the reality that your client will almost certainly be convicted of First Degree Murder. As you might guess, the client often has the opposite goal. By this I mean that your client is not really as concerned about their life, but instead their goal is to be found not guilty or to be found guilty of a lesser offense. Their "ultimate goal" is to get out of prison alive and they are willing to take the risks associated with trying to find a path to freedom even if that comes at the expense of their life. Clearly, these goals are not often in sync. In fact, more often than not, these goals are in direct contradiction to each other and for that reason they can create quite a conflict between the attorney and the client. That being said, laying the groundwork for such a conflict is not what you are looking to do when you first meet a new client.

One of the most important goals in an initial meeting with a capital defendant is to get to know them and establish a level of trust with that person. Why do I care if that person trusts me? I seek the trust of my clients because in order to accomplish the ultimate goal of saving that client's life, I must first have their trust. If my client trusts me they will allow me into their lives in a way that I could not obtain without their permission. Thus, my plan during an initial meeting is to listen to the client whatever, it is they want to say, I will simply sit back and listen. In listening to the client I try to learn as much as I can about them, I try to get to know them apart from the crime they are accused of committing. I try to learn where they are from, their family background. I try to get contact information for their family so that I can begin initiating a relationship with my client's family. This is very important because a client's family can also provide a lot of helpful information, information that could help spare the client's life. Listening to my client in this manner also helps me discern what is important to them. They might be angry about their inability to call their girlfriend; they might be worried about their car or their last paycheck from work it could be any number of things. Why do I care what is important to them? Learning what is important to them as soon as I can and responding as best I can is a way to build trust. Earning my client's trust makes my whole job (achieving my number one goal) a lot easier.

With these goals in mind you might correctly assume that I never talk to my clients about the charges themselves at all unless they bring them up. I never confront them about what they did or what they have said to anyone about what they did. In fact, I do all I can to avoid confrontation of any kind simply because I do not want my client to shut down or begin to question whose side I am on. I do not want them to be suspicious of my motives. I want to plant the seeds of trust.

Undoubtedly, when it came to Ms. Arias, because of the CBS program, I certainly knew some of the information that I typically seek during a normal initial meeting. I also assumed that the file would contain a great deal of other information so probing for information was not something that I needed to necessarily do. That being said I learned on day one that Ms. Arias can sure ramble on about all sorts of things, so I just listened to her for an hour or so. I learned a great deal about her that had nothing to do with the crime. Some of these things I would learn in the file but other things I would not because, as I alluded to previously, reviewing a file cannot give you a sense of a person; mere paper cannot provide you with a sense of a person's mannerisms or their disposition.

One thing that struck me about this initial meeting with Ms. Arias, though it took place in a jail and she was wearing jail clothing, her mannerisms and disposition were such that it was as if we were talking in a coffee shop. There were no conflicts, she did not press me on anything related to the case in fact Ms. Arias did not seem to care about the case at all. Consistent with this disposition, I never got the impression that she was treating me as if I were her lawyer. To be clear, I am not saying that Ms. Arias did not understand that I was her lawyer, what I am saying is rather than talking to me as one might talk to their lawyer, Ms. Arias spoke to me more like a person might talk to a stranger that she just met at a coffee shop. She was even more than a bit flirtatious at times. Undoubtedly, this was strange but once she realized that being flirtatious with me was not going to be a method through which she could manipulate me, she stopped flirting and switched to being polite and friendly without any signs of flirtation. Now certainly Ms. Arias being polite and friendly did make it easier for me to accomplish the goals I had going into this initial meeting with her in that I learned a great deal about Ms. Arias. However, in reflecting back on that day I can see that while I was attempting to get to know Ms. Arias apart from her crime and trying to lay the foundation needed to build a trusting attorney-client relationship, she was testing me. Ms. Arias was testing me because it was important to her to figure out how she could get me to follow her wishes. The fact that she tried flirting with me as a method of manipulation during our initial meeting did not come as a huge shock to me. The immature mannerisms she displayed in her CBS interview made me suspect that she was a victim of sexual abuse. Flirting with me was simply expected because I was well aware that women who were victims of childhood sexual abuse tend to learn at a very young age that flirting and/or being sexual with a man, was a way to get that man to do what the woman wanted. Certainly, I will expand on why I felt that Ms. Arias was a victim of sexual abuse elsewhere in this book, but for now let me just say that I had some pretty clear suspicions to that effect from the first day I became acquainted with Ms. Arias. Beyond all of my suspicions of my client being a victim of sexual abuse, I knew that I was dealing with a very disturbed woman. How did I know this? The best answer I can give you, in addition to the reasons I mentioned above, is that after years of practicing criminal law, one just gets a sense of these things and Ms. Arias appeared to me as a very disturbed woman.

CHAPTER 8

MY INITIAL REVIEW OF THE EVIDENCE RELATED TO THE CRIME

In the days that followed this initial meeting with Ms. Arias the evidence that the State had provided to Ms. Arias and the evidence Ms. Arias' former attorney had collected came pouring into the office. As you might guess there was a ton of stuff (little did I know that this "stuff," though plentiful, was just the proverbial tip of the iceberg). Most of the stuff that the State had disclosed included the police reports, videotapes of all the interviews related to those police reports and a ton of crime scene photos. Of note, is the fact that the disclosures that the State had made to Ms. Arias' former counsel did not include many of the text messages and emails that were destined to be shown in trial. Despite the rules, they had not been disclosed yet.

Ms. Arias' former attorney also provided me with a great deal of things that she had gathered including interviews that she had done with Ms. Arias' family as well as her school records and other things of that nature. Trust me it was a lot of stuff. Stuff that I, as the lead counsel, in the case had to review, stuff that I had to be aware of and had to digest to the point that I could determine how myself and the rest of the defense team were going to proceed with the case. In this regard, you have to keep in mind that the case itself appeared to be set in stone when I was assigned to take over. Remember, Ms. Arias' former counsel withdrew from the case only a few months before it was scheduled to go to trial. As I reviewed the evidence I could tell that my predecessor had a plan of sorts, but as it was my case now, it was now my responsibility. I had to come up with my own plan. Doing so meant that I had to begin by taking a hard objective look at the crime scene.

To that end, I had to admit to myself that it was one of the most gruesome crime scenes I have ever viewed. I further had to admit that if I found this crime scene to be gruesome the members of the jury, who were not accustomed to seeing such things, would be beyond repulsed. The scene, told a pretty clear story, a story of unmitigated rage. As Detective Flores said in his interview with Ms. Arias, whoever did this to Mr. Alexander was extremely angry. In fact, based on my experience, the killing of Mr. Alexander contained a level of emotion that one does not often see even within the brutal world of homicides. The other thing that stood out from the evidence is that this was one heck of a fight. Mr. Alexander and his attacker had quite the tussle. The fight had clearly gone from the bathroom to the bedroom and back again.

As it related to the crime scene, I had several questions. First and foremost was the question of who did this to Mr. Alexander. The State of Arizona says Ms. Arias did it and that is obvious now and I am not saying that I did not believe she did it at the time. Instead, what I am saying is that as a defense attorney I simply can't just accept the State's claims as fact and move on, I am instead obligated to explore alternative theories. Keep in mind Ms. Arias was still telling the "ninja story." Thus, much like when the Mesa Police Department first got the case I have to consider all possibilities.

One possibility, assuming that Ms. Arias was involved, was that Ms. Arias committed the crime alone. Another possibility was that she did it with the help of another person. Of course the police reports were full of interviews with people who thought Ms. Arias killed Mr. Alexander, but again, my job was to analyze the situation more deeply than that. In this regard, one prominent question was; if Ms. Arias was involved in doing this to Mr. Alexander could she have done it herself? The logical follow up to this question being; if she did do this by herself, how did she do it? Keeping in mind this was my first glance at the evidence related to the crime scene, initially it seemed difficult to believe that Ms. Arias could have done this alone. Mr. Alexander was bigger and stronger than Ms. Arias. Thus, it would make sense that he would likely prevail in a situation where the combat was hand to hand even if Ms. Arias had a knife. That being said, the logistics of the situation were such that it seemed highly improbable for Ms. Arias to have an accomplice. I say improbable because for her to have an accomplice this person would have either had to drive to Mesa with her or meet her there knowing that they were there to kill Mr. Alexander and it would seem hard for Ms. Arias to convince anyone to do that for her. This person would have had to then wait around several hours for some sort of signal from Ms. Arias. This person would have had to wait for Ms. Arias to let them know that it was time to effectuate her plan and kill Mr. Alexander. Given that Ms. Arias' cell phone was never on while she was in Mr. Alexander's house and given that Mr. Alexander's home and/or cell phone didn't contain a record of any calls to anyone during this time it would seem impossible to believe that any "signal" was ever sent to any possible helpers. So with no real evidence that there was an accomplice and with the logistical problem inherent in Ms. Arias utilizing an accomplice, I had to conclude that if Ms. Arias killed Mr. Alexander she acted alone.

Before moving forward, I realize that saying "if" Ms. Arias killed Mr. Alexander might be shocking to you. However, I ask you to keep in mind that you are reading this book several years later. You are reading this book after two trials on the issue have taken place. In contrast, when I was reviewing this evidence for the first time in August of 2009, I had to consider all possibilities. I had to consider the idea that Ms. Arias did not commit the crime and that perhaps Ms. Arias' "ninja story" was true. Now as I said before, when I talked about my review of the CBS program, the "ninja story" never made sense to me. In fact, when I initially heard this story, it made no sense to me at all. However, as I will say more than a few times in this book, what I thought was completely irrelevant. As Ms. Arias' attorney, I had to consider her story now that I had all the crime scene evidence in front of me. I had to do this for two reasons, one being to consider the merits of the story of which there truly were none and the other being to see if it could be disproven by any of the physical evidence so that I could either confront her with that evidence or be prepared if somebody else were to do the same.

In this regard, as it related to the "ninja story," as I alluded to previously, having looked at this evidence it did seem difficult to believe that one person committed this crime. However, at the same time there was no evidence that would support the idea that two "ninjas" came into Mr. Alexander's home and did this. The only relevant DNA found at the crime scene belonged to Mr. Alexander and Ms. Arias. Now you might think it is just that simple, that this lack of evidence proved that the "ninja story" was false. Not so fast, just because the crime scene did not contain evidence that two "ninjas" were in the house on June 4, 2008, that did not prove that this killing did not happen the way Ms. Arias described. Instead, disproving her story meant finding evidence that proved it to be false and in that regard, there was not a single bit of evidence that could definitively disprove this story either. Don't believe me? Don't you think if Detective Flores could have broken down or disproven Ms. Arias' "ninja story" during his interrogation of her that he would have? Don't you think if a piece of evidence that disproved her story existed that Detective Flores would have confronted her with this evidence? I certainly have no doubt that he would have. By doing so he would have begun the process of breaking Ms. Arias down to obtain a confession. Any cop would have done this. It is interrogation 101. Heck, he tried to break her down with false "facts" such as fictitious red light camera photos that proved she was in Mesa. Had he had real facts that would disprove the "ninja story" I don't doubt for a second he would have used these facts against his suspect. Instead, he only confronted Ms. Arias with the reality that there was no evidence to support her "ninja story" and that it made no sense.

Since the first trial concluded I have heard or seen many theories on what happened in Mr. Alexander's bathroom from many different people. Some of these people were well meaning attorneys or investigators who were either giving their perspective on television or who thought they were educating me on the case by detailing their theories in letters or emails. Other people, mostly supporters of Ms. Arias, also sent me letters detailing their theories on what really happened. As you might guess, almost all of these people had no background whatsoever from which to form an educated opinion. I also received many letters, again from Ms. Arias' supporters, that might be best described as conspiratorial. Lots of people seem to believe this was a Mormon conspiracy of sorts.

I could probably write a whole book responding to the various theories, but I won't (though maybe I will publish these letters someday). Instead, presently, I will simply detail the realities that this crime scene and the associated autopsy tell us. They are not complex and I could discern them easily from my initial assessment of the case. Mr. Alexander was shot in the face. The bullet traveled in a downward direction meaning that the gun was above his head when he was shot. He was stabbed in the chest and his throat was slashed. Combined, these reports also demonstrate that there was a serious struggle that the fatal blows (the stab in the chest and the slashing of the throat) came last. The defensive wounds on his hands and arms also demonstrate the fact that he was alive and struggling during this ordeal, that he was alive and struggling before the fatal blows were delivered. It was clear that Mr. Alexander was trying to fend off his attacker. We know that at some point in time he stood at his bathroom sink and aspirated blood. We also know that he ran down the hallway trying to escape his attacker. The autopsy specifically shows us that at some point during this confrontation that he suffered numerous stab wounds to his back. That is all the meaningful technical information that the crime scene tells us, period. Why doesn't it tell us more? Because the crime scene was altered by water and it was altered even further by the movement of the body, because the crime scene was altered by the desire of the person who killed Mr. Alexander to cover up the crime.

Certainly, I have more thoughts on what happened during this struggle. However, I will not go any farther with my discussion about my assessment of the crime scene in this chapter because this chapter deals only with that initial assessment and not the theories that I developed over time. However, do not worry, in Chapter 47 of this book I discuss what I believed happened on June 4, 2008. In this regard, let me point out that I used the word believed, as in the past tense of believe, intentionally. I did so because I want to be clear and I will repeat this in Chapter 47 that what I believe now is different from what I believed before the trial began. Furthermore, since this is a book about the happenings before the trial that is the only belief that I will be discussing in this book. Again do not worry my current beliefs will be part of the final book in my "Trapped with Ms. Arias" trilogy.

Having said all of this, at this point I don't want anyone to be under the impression that the clinical manner in which I'm analyzing this crime scene does not mean that I do so without thoughts of how terrible and painful the last few minutes of Mr. Alexander's life were. I know he suffered greatly but the reality is that those of us in this business: prosecutors, detectives and defense attorneys must analyze these crime scenes with a certain amount of objectivity so that we can discern what happened and do our jobs in the most effective manner.

Having said all of this, it is important to note that a crime scene does not exist in a vacuum. There are always people and physical evidence that, while not part of the crime scene per se, are relevant to determining what happened at the crime scene and perhaps even why the crime itself happened.

As it relates to the events of June 4, 2008, one obvious glaring fact stood out. Mr. Alexander's body was not found for about five days. This might not be overly surprising under other circumstances. However, it is downright shocking when you consider the fact that Mr. Alexander had two roommates, at least one of whom was present in the home on a daily basis. Certainly I was curious as to how this could occur. I found it highly suspicious that at least one of these roommates would not have detected the smell of Mr. Alexander's decomposing body when they were present in the home. Based on the reports written by the various police officers at the scene, they seemed curious about the same thing. They all had noticed this odor the second they entered the home, but the roommates were claiming that they did not notice or that perhaps some spoiled food had been left out. Based on the interviews the Mesa Police Department detectives conducted with these two roommates it seemed as if these detectives were very suspicious of Mr. Alexander's roommates as well. However, it was obvious from the interviews that these two had nothing to do with the crime. As stated earlier, the evidence pointed to this being a crime of passion, a crime of anger. One roommate was just an acquaintance and the other was more of a casual friend. They did not have the requisite anger, nor did they have any other reason to kill Mr. Alexander. The fact that they were ignorant to what had happened to Mr. Alexander and could not smell his rotting corpse for five days was certainly strange, but ultimately there was not much more that could be made of this fact.

As for who was at the home at the time Mr. Alexander was killed, the interviews with the roommates made it clear that they were not home. The only person who could be placed at the home besides Mr. Alexander was Ms. Arias. Ms. Arias was placed at the home in three different ways. First of all, she finally admitted she was there. Secondly, DNA proved she was there during the attack and of course, finally, nude pictures of her were found in Mr. Alexander's camera. Additionally, there were no signs that anyone who was not welcome in the home was actually in the home. Meaning there were no signs of forced entry but also that there was no evidence that Ms. Arias was unwelcome in Mr. Alexander's home. In fact the evidence, specifically the text message found on Mr. Alexander's phone, collected from his physical phone, the day his body was found, demonstrated that Mr. Alexander wanted Ms. Arias in his home. It also seemed to defy logic that anyone would take nude pictures of an unwanted guest.

The reports I initially received also detailed the amount of evidence that was being collected outside of the home. This evidence consisted almost exclusively of interviews that were conducted with friends and acquaintances of Mr. Alexander, many of whom described Ms. Arias as a stalker or a crazy ex-girlfriend who Mr. Alexander didn't want anything to do with.

So in terms of the evidence related to those initial police reports as it relates to the crime itself and/or the crime scene, the reality before me after my initial review was that my client was the only one known to be at the crime scene near the time of the victim's death. The further reality before me was that many people described her as a stalker ex-girlfriend. Not a good situation to be in from the perspective of the guy who was appointed to be lead counsel on the case. Not a good position to be in when you are the person who is duty bound to try to save the life of Mr. Alexander's ex-girlfriend.

CHAPTER 9

MY INITIAL REVIEW OF THE EVIDENCE RELATED TO MS. ARIAS

Because my number one goal in this case from the day I was handed the file was to earn a life sentence for my client, a key component of my initial analysis of this case was to understand who Ms. Arias was as a person. In fact, because of what my ultimate goal was who Ms. Arias was as a person, not as a murderer, was much more important to me than what she had to say about the crime. In my experience, I have found that the best way to get a sense of who someone truly is as a person is to observe them as much as possible. As it related to my clients, in most cases that would mean observations made while talking face to face with the client. With Ms. Arias I was not so limited. I had seen Ms. Arias' interview with CBS and that certainly gave me some sense of who Ms. Arias was. However, I knew that Ms. Arias had prepared for the interview and that what I saw online was only a portion of the interview. Thus, in reality, the CBS interview only provided me with a mere glimpse of who Ms. Arias was, a glimpse that made it obvious to me that if I had any hope of truly understanding Ms. Arias, I would need more. In an effort to increase my understanding, I wanted to view all I could so I could get a sense of her tone, her mannerism and to look for any signs of abnormal behavior. Fortunately for me, I had several hours of videotape to review as Ms. Arias had engaged in lengthy interviews with Detective Flores twice and a female detective from the Siskiyou County Sheriff's office once.

When I watched these videos what I saw was certainly strange. What made what I saw even more bizarre was that this strange behavior could not truly be defined psychologically. By this I mean that though I am not a psychologist, in most cases I am able to watch an interrogation and notice some form of psychological malady that I can define. For example, I might see signs that someone is delusional or perhaps paranoid. I could not do this in Ms. Arias' case instead the best I could discern is that she was strange. Certainly, this is not a true psychological term, but I based my imprecise conclusion on several observations.

This may surprise you but I took nothing from the fact that she denied being at Mr. Alexander's home on June 4, 2008. Though I knew that this was a lie, it is certainly not uncommon for someone who committed a crime to deny involvement when confronted by a detective's allegations. In fact, I think it's fair to say that an initial untruthful denial is sort of expected. Cops often use these stories as a way to break down a suspect and gain a confession later on in the interrogation. I did however take note of Ms. Arias' mannerisms when she lied. Based upon watching her on video for several hours it was abundantly clear to me that my client expected people to believe her lies. Why? At the time I wasn't sure but I had two theories as to why she might feel this way. The first being that she simply believed she could fool people, she believed that she was so smart that she could simply convince others that she was telling the truth regardless of how tall the tale might be. My other theory being that she had convinced herself that she had not killed Travis Alexander and/or her mind could not accept the reality of what had happened. This may sound strange to you but I have seen this happen with other defendants as well and at the time I certainly thought that this was a possibility.

I noticed something else about Ms. Arias when I watched these videos, Ms. Arias seemed very immature to me. Not the kind of teenage immaturity that Dr. DeMarte would testify to years later, but a child-like demeanor. In my mind when she was singing and doing handstands during interrogation she was acting like a restless child. I saw more childlike qualities when she voiced concerns about what the media might print about her arrest. Image would not be that important to a mature adult in that situation yet it was to Ms. Arias.

Having made these observations of Ms. Arias, I could certainly tell that something was off, she was strange. However, as I was still lacking any true more formal definition of who Ms. Arias was, I thought I would turn my attention to the videotaped interviews of others who knew her much better than I ever would from watching her on videotape. It was my hope that by watching these videos I would find the definition I was seeking. So I reviewed the interviews of her parents, Bill and Sandy Arias. Neither of them portrayed a very flattering picture of their daughter. Combined these interviews describe my client as being secretive, obsessed with Mr. Alexander and cold or crazy because she acted "so normal" when she returned home from Mesa. Now you may see all these things that Bill and Sandy said about their daughter as being true and they might be, but think about the fact that Ms. Arias had parents who cared so little about her that they went out of their way to throw her under the bus after her arrest. That spoke volumes to me in the sense that it did not seem as if her parents cared about her much at all. You might find this to be amusing but when you truly think about it it's very sad. Regardless of what you think about it, I hope you can see how this information did not aid me in my quest to truly define what was wrong with Ms. Arias.

While I certainly preferred videos, learning about Ms. Arias and trying to define what is wrong with her psychologically also meant reviewing all of the things that were said about her in written reports. To this end, I reviewed all of the statements that were made about Ms. Arias in the police reports related to the case and I also reviewed all of the interviews that Ms. Arias' former counsel had conducted with my client's family, friends and former co-workers. My initial observations of these interviews were that they didn't make a heck of a lot of sense to me in that they were often contradictory and perhaps more importantly they were not consistent with any specific mental health issue. Much like what I observed on tape reviewing these documents did not provide me with the definition I was seeking. What reviewing these documents did do for me is make me all the more certain that there was something wrong with my client from a psychological standpoint. The question still remained; what was wrong with her?

Keeping in mind that definitions like "strange" and "crazy" are insufficient, defining what was wrong with Ms. Arias is harder than you might think. In one interview she was a nice quiet shy girl and in the next she was some overly sexual wild woman. In some interviews she was portrayed as being clean and professional, in others she was described as lazy. The list of contradictions was nauseating and I could go on and on but I won't as doing so would serve no true purpose because I suspect it is now painfully obvious to you that what I had on my hands was a mess.

Despite this mess, despite my inability to review these materials and define what was wrong with my client, a few things stood out to me as being very important. Many who made observations on her childhood talked about Ms. Arias being "different" as a child. There was no true definition of what was meant by "different," but not playing with other children and instead preferring to draw or read were a few cited examples of how the young Ms. Arias was "different." Others who commented on her later in life talked about her being mean towards animals yet still somewhat of a loner. Additionally, as those of you who watched the trial know, these reports also contained information that Ms. Arias smoked marijuana at around 14 years of age and that she would not take showers for several days.

To some these behaviors might seem like random acts of weirdness or evidence that Ms. Arias is a "psychopath." To me it meant something completely different. Though not a definable psychological disorder, to me these observations made by Ms. Arias' loved ones and the behaviors I observed while watching Ms. Arias on video demonstrated to me that it was very likely that Ms. Arias was a victim of sexual abuse at some point in her childhood. Could I prove it with actual evidence? No. This simply became my theory based upon my observations of her.

As you might guess, absent any sort of tangible evidence, I couldn't be certain that my theory was correct nor could I be certain of when this abuse began or when it ended. Despite these limitations, I was still pretty sure that this abuse had occurred. I also felt secure in the belief that the person who victimized her was a family member or someone who was very close to her family. To be clear I'm not talking about the incident you heard about during trial when Ms. Arias was about two years of age and she was touched and/or grinded on by a slightly older male family member. Although this incident was sexual abuse, I did not believe that this incident was impactful enough to cause the sort of strange behavior that I observed during her interviews and the behavior that her family documented in other interviews. To me this incident just served as evidence that something more was going on within this family. Why? Because young children typically do not touch other children in this manner unless someone taught them to do this or told them such behavior was okay. What this incident told me was that the young family member that had done this to Ms. Arias was almost certainly, a victim of sexual abuse. Having had experience in dealing with sexual deviants my suspicion was that if there was one victim in the family there were likely more because victimizers tend to be close to their victims. Sexual abusers tend to be a person their victim trusts. Oftentimes these trusted victimizers are family members.   It was my theory that whoever victimized this child also victimized Ms. Arias and possibly other members of her family.

Again I will concede that despite the facts discussed above, I still did not have any actual proof that Ms. Arias was sexually abused in her childhood. However, other undisputable facts play a prominent role in why I feel this way. During my several years of defending those who were accused of sex crimes I learned that most, if not all of these people, the ones who actually did it, were victims of sexual abuse as a child and that this victimization tended to impose a victim mentality upon the person. Meaning after being abused sexually, the person became a victim of the entire world and whenever something bad happened to that person it was not their fault, but instead the fault of another person or the world at large. This fit Ms. Arias to a tee. The other thing I have learned over my years of dealing with sexual abuse victims who have turned into sexual offenders is that they tend to be very manipulative people. They have all these psychological issues (though no definable disorder) but they were able to blend into society, they were able to make everyone think that they were normal and trustworthy. In my mind this also fit the profile of Ms. Arias to a tee.

There was one other factor as well, that in my mind, clearly supported the idea that Ms. Arias was sexually abused as a child. Angela, Ms. Arias' sister went to rehab for substance abuse as a teenager (I can note this because she recently tweeted about being sober for 7 years and I can do simple math). Clearly, something was going on with the Arias girls, something that wasn't normal. Did Angela's situation provide me with actual proof that my client was victimized sexually as a child? No. However, as the saying goes "where there is smoke there is fire" and there sure was a lot of smoke signaling that my client had been sexually abused as a child.

This became my working theory after obtaining an initial sense of who my client was at the time she came to be my client. For those of you who are curious, over the course of time, I must admit that I did not find any evidence that proved my suspicions to be true. Unfortunately, there are no diagnostic tools that can discern who has been a victim of childhood sexual abuse. If there were I certainly would have used them on Ms. Arias before trial began.

CHAPTER 10

MY INITIAL THOUGHTS ON THE BOOKING PHOTO

Recently, I was driving home from the office and I heard the old Rod Stewart song "Every Picture Tells a Story." Great song, but that is not why I bring it up. I am bringing it up because as I listened to the song on this occasion, I did not just enjoy it, I also reflected on what a true statement Mr. Stewart was making. Every picture does tell a story. Think about it, I suspect that most of you have seen pictures of someone and feel quite comfortable about making a least some assessments about the person in the picture. For whatever reason, all of us feel as if we can make some judgment about an individual based merely on what you see in his or her picture. Why we feel we can do this, is probably beyond the scope of this book, but let's face it we do it all the time. Should you have any doubts about what I am saying, pick up any magazine, I suspect it will be full of photographs placed there by advertisers who are hoping that the story that the viewer creates from the advertiser's picture will motivate us to buy their product. However, as this is not a book about the psychology behind advertising and instead is a book about Ms. Arias and her case you may be beginning to wonder, why I am bringing any of this up. Simple, because I think it provides a great context for how I had to view Ms. Arias' booking photo when I first reviewed the evidence. I had to be concerned about what story this picture would tell the world at large as well as Ms. Arias' jury.

I'm sure most of you have seen it. You have seen the tilted head, the smile and the wide open eyes. If by chance you have not seen this photo in a while you may want to search online for it before reading on so you know exactly what I am talking about. Of course, now that many of you have just looked at this photo with Rod Stewart's song in mind, I suspect that you have either created your own story or you are working on it.

As for my initial thoughts on this photo, I first have to confess that the oddness of this photo was overpowering. What I mean by this is that this booking photo was so distinct from any other booking photo I have seen during my career, which is saying something because I have seen a lot of booking photos. As you might guess, most booking photos are taken of people who are at a low point in their life. They may be scared, angry, drunk, high, ashamed or some combination of all of the above. What they are not is happy. Until I saw Ms. Arias' booking photo, I had not seen a single one in which the arrested person looked so darn happy. It was the joy that Ms. Arias seems to be expressing in this photo that stood out to me when I initially saw this photograph, when I let this picture begin to tell its story to me. Moving forward, the story this picture seemed to tell was that my client was thrilled to be taking the photograph. That Ms. Arias was thrilled with the idea that people worldwide would see this photo. She seemed thrilled that she would be known world-wide for something, even if that something was being arrested for murder. Likewise, in this photo Ms. Arias showed no sign of shame for what she had done to place her in this position. In fact, it seemed to me as if Ms. Arias posed for this photo with a sense of pride that would only be seen in a person who was severely mentally ill.

However, as I have often said in this book what I thought would not matter in the end. The only people whose thoughts would matter in the end would be those people who were on the jury. As it related to the story that this picture would tell the jury, I assumed that they would likely draw the same conclusions I just described, my only hope was that the amount of mental illness that this photograph depicted would save her life.

CHAPTER 11

MY INITIAL REVIEW OF THE EVIDENCE RELATED TO MR. ALEXANDER

In all capital cases the defense attorney will learn, at the very least, a bit about the person who was killed. However, when a capital defense attorney has a case in which the victim and his or her alleged killer had a relationship of some kind that attorney will learn a lot about the victim. That attorney will learn a lot about the victim in such situations because it is that attorney's job to make sure the jury understands why the killing took place so that the jury can decide what the defendant's fate should be if they convict that person of First Degree Murder.

Many might say that this amounts to "dragging the victim through the mud." In fact, this mantra seems to be the rally-cry of many a pundit who gets on television and launches into a verbal tirade about defense attorneys or our criminal justice system. What those who feel this way seem to be forgetting is that the United States Supreme Court clearly disagrees with them. So let me remind those of you who feel this way, that in the years that have followed the legalization of the death penalty by this same court, the Supreme Court has mandated that the jury must consider the circumstances of the offense when considering a sentence of death. Thus, as it related to Ms. Arias' case her jury needed to consider the dynamics of the relationship she shared with Mr. Alexander before a lawful sentence could be rendered. In fact, as I will often repeat in this book, if I had not presented such evidence Ms. Arias would likely be getting a new trial.

Having offered all this information to you, those waiting for me to apologize for doing my job had best not hold their breath because they will be waiting a long time, in fact, such an apology will never come. Furthermore, I will make no apologies about repeating the reality of the evidence that had to be collected and/or presented throughout this book. "Facts are stubborn things."

As it relates to Mr. Alexander, the hard part about trying to get an accurate assessment of who he truly was in the early stages of the case had nothing to do with a lack of information. Instead, the problem was that so much of the information was either inaccurate or contradictory to other evidence. Thus, as I made my initial assessment of him, I had to question the accuracy of all information related to who he was. For example, as it related to something as basic as his job, some said he was a motivational speaker, others described him as an insurance salesman and he was also described as an Executive Director for a company known as Pre-Paid Legal.

As I digested all of this I surmised that all these descriptions were about half right. While Mr. Alexander had the title of "Executive Director" that title seemed to me to be a temporary title because this title had to be earned in that having such a title was not a "job" per se but ultimately related to how many legal insurance policies he got others in his "down line" to sell. To explain further my initial assessment of Mr. Alexander's employment situation led me to understand that ultimately Pre-Paid Legal is a multi-level marketing company that bestows money and titles to those who begin by selling the product themselves and then move into various positions where they motivate their onetime customer to sell the policies. When you understand this pyramid and/or structure you can see how Mr. Alexander was not truly just an insurance salesman. Furthermore, by understanding this structure you can also see that using the term "motivational speaker" to describe his career is also a tad misleading in that he was not giving motivation speeches to the masses. Instead, these motivational talks were made towards a captive audience in an attempt to motivate those in the audience to sell these insurance policies to others so that they, as individuals, and those higher up on the pyramid would make more money. So what was Mr. Alexander's job? He worked for a multi-level marketing company whose product was legal insurance.

Beyond what he did for work, it was clear to me early on, as I reviewed the evidence in this case, that Mr. Alexander had a rough childhood. While rough might be a relative term. I doubt many would dispute that being raised by drug addicts and not having food to eat would qualify as rough. It was universally believed that he had overcome his rough childhood to become a successful person. As an adult Mr. Alexander was described as a flirt, a player and also a 30 year old virgin. It was also said that on a personal level he was very generous, very charismatic and very kind. It was readily apparent to me that Mr. Alexander was almost universally thought of as a great guy to be around and a good friend. During my initial assessment of Mr. Alexander I had no reason to believe that most, if not all, of these things were not true and frankly time has not changed that assessment. That being said, it was obvious from the beginning that there was another side to Mr. Alexander, a side that many of his friends and family did not know.

On a spiritual level he was described as a devout Mormon who was living by the dictates of the church to such a degree that he wouldn't even drink caffeine. Most people also thought that he was very well off financially because he had a big house and drove a BMW. In contrast to these descriptions, the bank statements I saw during my initial review of the evidence showed me that his financial situation was far from what many thought it was. Likewise, the nude pictures of Ms. Arias that he took on the day of his death demonstrated the clear reality that he was not a 30 year old virgin. These pictures further demonstrated that despite the fact that most of his peers thought he was living a chaste life, he was not, in fact, these pictures demonstrated that his lifestyle was far from chaste.

So what did all this mean to me? I saw him as a person who was loved by many but who, at the same time, was not who people thought he was. He was a guy who was hiding more than a few things from most of the people who cared about him. Not just in a way that involves not telling everyone you meet your deepest darkest secret. Instead, he seemed to be living a lie. He seemed to be living the sort of lie that placed him in a position where he could not be himself because that would damage the image others had of him. Certainly this was just my opinion, my initial assessment of this man and frankly, I found it to be very sad.

CHAPTER 12

MY INITIAL REVIEW OF THE EVIDENCE RELATED TO THE RELATIONSHIP

It is not typical in a capital case for the alleged killer and the victim to have much of a relationship at all. It is even more atypical for them to be romantic partners and/or lovers. That is not to say that former romantic partners and/or lovers do not have disputes that end in the tragedy known as murder. Sadly, killings of this nature happen all the time. However, such killings are most often considered second degree murder or manslaughter. Rarely are such killings charged as First Degree Murders. It is even rarer for such crimes to be charged as a capital offense.

Rare or not, the State wanted to kill my client because she had killed her lover. However offended I was by this disparity, I realized that how they charged other cases of a similar nature or the penalties that other defendants received under such circumstances would not matter in the end for Ms. Arias. Instead, I knew that the relationship she shared with Mr. Alexander would play an important role in whether or not the State would be successful in their quest to kill my client. I say this because I knew that beyond the legal requirements that I referenced throughout this book, related to the circumstances of the offense, when the jury was at that point in time when they were going to choose between life or death that these twelve people would almost certainly like to know what happened within the context of this relationship that would lead it to end in such a brutal killing. So what did I know about this relationship after making my initial assessment of the evidence?

I knew that nearly every person who spoke to the police about the relationship told a different story. To elaborate, as I mentioned earlier, I reviewed the interview Ms. Arias had given to the CBS program "48 Hours." If you recall, as it relates to the relationship, she described it as a sexual relationship and described it in a way that made it sound as if they were boyfriend and girlfriend. However, when asked to label the relationship, the label Ms. Arias used was a "friendship." Hearing Ms. Arias describe the relationship and the label she put on it made it hard to tell if these two were in love with each other or friends who also happened to be secret "sex buddies." Adding to the confusion were the statements of many of Mr. Alexander's friends and in particular, the comments made by Chris and Sky Hughes.

In the interviews with CBS, Chris and Sky described the relationship and how it began at a convention that took place in the fall of 2006, how Ms. Arias borrowed a dress from Ms. Hughes and how they all went to the "Executive Ball." The Hughes described how their home served as a rendezvous point for Ms. Arias and Mr. Alexander after the convention was over. They went on to describe how in their eyes Ms. Arias was being clingy and obsessive towards Mr. Alexander and how this sort of behavior led them to feel scared to have Ms. Arias in their home. Without shedding a tremendous amount of light on the topic they also described how after asking Ms. Arias to leave their home the relationship she shared with Mr. Alexander went "underground" and that from this point forward they did not know the full extent of it.

In their interviews with Detective Flores they told a substantially similar story about this relationship. However, in this interview, they said something that they had not mentioned before, something that I found to be particularly interesting. In October of 2008, when they were being questioned about Mr. Alexander's temper and/or the possibility that there might have been domestic violence of some sort in his relationship with Ms. Arias, the Hughes talked about Mr. Alexander hitting things but not people. Not terribly interesting in and of itself but then Chris Hughes expanded on that thought by making the comment that he could see Mr. Alexander pushing Ms. Arias if he really got mad. I found this comment interesting because here was one of Mr. Alexander's best friends telling the lead detective in the case that he could see Mr. Alexander pushing Ms. Arias around. Perhaps Detective Flores did not share my interest in this comment because he did not follow up on that comment. Perhaps he knew that any follow up would not serve him well.

Apart from Chris and Sky Hughes, Mr. Alexander's other friends and/ or roommates that were interviewed by the police during the early stages of the case each had their own thoughts. These thoughts pretty much revolved around the same theme. That theme being that Ms. Arias was a crazy exgirlfriend that Mr. Alexander wanted nothing to do with. The theme continued to include that the two did not have a sexual relationship because Mr. Alexander followed the principles of his faith which would not allow for him to engage in premarital sexual relations.

In addition to all the statements Ms. Arias and others had made about this relationship, there was also some objective evidence that spoke volumes about the relationship that Mr. Alexander and Ms. Arias shared. To be clear, I am not talking about the bulk of the text messages and emails that came out at trial. Nor am I talking about the "sex tape." Remember that in August of 2009, I had yet to obtain this evidence. Instead, what I am talking about is the nude photographs of Ms. Arias and Mr. Alexander that were recovered from Mr. Alexander's camera. Why were these photographs important to my initial assessment of the relationship? Remember my earlier reference to the Rod Stewart song "Every Picture Tells a Story?" Well to me these pictures certainly told a story. First, they told me that in direct contrast to what many of Mr. Alexander's friends believed, Mr. Alexander was having a sexual relationship with Ms. Arias. Secondly, the fact that these people had no idea that Mr. Alexander and Ms. Arias were seeing each other told me that the realities of this relationship were a secret to others besides Chris and Sky Hughes. Perhaps the most important thing that these pictures told me was that if Mr. Alexander told others that he wanted nothing to do with Ms. Arias he wasn't being truthful, that this relationship was part of the lie he was living. I felt this way because if one does not want anything to do with a former romantic partner one does not have a sexual interaction with them and take photographs of the encounter. These photographs also told me that Mr. Alexander was not acting consistent with the beliefs he professed to follow because he was having sex with Ms. Arias. Finally, the fact that nude pictures were being taken and that these photos were very graphic gave me a strong suspicion that this sexual relationship did not start on the day the photographs were taken, but rather, that this sexual relationship was longstanding, intense and unrestrained.

So what were my initial beliefs about this relationship? That Ms. Arias and Mr. Alexander had a very intense relationship and that sex played a huge role in this relationship. That because this relationship was so sexually charged, the full extent of the relationship had to be kept a secret. To be clear, I don't mean that it was a secret because they didn't broadcast their sex lives to the world around them. Instead, what I am saying is that their relationship had to be broadcast to the world in a way that nobody would suspect that sexual relations were taking place. What I am saying is that due to their shared faith the sexual aspects to their relationship was the couple's dirty little secret (on a side note, I am not stealing this line from Lifetime, it was a line I wrote and later gave to Ms. Willmott for her opening that Lifetime took and used as their movie title).

I also suspected that love played a part in this relationship. It seemed to me that if this was simply a relationship between secret "sex-buddies" that these two would not have interacted so much in non-sexual settings or in so many non-sexual ways. Had the two just been "sex-buddies," there would not have been so much passion between them. In my mind the clear reality of this relationship seemed to be that on some level they either loved one another or were mutually addicted to the relationship.

CHAPTER 13

My Initial Review of Mr. Martinez

At the time I got the case in 2009, for whatever reason I had never had the opportunity to have a case against Juan Martinez. However, the fact that I had not done battle with Mr. Martinez before I was assigned this case did not mean that I did not have other sources of information about him. There were court opinions that mentioned him by name talking about how it was always nuclear war with him and how if the court sustained an objection he would merely repeat the same question. I took from this that the guy did what he wanted and didn't care about what others thought of him, including the court.

I had also heard stories of him referring to a former colleague, a man who happened to be Jewish, as Hitler. I had heard stories of him arguing that the defendant was into necrophilia with no evidence whatsoever supporting such a claim just because he thought making this claim would help get the person sentenced to death. I had heard stories of him claiming that certain evidence did not exist when he knew that this evidence did in fact exist. These were just a few of the stories but suffice it to say he was not well thought of within the defense community, not because of the convictions he obtained but because of the way he operated.

All of this left me with the impression that Juan Martinez was a no holds barred kind of guy. The kind of guy who feels like the ends justify the means and for that reason he feels comfortable with being so caustic in the courtroom.

SECTION 3

PREPARING FOR THE GUILT PHASE

E arlier in this book I referenced that when I got the file in August of 2009, that it appeared to me that the case was pretty much set in stone. While certainly that was true of some aspects of the case, as it related to other aspects of the case my original assessment could not have been more wrong. Why was I so wrong? Because as time went on new evidence emerged that mandated further investigation and caused the case to go in many directions that I could not have accounted for in August of 2009. In this section I discuss obtaining that new evidence. Specifically, in Chapter 14, I talk about obtaining the text messages and the significance of this evidence. In Chapter 15, I talk about obtaining the e-mails and the significance of this evidence. In Chapter 16, I talk about the ordeal that was "The Letters." In Chapter 17, I discuss obtaining the infamous "sex tape." In Chapter 18, I talk about what more I had learned about Travis Alexander since I first received the file. In Chapter 19, I talk about reviewing Ms. Arias' jail calls. In Chapter 20, I talk about getting past the infamous "ninja story". In Chapter 21, I talk about the importance or lack thereof of the murder weapons. In Chapter 22, I talk about Ms. Arias' Supposed guilt phase witnesses and I end this section with Chapters 23 and 24 wherein I discus the important interviews that took place since I had obtained the file. A new stone had indeed emerged.

CHAPTER 14

THE TEXT MESSAGES

When I first got the case there were a few text messages but not many. The few text messages that I had were part of the initial discovery and in essence were what the Mesa Police Department actually found on Mr. Alexander's phone when they recovered it from his house. If you recall, they would have found this phone within a day or two of Mr. Alexander's body being found, so this phone would have been recovered between June 9, 2008 and June 11, 2008. At that time, the case was a "who-done-it," as the Mesa Police Department was trying to figure out who had committed this crime. Thus, it would be understandable at that point in time that the text messages of interest to the Mesa Police Department were those that might aid them in figuring out "who-done-it." Their interest was to learn who Mr. Alexander was communicating with via text message in the days before his death with the hope of learning who might have had the motivation to kill Mr. Alexander. They were looking for evidence of an argument, threats and that sort of thing. They were not looking to get into the complete history of Mr. Alexander's relationship with Ms. Arias.

When I got the case a year or so later, the case was not a "who-done-it." As I never believed the "ninja story," I did not need to determine who did it. Instead, I needed to present the circumstances of the offense to the jury not only as it related to any legal defenses Ms. Arias might have but also as it related to the sentence she was to receive. Thus, I needed whatever evidence

I could get my hands on that would demonstrate to a jury the history of the relationship these two people shared. Not only that but if the relationship itself gave rise to any psychological issues or conditions I needed to explore those issues and then decide if I wanted to present that evidence to the jury. These are just a few of the reasons that I needed the text messages. To be clear, without going into too much legal detail, I do mean that I needed these text messages because if evidence existed that helped to demonstrate the dynamics of this relationship and I did not seek out such evidence, that would be the kind of thing that would likely result in a conviction and/or sentence being overturned for ineffective assistance of counsel. In conjunction with my need for these messages, the law on Ms. Arias' right to have these messages is pretty clear, I was entitled to have these text messages, in fact the law said that the State was obligated to give them to the defense. The fact that the State had not given them to me meant one of two things, either there were no text messages or the State was not complying with the law. In this regard, I knew that the text messages existed. So the issue became forcing the State to comply with the law. Yes, I do mean force because had the State been complying with the law, they would have been turned over already.

Given the State's failure to follow the rules, it became obvious to me that I would not obtain these text messages without court intervention. So, as you might guess, I sought such intervention from the court. I filed a Motion to Compel the text messages (this was just one of many such motions I filed). The response from the State was that these messages did not exist. Eventually, after several weeks of litigation, the State, motivated by court intervention, served a search warrant on the cell phone companies and wouldn't you know it the results came back and there were hundreds of text messages. So it appears that they did exist, not shocking to me at all.

When I finally received these text messages, I did not receive them directly from the phone companies themselves. Certainly, I would have preferred this so that I could feel more confident that the messages themselves were unaltered. However, it is amazing how the State when called out for violating the rules suddenly cares about them when it is to their advantage.

So instead of my preferred course, the phone companies sent their data to the State, then the State gave them to the defense. Thus, after several weeks of litigation and several weeks of waiting, I had the information that I needed and the information that should have been automatically handed over to me when I first received the file.

Once all was said and done with this superfluous litigation, as I alluded to earlier, I ultimately received hundreds and hundreds of messages many of which were not spelled out in a cohesive manner. As you might guess, it took several days, if not weeks to go through these conversations and make sense of them. These two texted each other a lot, almost every day and in fact they often texted several times a day. This fact in and of itself spoke volumes to me, regardless of the content of the messages because it demonstrated to me that these two were really involved in each other's lives on so many levels. The frequency of the text communication between these two also demonstrated to me that there was no point in time where Mr. Alexander tried to disengage from Ms. Arias by actually not communicating with her, he always either responded to her text messages or initiated a conversation. Thus, these messages, even putting their content aside, made it obvious that, instead of wanting nothing to do with Ms. Arias as he told others, the objective data told a much different story, that he was very into Ms. Arias. These text messages were thus further evidence of the reality that Ms. Arias was not a "stalker ex-girlfriend" but at the very least she was Mr. Alexander's friend and sexual partner.

Before we talk about the content of these messages, I think it is important to note the value of these text messages as evidence. In my mind, these text messages were so valuable because, they were very genuine and objective. By genuine and objective, I mean that both Ms. Arias and Mr. Alexander wrote these text messages at a time when neither had an incentive to fabricate these messages or send messages with any kind of secret motive behind them. In fact, just the opposite was true in that both of them were likely authoring these text messages thinking that nobody but themselves would ever read them. Sadly, they were wrong but the fact that they both wrote with such a mindset would make the content even more valuable because they were genuine and objective.

Moving on to the content, the thought that repeatedly popped in my head was "Wow this stuff is amazing." I was quite amazed by the content of these messages in that these text messages provided me with a greater insight into this relationship than I ever would have assumed to be possible. Because these two communicated so frequently and substantively via text message, these text messages, rather than containing a few bits of supplementary information, were instead a treasure trove of substantive information that was highly instructive to me both because of the content and because this content was created at a time when neither of the parties could have contemplated that I, or anyone else, would be reading them. Nor was this content created at a time when either party would be aware of the reasons why I was reading them. Reading these text messages as a whole really illustrated the chaos inherent in this relationship. In one text Mr. Alexander might tell Ms. Arias that he didn't want anything to do with her then the next text message, that would likely be sent within a few hours, he would say how beautiful he thought she was. In some messages to Ms. Arias, Mr. Alexander classified her as an evil liar and in others he loved her and she was awesome. The chaos was so extreme that Mr. Alexander even threatened to destroy Ms. Arias by turning everyone she cared about against her. This in and of itself was remarkable but what was even more remarkable was that for whatever reason the two kept talking to each other after Mr. Alexander made this threat, after this intense fight they had over text messages. Thus, one of the clear bits of insight that I gained from these text messages was the relationship that these two shared was chaotic to say the least and that during his arguments with Ms. Arias, Mr. Alexander certainly did not hold back, it was obvious that he was comfortable articulating his anger.

The text messages also clearly illustrated the fact that this relationship was about more than what the two would likely call a friendship and chaos that was inherent in this "friendship." These text messages demonstrated that sex was an important part of this relationship, a very important part of the relationship. They would talk of "BJs," talk of "mouth hugs" both of which were references to oral sex. There were references to Ms. Arias being spanked by Mr. Alexander and other references to anal sex. There were text messages about sexual intercourse and references to each other's genitalia. In fact, there were so many of these that they tended to blend together but to this day one conversation stands out just because I remember how funny I found it. Funny because in one text Ms. Arias was talking about how she groomed her vagina for Mr. Alexander and in the next text she asserted her support for Mitt Romney in the upcoming election. To my knowledge Mr. Romney did not accept Ms. Arias' endorsement.

Keep in mind too that there were other text messages that were found on Ms. Arias' Helio phone, the phone that she had believed to be stolen. Once in my possession, my analysis uncovered many things but limiting my discourse to the subject of the chapter, we found some text messages that were quite graphic. Text messages from Mr. Alexander sent to Ms. Arias in which he talked about nude photo shoots he wanted her to participate in and how she would feel like she had been raped after they were done, really very graphic stuff.

So what did all this mean to me? What conclusions did I draw from all of these text messages? My overarching thought was one of sadness. Why sadness? Well you see, apart from the sensational texts, the sexual texts and those texts filled with anger, there were also many texts that were non-sexual, loving or downright mundane. Thus, when taken as a whole, on a personal level reviewing these messages just made me feel sad. It was as if I was watching two people running towards a cliff that neither of them could see but not being able to warn them because it was too late, they had already fallen.

As a professional analyzing this relationship, it was clear to me that no matter how badly Mr. Alexander and Ms. Arias treated each other they were, for whatever reason, dedicated to this relationship regardless of how unhealthy it was. Thus, as a professional my initial review of these messages did not just provide me with insight, it also gave rise to more questions, all of which focused around the dedication these two seemed to have to their relationship. The most prominent question in my mind was; why did these people still interact with each other? Think about it, in some of these text messages Mr. Alexander expressed such disdain for Ms. Arias that you might conclude that he would want nothing more to do with her. Conversely, why did Ms. Arias continue interacting with Mr. Alexander after he expressed so much disdain for her? Why didn't she simply move on? She had other options, like Ryan and probably many others. I guess we will never really know the actual reasons but it is obvious from these text messages that they were connected and/or addicted to each other in some way. Another question that came to my mind was; why did their sexual relationship continue after they broke up, after Mr. Alexander was dating other women? I suppose many have asked this question. I suspect many have wondered why didn't Mr. Alexander just walk away from Ms. Arias? One answer might be that it was the sexual component of their relationship that was at the heart of this connection and/or addiction and that could be the reality of the situation. However, I suspect this is another of those questions for which there is not one undisputable answer. I suspect many of you have theories as to why Ms. Arias didn't just walk away from Mr. Alexander and visa-versa but ultimately, they are just that, theories.

Certainly, the focus of my interest when I reviewed these text messages related to the text messages that were exchanged between Mr. Alexander and Ms. Arias but as you might guess, these two sent text messages to other people as well. These messages were also of interest to me simply because they could shed some light on both of these individuals in terms of how they interacted with other people. Most of these messages were not of interest to me because they just did not hold any relevance to the case. You see I did not have any interest in Mr. Alexander's business activities, his meeting schedule, things of that nature. Likewise, I had no real interest in Ms. Arias' activities of this nature as these things did not really matter they did not provide insight into the story I need to tell.

That is not to say that all of the text messages that these two sent to others were irrelevant, in fact, far from it. Instead of being irrelevant, many of these messages were highly relevant to the story I needed to tell as these messages gave a great deal of insight about one party to the relationship, Travis Alexander. What I am referring to specifically are those text messages which demonstrate the clear undisputable reality that Mr. Alexander was sending text messages of a sexual nature to other women. When I bring these messages up I suspect that many of you may think that I was interested in these messages so I could "trash Mr. Alexander" or otherwise "bash the victim." I hear accusations of this type all the time and I will certainly address these accusations in greater detail in future books but for now let me pose this question to you; is it "bashing the victim" if it is the truth? My answer to that question is "No." You may have a different answer but you cannot legitimately dispute that the content of these messages are the truth in that these are the texts Mr. Alexander sent to other women. I realize that this may upset some of you but as is one of my mantras in this book, "facts are stubborn things" and the facts are that Mr. Alexander sent graphically sexual messages to other women and in so doing Mr. Alexander revealed that he was certainly not a one woman man. These messages also revealed the clear reality that Ms. Arias was not his only sexual partner and that if he had it his way Ms. Arias would be just one of many. To be clear, I don't say this to judge the activity but these text messages did in fact reveal that Mr. Alexander was much more active with the other sex than was Ms. Arias. There is no doubt about it Ms. Arias did flirt with Ryan over text messages. However, rather than sending flirtatious emails to members of the opposite sex Mr. Alexander was sending messages describing the sexual acts he wanted to engage in with the recipients of these messages or reliving the moments when he was between their legs.

Undoubtedly, as you read my words, many of you might now be thinking, so what? You might be questioning why this is important. You might be thinking that Mr. Alexander was free to have sex with whomever he wanted and that he did not deserve to be killed for acting in such a manner. To that I would say that you are right for the most part in that he was free to have sex with whomever he wanted and he did not deserve to be killed for engaging in this behavior. However, you are wrong when you say it is not relevant in the sense that the Supreme Court says it is highly relevant to present the circumstances of the offense to the jury in a death penalty case, so relevant in fact that my failure to do so could have led to a reversal. Furthermore, I would assert that if you are of the mindset that I mentioned above, you are also wrong as it relates to this case specifically in the sense that these text messages negate any argument that Ms. Arias is responsible for luring Mr. Alexander into the evils of sex. Now you may believe that is what she did but the facts, those stubborn things that they are, demonstrate that this is not true.

Before I end my discussion about these messages, I think it is important to note that one more alarming thing about these messages stood out to me right away and still stands out to me today. You see when I began reviewing these messages it was readily apparent that, apart from those found on Ms. Arias' Helio phone, several text messages were missing from certain conversations. Was this intentional? If it was, I will never know but I certainly had my concerns that someone had deleted some data, but I could never prove it at the time, but who knows what will come to light in the days to come, perhaps someone will uncover more messages.

CHAPTER 15

THE EMAILS AND OTHER ONLINE COMMUNICATIONS

M uch like was the case with the text messages, the e-mails and other online communications that played a role in this case fit into a category of evidence that under the law the State was required to automatically provide Ms. Arias. However, just as was the case with the text messages, when it favored Ms. Arias the State seemed to lack interest in complying with the rules. I guess maybe the State was hoping I would just sit back and ignore this situation and/or assumed that I would simply accept the idea that the law was being followed. However, that is not the kind of defense attorney I am. I know that certain prosecutors try to skirt the rules and I never stand for it, so after I filed another Motion to Compel and went through the requisite wrangling, I once again obtained information that I should have been given without having to raise the issue. The payoff was big.

The payoff was big in many ways. Certainly, there were a ton of e-mails and online "chats" but it was not the amount that created the big payoff but rather the content of these exchanges or conversations. That is to say that the number of exchanges was far less important than the content of these communications because it was the content that provided me with a great deal of insight into not only the relationship that Mr. Alexander and Ms. Arias shared but also provided insight into the relationship that Mr. Alexander had with other people. Furthermore, much like was the case with the text messages I found these online communications of particular importance because they were written at a time when the writer never thought they would be seen by anyone other than the person they were talking with. In this regard, they were pure, they were objective.

As it relates to these online communications, I always found it strange that two people who had an intimate relationship would spend so much time conversing with each other by e-mail or in online chats. Perhaps it is a generational thing but I have been married over 20 years and I have never had an online chat with my wife, not even one, she and I actually talk in person or on the phone. So I guess it would be natural for me to wonder; why didn't they just talk to each other? I always assumed that my questions about this were related to the fact that I was an old guy who just did not realize that this is how things are done by a younger generation. Certainly, there is an element of truth to that theory, however, even as I write this book and reflect back on these communications, I cannot help but consider the possibility that perhaps there were deeper psychological issues that motivated this choice that perhaps "talking" over the computer made them less vulnerable to each other's words. Perhaps I was thinking about it too much and I guess ultimately that this might be one of the things we will just never completely understand about this relationship.

As to the content of these messages, they were obviously very enlightening as to the relationship and what was going on between these two people. Like with the text messages many of them blend together but a few of them stood out.

One e-mail that stands out to me still to this day is the e-mail that Ms. Arias sent to her friend Abe. If you recall, this e-mail became a big deal during the second trial. However, to me this e-mail was a big deal on the day I read it, for reasons that were far different from those that were discussed on social media during the second trial. Instead, upon my initial reading of the e-mail it was significant to me because Ms. Arias was sending an e-mail to Mr. Alexander in an effort to demonstrate to him that she was telling her friend Abe that it was best for them not to hug or spend time together. Why was this important? Because this e-mail made it clear that at some point in time Mr. Alexander and Ms. Arias had a conversation or conversations about the interactions and/or relationship that Ms. Arias had with Abe. Just as clear was the fact that Mr. Alexander did not approve of any continued interaction between Ms. Arias and Abe. In my mind, this e-mail evidenced the fact that Mr. Alexander wanted some sort of proof that Ms. Arias had taken steps to alter and/or terminate that relationship and that he felt as if he had the power to ask for it. Why were these things important? Primarily because Ms. Arias wrote the e-mail rather than tell Mr. Alexander, who at the time was not her boyfriend, that she was free to talk with whomever she wanted. Her choice to write this e-mail then told me that Ms. Arias was very inclined to do what Mr. Alexander wanted thereby proving to him that he was right, he did have a fair amount of power and control over Ms. Arias.

Additionally, we also have the online "chats" that Ms. Arias and Mr. Alexander engaged in over the course of their relationship. As was the case with the text messages these conversations were worth their weight in gold because they were written with the idea that nobody would ever see them. There were several of these chats. The most important chats from my perspective took place in May of 2008. I see these chats as the most important between the two because it is during these chats that Mr. Alexander refers to Ms. Arias as a "whore," a "slut," a "three whole wonder" and a "corrupted carcass." Granted, these are just the highlights but obviously these are horrible things to say to a person. What was amazing to me at the time I reviewed these chats is how Ms. Arias simply took it and did not return fire by calling him names. Heck, she did not even stand up for herself enough to put an end to the conversations. Instead of logging off, she just took it. It was also amazing to me that conversations that included such verbal venom continued after such venom was vocalized. If Mr. Alexander really thought Ms. Arias was a whore and a slut why was he still talking to her and why was Ms. Arias willing to keep talking to Mr. Alexander after he said these things to her. Even trained experts can only speculate as to why this was the case but it was definitely becoming even clearer to me that these two were, for lack of a better way of saying it, addicted to each other.

As those of you who watched the trial likely know, another set of e-mails was important to understanding the relationship that Mr. Alexander and Ms. Arias shared and these e-mails certainly stood out to me right away as well. If you have not guessed already, I am referring to the e-mails that Mr. Alexander exchanged with Chris and Sky Hughes in January of 2007. If you are unfamiliar with these conversations or need some refreshing, this e-mail conversation followed a conversation that Chris and Sky had with Ms. Arias in which they collectively advised her to move on from Travis because he was in love with Deana Reid and because he was not treating her well. A few days later Ms. Arias advised Mr. Alexander of this conversation and he then sent an e-mail to Chris and Sky Hughes to express his feelings to them.

Mr. Alexander begins this conversation by blaming Chris and Sky for speaking ill of him and/or bashing him in front of Ms. Arias. He expressed his unhappiness that Chris and Sky Hughes had called him a jerk who was abusive to women. Mr. Alexander also seemed upset that the Hughes had told Ms. Arias that he was using her as a booty call and that he would never commit to her until he was over his feelings for Ms. Reid. Admittedly, this is a quick summation of the conversation but I believe this summary captures the essence of the conversation. If you want to read the whole thing I strongly suspect you can find it online somewhere and that when you do you can take no legitimate issue with my summation. This is what Chris and Sky said to Mr. Alexander and "facts are stubborn things."

In saying this, I believe that after the killing the Hughes decided that they said all these things to Jodi because she lied to them about how Mr. Alexander was treating her but "facts are stubborn things." The Hughes had the opportunity to tell Ms. Arias that what she was saying didn't make sense and they had the opportunity to respond to Mr. Alexander's e-mail by saying that her story didn't make sense. That is a fact and it is a fact that they did not respond in this manner.

For his part Mr. Hughes laid out his reasons for saying what he said to Ms. Arias. To put it in his words "it's just stating the facts." The facts as Mr. Hughes put it were that; during the past 5 years Mr. Alexander had not committed to one woman, that Deana was always in the background as part of some undefinable relationship, that he told Deana that he loved her but there was no commitment and he told Mr. Alexander that he was the "biggest flirt this side of the Mississippi." Mr. Hughes also reminded Mr. Alexander how he likes to claim that "the T-Dogg pulls chicks." Mr. Hughes completed this section of his dialogue by expressing amusement about the way Mr. Alexander would hook up with chicks, get in their hearts and then become disinterested. I'm not sure why Mr. Hughes finds treating women this way so amusing but it is what he said. "Facts are stubborn things."

As for her part Ms. Hughes talked about how Ms. Arias was in love with Mr. Alexander and that to him she was just a "booty call." Ms. Hughes referenced how Mr. Alexander had referred to Ms. Arias as a "skank." Never did she express to Mr. Alexander how such claims did not make any sense to her, that this did not sound like the Travis Alexander she knew, not once. Certainly, while one could assert that Ms. Hughes' reaction to these accusations against her dear friend was a result of Ms. Arias' lies, the same cannot be said for what follows. "Facts are stubborn things."

Completely independent of Ms. Arias, Ms. Hughes called Mr. Alexander a "heart predator." She talked about how Mr. Alexander, referring to him as the "T-Dogg" took great joy in making women fall for him and laughs about what he could get away with. Ms. Hughes also asserts that she would be fearful if her sister were fond of Mr. Alexander. She went on to say that she would not even allow her sister to have an interest in Mr. Alexander. Think about that statement for a minute, one of Mr. Alexander's closest friends would be fearful of how he would treat her sister. I ask you to put aside the zeal and your loathing for Ms. Arias and ponder that statement for a minute and as you do I would ask you to ask yourself; would I want Travis Alexander dating my sister?

CHAPTER 16

"THE LETTERS"

Those of you who followed the trial closely know that there were some letters that Mr. Alexander supposedly wrote to Ms. Arias. These letters were relegated to the sidelines because of the fact that after a hearing on the issue, the State prevailed in its attempt to keep the letters out of evidence. Meaning, the jury would never hear about them in any phase of the trial. In Chapter 40 I talk about that hearing. In this Chapter I limit myself to speaking about how I received "The Letters" and what steps I took after I received them. With this disclaimer aside, here is that portion of the story.

I don't know how many of you have had moments in life when you feel like what is happening to you can't be real, one of those moments like your living inside a movie. I certainly never had such an experience until Ms. Arias came into my life. Then, despite my best efforts to avoid such moments, several of these surreal moments came into my life, literally in some cases, but the first I can recall occurred in April of 2010 and it was related to a piece of evidence that would later come to be known as "The Letters."

It was a Monday and I was begrudgingly coming into the office on a Monday like most of us with nine to five jobs do on Monday mornings. After going through my customary ritual of setting my stuff down and turning on the radio to the local sports talk station I turned on my computer and checked my e-mail. Typically, nothing much of note was ever sent to me over the weekend because my typical correspondence was with other government employees who also did not work over the weekend. However, as we all know now, Ms. Arias' case was far from typical. You did not see this until January of 2103, but it was certainly becoming clearer to me with each passing day. In this regard, I guess that I should not have been too surprised when, in contrast to the typical collection of junk e-mails headed for the trash can, I instead reviewed my e-mail and found an email that was sent from a person named "Bob White." The subject of the email was "you might be interested in these" and it contained an attachment. "Mr. White's" email stated that he didn't want to get involved with the case but he thought I might be interested in the attached documents. The email was from a Yahoo account and the attachment(s) contained 10 letters. For reasons that will become clear later on, it is important to note that the attachment(s) were in PDF format and the PDF images appeared to be letters that Mr. Alexander wrote to Ms. Arias. What I received then appeared to be scanned copies of the original letters, but at the same time could also have been scans of a copy. I could not tell, nor was there any accurate way to determine, which I had received.

After the verdict and before sentencing Ms. Arias released these letters on her fan page. How or why she did it, I have some thoughts, but as far as the case went I really did not care at that point. I only point this fact out to you now to advise you that if you want to read them word for word, they are all over the internet. For our purposes, it is sufficient to say that these letters contained admissions by "Mr. Alexander" about his sexual interest in children and in particular his sexual interest in the son of his friends Chris and Sky Hughes. These letters also contained apologies from "Mr. Alexander" for breaking Ms. Arias' finger. You may have noticed that I put quotation marks around the name of the purported author. I did this because I cannot currently definitively identify the true author of these letters. However, as you might guess figuring out who authored these letters and who sent them to me was very important to me back in April of 2010 when I received them. If we were going to have these letters admitted at trial we needed to be able to prove that it was Mr. Alexander who authored these letters, if we could not prove that, they would have been worthless or even potentially harmful.

My first step in this regard was to discuss these documents with my team and Ms. Arias and I did just that. As it relates to Ms. Arias, I'm not sure if we spoke on the phone first or not. I suspect we did because she called nearly every day. However, I will concede that I cannot be certain. Either way I know that we discussed the letters at the jail within a day or so of me receiving them. They were described as letters that Mr. Alexander wrote to her during the course of their relationship. As you might guess one important question that came to my mind was "Why would Mr. Alexander hand write letters and mail them to you when you corresponded so much via a computer?" The answer I received is one that I wish I could share with you, but I cannot due to privilege. Another question that I contemplated was; who is Bob White and how did this person get these letters? I didn't realize it at the time but my efforts to answer the latter question through my own investigation was the moment in time that served as the beginning of the end of the relatively harmonious relationship I had with Ms. Arias.

Having read this you might be asking yourself; why it was so important to me to know who "Bob White" is and how "Bob" got the letters? The answer is relatively simple as Ms. Arias' lawyer I could simply not ignore these letters, I was duty bound to investigate them and use them at trial if they could be authenticated as being written by Mr. Alexander and it was wise for me to do so. To this end, knowing who "Bob" was and learning how he got these letters would potentially lead me to obtaining the original copies of these letters. Obtaining the originals was important because a handwriting expert could do a much better job of determining if Mr. Alexander was the author of these letters if he or she had the original documents to work with. If on the other hand the handwriting expert was limited to performing a comparison based upon the PDFs I received, her ability to draw her conclusions would be limited.

It is for these reasons that obtaining the originals became the ultimate priority for me and the entire defense team. Apart from the obvious question of; who was Bob White? How to best pursue the originals gave rise to many questions. At this time the pertinent questions in my mind were; where did Ms. Arias last see the originals? Where could they have been stored? Who could have found them? If they were found how would the person who found them know to email the letters to me? Of course I know the answers to all of these questions, but the answers are privileged. What is not privileged is the analysis we had performed on the letters. This is not privileged because Ms. Arias allowed me to advise Sky Hughes of the results and because we turned over the reports to the State.

Our expert's report showed that it was "highly probable" that Travis Alexander was the author of the letters. It was the most she could conclude without the originals, the highest standard she could apply when working from the PDF files I gave her. For the sake of clarity "highly probable" is the highest level of proof in the field of handwriting analysis. Handwriting experts never say that they have absolute proof. "Highly probable" is the closest thing they can offer but within that range they can make more powerful conclusions when they have the originals. In this regard, having the originals would have made all the difference in the world one way or the other as with the originals, the letters could have been exposed as fakes or determined authentic. Had these letters been determined to be fakes that would have been the end of "The Letters." These letters would never have seen the light of day in that they would have been privileged information that would be sealed away in her file forever, but of course this is not what happened.

With the "highly probable" analysis in hand I decided to disclose the letters to the State because at the time it was my intent to use them at trial as the content supported Ms. Arias' claims of physical abuse and her claim that Mr. Alexander had a sexual interest in young children.

However, before we disclosed the letters to the State I felt as if Chris and Sky Hughes should be allowed to see at least one of the letters before the world did. Advising Chris and Sky Hughes of the content of the letters was important to me because in these letters "Mr. Alexander" expresses a sexual interest in their son and further explains how easily he could act on his desires. I did not want them to learn of these things for the first time at trial or in some other public setting but instead to learn of them in the privacy of their own home. I realize that Ms. Hughes has made public comments about my disclosure of the letters to them and that in these comments she claimed I told her we had absolute proof that the letters were genuine. It is my further understanding that she is claiming that I disclosed this letter to her so that she and her husband would testify for the defense. Let me be clear that neither of these claims reflect my true motivations for sending the letter to her.

That being said, I do not blame Ms. Hughes for recalling that I claimed to have absolute proof that Mr. Alexander wrote the letter. I say this because based on my reading of Ms. Hughes, she was understandably emotional when she reviewed this information and perhaps she does not recall the fact that what I actually said was that the analysis performed was as close to absolute proof as the field of handwriting analysis can offer.

As to the claim that I gave this letter to her in order to trick her or induce her into testifying for the defense, I am not sure why she feels as if she can read my mind and thus know my intentions. Only I knew my intentions that day and they were only to make sure that the Hughes did not hear or see this letter for the first time in trial. For those skeptics out there who might not believe my claims, I offer you another one of those stubborn things, a fact. That fact being that when Ms. Hughes sent me an e-mail in which she expressed the fact that she knew Mr. Alexander had problems but not to this extent, I did not follow up on that e-mail, I did not ask her to tell me what Mr. Alexander's issues were. If my goal was to pursue such evidence I clearly could have obtained it from her.

As for what else the Hughes have said publicly, I have yet to hear Ms. Hughes discuss how grateful she was at the time that I sent the letter to her and how that at no time did I ask her to testify for the defense. In fact I remember staying at the office late so that I could calm her down, assure her that this did not mean that Mr. Alexander had actually touched her son and that perhaps they should talk to their son and/or seek counseling for him. I have also not seen Ms. Hughes publicly admit that she sent me an e-mail advising me that she knew Mr. Alexander had problems but she was unaware that he was dealing with this issue. Perhaps Ms. Hughes forgot about that e-mail or thought I might not have it, but I do. Ms. Hughes must also not be aware of the fact that if I wanted her as a witness for Ms. Arias I could have called her as a witness I did not need to garner her cooperation.

Again, Ms. Hughes, her husband and the supporters of Mr. Alexander may not believe me, but having handled many a case where children are victims of these types of crimes, my only motivation was to provide this information to them out of human compassion and concern for their son. Had I been doing so for the reasons she speculates, I could have recorded our conversation or responded to the e-mail I referenced above and asked her to elaborate in writing, I simply spoke with her and left it at that. "Facts are stubborn things." Note should also be made of the fact that at the time I spoke to Ms. Hughes, I had no reason to believe that Mr. Alexander did not write the letters. The information available to me at the time was that an expert had said that it was "highly probable" that Mr. Alexander was the author.

Later on when more information became available, I became much more suspect of who wrote these letters. Why? Ms. Arias' cell was searched by deputies at the jail and pens were found (it was a violation of the rules for an inmate to have a pen). That small rule violation in and of itself was not a big deal to me what was a big deal to me was the fact that during this search a 3 by 5 note card was found in the cell with handwriting on it. The State's expert concluded it was handwriting that was an attempt to simulate the hand writing of Travis Alexander. I'm not sure how such a conclusion was reached as it sounds more like mind reading than handwriting analysis but be that as it may that would have been his testimony and the link would be obvious that Ms. Arias wrote the letters. In realizing this I also began to question how, if Ms. Arias did write these letters she was able to author them, get them out of the jail and have them e-mailed to me? This is a more difficult task than you might think given that she was living at the jail and everything she sent out was inspected and her phone calls were all recorded. Adding on to the difficulty of the task of Ms. Arias creating these letters would be the fact that she would have to do a good enough job at simulating Mr. Alexander's writings to fool a handwriting expert. She could review the portions of Mr. Alexander's journals but still a tough task you have to admit.

Putting these difficulties aside, once the 3 by 5 card was found, it was my belief that Ms. Arias wrote the letters. However as what I personally believed was irrelevant, as her attorney I had to consider how this evidence would sit with a jury. My reasoning was that if I believed that she wrote the letters it certainly would not be too hard for the State to convince the jury that Ms. Arias wrote these letters. The argument that would follow from this premise would then be that Ms. Arias wrote these letters as a way to further defame Mr. Alexander. A fairly simple argument to make in that the jury would not need a lot of convincing as to Ms. Arias' motives. Once convinced that Ms. Arias wrote these letters to defame Mr. Alexander the jury would then have had yet another reason to detest Ms. Arias and the more they detested Ms. Arias the more motivated they would be to sentence her to death.

Certainly, when we look at this issue closer the issue becomes, could the State prove that these letters were forgeries? The answer was that they could not. The State's handwriting expert never could conclude that these letters were actually forgeries. Instead it was the opinion of the State's experts that the conclusions about their authenticity that Ms. Arias' expert made could not be made because the analysis was being done from a copy. Perhaps this is why the State sought to have them excluded. I am not sure but in my mind this was a huge mistake for the State, given what they knew at the time I believe that they could have convinced the jury that these letters were forged and I believe if they had Ms. Arias would be on death row as you read this.

CHAPTER 17

THE PHONE SEX TAPE

Those who paid close attention to the trials might recall that at some point in time Ms. Arias had lost her old Helio phone and her friend Gus Searcy gave her a new Helio phone. Those who followed particularly close might recall that at some point in time Ms. Arias reported that her old Helio phone was stolen from a car belonging to Ms. Arias' grandfather in Yreka in the spring of 2008. This fact in and of itself would really not be much of a big deal, but what was on that old Helio phone, the phone that was reported stolen, turned out to be a huge deal.

At some point in 2010 I was advised that this phone was found by a family member in that car. Apparently rather than being stolen this phone had simply been lost in the car. Once I learned of its existence of course I wanted to have it. I knew that this phone would likely contain photographs and/or text messages relevant to the case. I thus advised Ms. Arias' family to send this phone to my investigator so that it could be delivered to a computer expert who could then recover all the evidence from the phone.

As anxious as I was to know what was on this phone, I knew that I could not run the risk of altering the evidence by turning it on and taking a look, so off it went to our expert. When the results came back I realized that I was correct to presume that the phone contained evidence but at the same time I had no clue that I was about to encounter the type of evidence that I heard on that phone. To be honest, I didn't expect to hear anything on that phone, maybe an old voicemail but that was it. I suspected that maybe there would be a racy text or two, which there was. I suspected that there might be a few nude pictures, there were none. What I got was unbelievable.

What I got was unbelievable in many regards. First, it is truly a rare case when there are any sort of recordings, be they audio or video of the victim to which I would ever have access. Typically I do not see things or hear things of this nature until we get to victim impact statements. Of course, as is my mantra, this case was far from typical. In this case Mr. Alexander had a few videos of his presentations that were posted online, but what I found in the voice notes section of this phone was immediately recognizable as something different. This was a recording of a conversation Mr. Alexander had with Ms. Arias, the woman who would wind up killing him within a month of having this conversation with her. I was immediately fascinated, as listening to such a conversation could provide great insight into the relationship that these two were having just before the killing took place. To be clear, my fascination did not come from the sexual aspects of the conversation, in fact, those aspects did not arise until much later during the call. Perhaps I should set the scene for you.

I was sitting in my office at the Public Defender's Office with my door open. Having my door open meant that people walking down the hallway might hear what is said in my office. At the time this was not a huge concern to me because I was not planning on cussing. You see, at the time the administration was cracking down on swearing, the seven dirty words were proclaimed to be off limits. Yes, however ridiculous it was, the office that represented baby killers, child molesters and people who have committed a wide variety of vile acts was concerned about swear words being heard in the hallway. But like I said earlier, I was just looking through the evidence found on Ms. Arias' old Helio phone, no big deal right? Wrong. After looking through the expected items I noticed a folder containing voice notes so I opened it up. The first note was Ms. Arias talking to some person about a business matter of some sort, completely unimportant. The next note was not so trivial. It was Ms. Arias and Mr. Alexander talking. This stunned me because never before in my career had I heard a murder victim and the accused talking a few weeks before one would end up killing the other. This tape was thus chilling on a personal level and dynamic as a piece of evidence. Of course, this evidence was even more dynamic than I would have guessed as I listened to the first few minutes.

During these first few minutes the couple spoke about traveling, business and a few other mundane things. However, when I say mundane I mean mundane in comparison to what was to come. Additionally do not take this to mean that this mundane talk was of no value, instead it was of enormous value. The value in this part of the conversation was that when travel was discussed, Mr. Alexander talked about his intentions to come visit Ms. Arias in Yreka. Does one visit their crazy ex-girlfriend who is stalking them? Granted, I had several pieces of evidence that indicated this, but this was in Mr. Alexander's own words, powerful evidence.

The conversation moved from the mundane to the interesting when the subject of Abe came up. At the time I didn't know much about Abe but from the call I could tell that Abe was someone who likely dated Ms. Arias at some point in time and had kissed her. Mr. Alexander clearly was not happy about this event. He talked about giving Abe a look that indicated his desire to whip Abe's "A" because Abe had kissed his girlfriend. The fact that Ms. Arias was not Mr. Alexander's girlfriend at the time of the kiss didn't seem to matter to Mr. Alexander. This dialogue was very important to me and was perhaps one of the most important portions of this recording that would become known as "the sex tape." As you read this you might wonder why this portion of "the sex tape" was so important to me. It was important because it told me that Mr. Alexander seemingly had a violent streak because he expressed a desire to be violent with Abe. Mr. Alexander also seemed to be evidencing either one of two things. He was either a jealous person when it came to Ms. Arias or he viewed her as a possession, perhaps both were true.

Directly after this bit of contention the conversation went from interesting to downright salacious when the conversation quickly turned to sex and when I say quickly, I do mean quickly. It was amazing to me how quickly the two went from a mild argument about Abe to talking about sex in graphic terms. That quick shift is telling by itself but at the time I think my state of shock at the content may have prevented me from picking up how fast they shifted to sex during my initial review of this recording, but I noticed it the second time around. Having told you what I told you about how rare having evidence like this in a murder case is I suspect you could understand why I was in a sense of shock. My client and the man she killed were recounting numerous details of their sex life in somewhat graphic detail. I was in such shock from hearing all of this that I totally forgot my door was open. Anyone walking down the hallway could undoubtedly hear these two talking about their shared desire to have a "F***fest" amongst other things and that, as I mentioned earlier, was now a no-no in my office. I snapped out of my shock when I heard Ms. Arias' howling while supposedly in the midst of an orgasm. I use the word howling because what I heard reminded me of an old movie "Porky's." Some of you may know it was a big hit in 1982 and it contained a scene in which two gym teachers had sex and the female teacher whose nickname was "Lassie" howled so loud that a gym full of students could hear her. Anyway, putting old 1980's movies aside for now, after I heard this loud "orgasm" I jumped up and shut my door out of concern that I would have to explain this to somebody. Fortunately I never had to offer such an explanation. Looking back on it, perhaps had I blasted this recording with the door open perhaps I would have gotten fired. In retrospect that might have been nice as it would have meant that I was off the case for good.

Returning your attention back to the tape itself, just when I thought it could not get any more shocking I heard Mr. Alexander say something I could absolutely not believe. He said that Ms. Arias' orgasm sounded like a 12 year old girl having her first orgasm. I was in such disbelief that I wasn't sure that I had heard him correctly, obviously Ms. Arias was shocked as well when she heard these words, but then clarity came when Mr. Alexander repeated himself. A few seconds later he said something to the effect of "it was like corking the pot of a 12 year old girl." Now I know that many of you believe that the defense team "lied" about Travis Alexander being a pedophile and I will discuss this more fully later and in subsequent books but putting all the emotions aside and putting whatever you think about Ms. Arias aside,

Mr. Alexander said this on tape. When you further contemplate these statements bear in mind that this was before the trial, before the world was paying attention and before the world universally hated Ms. Arias. What would you think if you heard Mr. Alexander saying this on tape before he had been killed? In fact, what would you think about anyone who said this? What would you think of that person? Would you think they were a pedophile? Based on news reports it was comments such as this that brought former Subway pitchman Jared Foggle to justice because a woman reported that he had made similar comments to her. If someone made these comments to you would you let them be alone with your daughter?

As our second president John Adams is alleged to have said while defending a British soldier accused of murder in a trial, related to the events that are now known as the Boston Massacre, "facts are stubborn things." It is a fact that Travis Alexander said these things on tape. I say that it was a fact that Mr. Alexander said these things on tape because before I did anything with this tape I had the voices on the tape verified so there could be no legitimate argument that it was anybody other than Mr. Alexander that Ms. Arias was talking to on this tape.

So putting the sensational aspects of the "sex tape" aside, putting the bombastic commentary aside. I had this recording. I had a piece of evidence that supported Ms. Arias' contention that Mr. Alexander had a sexual interest in children. I also had a piece of evidence in which Mr. Alexander exhibited some violent tendencies. This was evidence that had to be used, regardless of who it upset.

CHAPTER 18

LEARNING MORE ABOUT MR. ALEXANDER

As you might guess, as I reviewed the text messages, e-mails, online chats, the phone sex tape and other items of evidence I learned more about Mr. Alexander. Did reviewing these items change my opinion of Mr. Alexander? Yes and No is the best answer I can give.

Earlier when I spoke about my initial assessment of Mr. Alexander I talked about how I looked upon him with sadness, not just because of how he died but because of how he lived. Having reviewed all the materials and before learning some additional information after the first trial, reviewing more materials merely served to increase my sadness. My sadness increased the more I learned because it seemed to me that during his life Mr. Alexander never truly got to be who he wanted to be because it appeared to me that he was a slave to his image. When I say he was a slave to his image I mean that he seemed to care so much about what others thought of him. It appeared that he wanted others to think he was doing well financially when he was not doing so well. Not doing well financially does not make someone a bad person, far from it, but it seemed to me as if he wanted to hide the realities of his financial troubles from as many people as he could so that others would think he was well off. Beyond hiding his financial struggles he would do things to demonstrate his wealth like hosting fight night parties and things of that nature. It seemed to me as if he feared that people would think less of him if they knew he was struggling financially like most of us do during different points in our lives, sad.

When I thought about Mr. Alexander and who he was as a person, his morals and his spiritual beliefs, I also felt a sense of sadness. I felt sadness because I could tell that he was not truly living in the way he wanted to live. Before you get angry with me for making such a statement let me explain what I mean. I tend to be the kind of person who looks at a person's behavior to assess the kind of person they are. For example if a person professes that homosexuality is a sin, yet they are engaging in homosexual activities, I tend to see that person as someone that does not truly believe that it is a sin because if they did they would not engage in that behavior. This correlated to the sadness I felt for Mr. Alexander because based on his behavior he was a guy who did not act as if he wanted to be Mormon. Putting Ms. Arias' allegations about Mr. Alexander having a sexual interest in children aside, like many young men in their twenties, he seemed highly motivated by sex. Evidence of such motivations can be seen in his communications and conduct not only with Ms. Arias but with other women as well. By in large these communications were not outside the norm if a person is not a member of the Mormon faith, but are obviously well outside the norm if someone is an adherent to that faith. His actions were that of a guy who wanted to live a less restrictive more normal sexual existence. Seeing nothing wrong with that choice the sadness I felt for Mr. Alexander in that regard was related to the idea that if he shared his feelings with his friends that he would lose their love and friendship. From what I know of these people that would not have been the case, but it made me sad to think that he would fear that.

Certainly, I will concede that I could also be dead wrong about Mr. Alexander not wanting to be Mormon and live by the dictates of the LDS Church. It could have been the case that he truly wanted to live his life in a way that was consistent with the dictates of the church but, for whatever reason, he could not. If this was the case, think about the guilt and shame he must have lived with. To me living with such guilt and/or shame would be a very sad way to live.

CHAPTER 19

MS. ARIAS' JAIL CALLS

When people are in the jail they have access to a phone from which they can call friends, family and/or loved ones. Now you might think this is nice for the inmates and it is, but the real winner in this deal is Maricopa County. Why is Maricopa County the winner in this situation? Because the jail charges a hefty price to those who accept the inmates calls which can only be up to twelve minutes in length before another call must be made (thereby incurring more charges) and the Deputy County Attorney's oftentimes get lots of good evidence because many defendants oftentimes say things in the course of these twelve minute calls that hurt them in their criminal cases. As you might guess before these defendants make these harmful statements they are warned by their lawyers not to talk about their case with anyone because it can be used against them in court. However, as most of these people are "smarter than their attorneys" they do not listen to this advice. Despite the fact that such advice is almost always ignored, I still give it to all my clients.

In a non-death penalty case more often than not I would not listen to the client's jail calls because I know that they will likely not be important. You see, when a client gives a confession or enters a plea and their life is not on the line, what they say on the phone does not really matter. However, in a death penalty case everything is important thus I almost always listened to these calls. At the very least listening to these calls gives me great insight into who my client is apart from their criminal conduct, because I could hear them relating to people they cared about and furthermore, talking about things that they cared about that had nothing to do with the case. This may sound taxing, but even in a typical death penalty case listening to a client's phone calls is not that much of a burden. The typical client might call his or her family and friends a few times a week, primarily because these calls were expensive, thus there were not a huge number of calls to listen to. In contrast to the norm, Ms. Arias was prolific on the phone. She would call friends, she would call family, she would call people to ask why other people were not picking up their phone and calls of this nature would happen several times a day and on a daily basis. Certainly, I will concede that there might have been a day or two that Ms. Arias, over the course of the years that I had her case that she did not call anyone, but such days were truly rare.

It was amazing how much time she spent on the phone if you consider that the people she called had to pay for the calls and they were typically pointless. However amazed I was about the number of calls and their content, my amazement did not alter the reality that I had a certain obligation to listen to these calls regardless of how many hours of my time it took. To add insult to injury, I even had to go online and seek out a computer that worked with "Windows 2000" because that was the only system compatible with the jails outdated recording system.

Why was listening to Ms. Arias' calls so important to me in her case given what I have said about her calls? First of all, I had the strong suspicion that if Juan Martinez was not listening to these calls very closely, someone working on his behalf was certainly doing that job for him. Furthermore, I had little doubt in my mind that Mr. Martinez would use these calls in whatever point in the proceedings that he felt would help him make his case for death. Furthermore, I was also well aware that I had a self-destructive client who thought she was smarter than anyone. So I assumed that she would try and pull something off during one of these calls, something that she thought might help her cause.

Preparing for all three phases of this death penalty trial meant that I would need to be aware of what was on these tapes because given that the

State, by in large, could have used them at almost any point in time during the trial without any advance notice. It would be unwise of me not to know what my client may have said during her many phone calls. To her credit Ms. Arias did not talk about her case much at all during these calls. However, she said so many other damaging things that I was sure that the State would bring them up during sentencing because these calls did not portray Ms. Arias in a good light. During these calls she would yell or otherwise act in mean spirited ways towards her mother. She would call her mother stupid and/or guilt her into sending her money because she was starving. Ms. Arias would get angry with her mother for not sending her money or a book in a timely fashion. Ms. Arias did not seem to care that her mother did not have the money to buy the books or send the cash she was demanding. The narcissism and arrogance Ms. Arias displayed during these calls was amazing. Ms. Arias would even go so far as to tell her mother how to budget her money so that she would have enough to send to her and if Bill Arias objected she would instruct her mother to ignore that as well. Beyond that Ms. Arias had the unmitigated gall to give some canteen items to other inmates and thus ask her mother for more money. It was pretty repulsive to listen to, I must admit. During these calls I found myself rooting for Sandy Arias to hang up on my client or stand up to her, to my recollection she only did once. Apart from that one occasion she always gave into Ms. Arias' whining about how she was suffering in jail and how she would starve to death if she did not have enough money. I found it strange that absent the one occasion that I referenced, that Sandy never stood up to her daughter. At most she might question what other inmates who did not have money on their "books" would eat since they could not buy things from the "canteen," but those questions were rare and not vigorously pursued. Sandy was the parent but she never seemed to act like it at all. However, at the same time, I tried not to read too much into it because Sandy was Ms. Arias' mother and I cut her some slack because she was empathetic to her daughter's situation.

As you might be able to guess, apart from being aware of the evidence that the State could use at trial, listening to these calls also gave me insight into Ms. Arias and her relationships with people. She would degrade her mother directly and to others. She felt comfortable ordering her siblings and friends around while at the same time acting superior to all of them even though she was in jail. The psychology of this was truly unique but it certainly led me to believe that Ms. Arias felt as if the world owed her something and that she was very angry with her mother for no reason that was ever vocalized. To me this was something I saw a fair amount of in former clients who had been sexually abused. Thus, to me it was more evidence that Ms. Arias was sexually abused as a child, more evidence that Ms. Arias was mad at her mother for not caring for her enough to stop the abuse, more evidence that she was mad at her mother for not protecting her from the person who sexually abused her as a child.

The only person who did seem to escape Ms. Arias' wrath was dear old dad, Bill Arias. When she spoke to her Dad she was typically kind and respectful. That being said, the conversations seemed very cold. She did not talk to her Dad often but when she did neither seemed to want to be talking to the other. It seemed as if both were doing it out of obligation to the other because of the biological link they shared. This is not to say that Dad did not receive any of Ms. Arias' wrath, but is to say that it was almost always indirect in that she would talk badly about him to her mother and/or manipulate her mother into doing things behind Bill's back because he was such a "jerk." You see, Bill did not like it that Sandy sent so much money to Ms. Arias and as you might guess she was not going to tolerate that.

Listening to Ms. Arias made it clear to me that money was a big deal to her and that she was more than willing to do what she could to pad her bank account, even when she was in jail (even before the art business took off). Ms. Arias did this by communicating with her fan base. Where did this fan base come from? Well for the most part before trial began Ms. Arias' fan base came from those who watched her on "48 Hours." After she was on that show Ms. Arias received a ton of fan mail. Trust me, I have seen a decent amount of it. If I were to break her fan mail into categories the biggest category would be men who wanted to have sex with her. Men who believed that once Ms. Arias was set free that she would come running into their arms and eventually into their beds. I will politely call them her "suitors." To be fair, there was also just your general assortment of weird people as well. I remember one woman who saw Ms. Arias on television and was thus motivated to share her whole sexual history with Ms. Arias, all of this was very strange to me, but to Ms. Arias these people were potential sources of income, people who might put money on her books and/or do things for her. However, as you might guess the people Ms. Arias thought she could get the most money and/or assistance from were her "suitors" so it was with these people that she dedicated most of her time.

What this translated into as far as the work I had to do was that I had to listen very carefully to the calls Ms. Arias made to her "suitors" so I could discern if she was engaging in any shenanigans. I never did. I assume that Mr. Martinez never did either because he never played such a call in court. Shenanigans aside she was definitely working these guys for money. I remember one such "suitor" who sounded like he was in his sixties, an age that does not sound so old to me now that I am approaching fifty but certainly he was much older than Ms. Arias and he was so thrilled that she called. If I recall correctly he lived in Missouri and worked on a farm. He would tell Ms. Arias about what he was doing on the farm. This man would tell her how he had a room for her once she got out of jail that sort of thing. It was so obvious what this guy was up to, he had a sexual interest in Ms. Arias and she knew it. To capitalize on this situation Ms. Arias would feign interest in what he was saying and without fail he would eventually ask Ms. Arias if she needed anything and she would pretend that she was okay and that she did not need anything. Then he would ask a little bit more until it got to the point where Ms. Arias was practically doing him a favor by allowing him to send her money or send her a specific book. In this regard, she was amazing.

As you might guess, this guy was not the only "suitor", there were plenty of others, but this man stood out to me because it was just so pathetic. I do not know how much money this man gave Ms. Arias over time but I know that between this guy and the other "suitors" Ms. Arias had plenty of books to read and plenty of money to order candy bars and other junk from the jail "canteen."

Before I conclude this chapter on the jail calls, one final thought might be of interest to you. Even as I sit here today, writing this book, months after the trials concluded, I am amazed that the State never used these calls during the third phase of the trial. I may never know why the State did not use these calls. If I was trying the case for the State I certainly would have. I would have used them because there was never a time when I thought Ms. Arias was deserving of the death penalty more than when I listened to her on these calls. Keeping in mind that I am against the death penalty under any circumstance these calls made Ms. Arias sound like a monster. The way Ms. Arias talked to her mother, the way she demanded things from everyone that she felt that she could control was truly sickening to me. For example, she would often call her friend Donovan, those who watched the trial closely would recall that this was a woman who came to the trial nearly every day and served as a quasi-spokesperson for Ms. Arias throughout the trial. To be clear when I say that Ms. Arias and Donovan were friends this was not some life-long friendship, instead, they met in jail. Whatever relationship they had it was formed at the jail during the months that they were housed together. I do not know how she did it, but in listening to these calls it was obvious that Ms. Arias had found a way to manipulate this person into being her personal assistant on the outside. Donovan became the person who would help Ms. Arias do the things she could not do for herself. Listening to her calls with Donovan made Ms. Arias seem like a very scary person in her ability to manipulate others.

I thought if the jurors heard these calls that they too would despise Ms. Arias, not just for her crime but also on a personal level. I thought that they too would be sickened by how she treated her mother and I thought listening to these calls would have illustrated to the jury how Ms. Arias truly had an ability to manipulate others. If I was the prosecutor on the case, I would have had Dr. DeMarte speak about Ms. Arias' behavior during these calls. I would have had Dr. DeMarte refer to these calls as examples that supported her diagnosis as doing so would have been a way to illustrate to the jury, perhaps without saying so, that Ms. Arias was a monster whose life needed to end. Fortunately for Ms. Arias, that never happened.

CHAPTER 20

MS. ARIAS' "NINJA STORY"

Keeping in mind that it is not feasible for me to tell this story in a perfect chrono-logical order, amongst all this new evidence, we still had Ms. Arias' story that Mr. Alexander was killed by these two masked intruders. This story later became known as the "ninja story." Not sure how this story was labeled in such a manner, but I guess that is not important. Back when I was preparing the case it sure seemed like a bull**** story to me, but as I discuss elsewhere in this book, I could not prove that it was bull**** so if that was Ms. Arias' story I would have to figure out how to work around it. At the same time she was telling me this supposed "ninja story" I also had to be prepared for her to drop this story and tell me another version of events.

As the case moved forward I could never be certain that she was going to drop the "ninja story" and I could not hold up the proceedings and ask for a continuance based on the fact that the "ninja story" was bull****. Criminal cases do not work that way. I had to prepare my case, I had to have her talk to experts even if she was going to tell this bull**** story and see what could be made of it. I knew that this would hurt her but at the same time I had to be ready for trial and doing nothing or simply sitting around waiting for her story to change was not an option. I had to be prepared for trial either way. I could not simply forgo expert examinations in anticipation of her changing her story they had to be done in advance of trial. At the same time, think-ing that a story change was quite possible I had to be prepared as much as was possible for whatever version of events that she would tell. In essence I had to do the best I could with what I had and try to minimize how much the change in story would be harmed by what had already been done. Put another way I had to try to minimize the damage that my client was doing to her own case.

As I explain this to you I am not expecting sympathy from you but I would ask you to consider these issues from a defense attorney's perspective for a minute. As her defense attorney, I was in a position where I was preparing to defend this case and my client's life on two different theories. One being the bull**** "ninja story" and the other one being a story I had yet to hear. Not a good position for a defense attorney. As you might guess a defense attorney typically likes to know what story their client will tell if they take the stand. So I obviously wanted to do something about this situation. If Ms. Arias' story was going to change, if she was going to admit that the "ninja story" was not true, from my perspective, the sooner the better. I needed to know as soon as possible what the story was going to be if I had any chance of saving my client's life. So what was I going to do?

As you might guess by this time I had some pretty clear beliefs about what happened on June 4, 2008, and I will discuss those beliefs in Chapter 47, but for now let me just say that those beliefs certainly did not include the presence of ninjas or any other person for that matter. Did I vocalize these beliefs to Ms. Arias? No, I did not. Knowing Ms. Arias as I did, there would not be much point to that as doing so would likely result in Ms. Arias becoming more steadfast in asserting this story, just to prove me wrong. All this being said I did not in any way shape or form assert to her that I believed her "ninja story" and I think Ms. Arias over time began to sense that I did not believe this story. At the same time I got the sense that because she knew I did not believe her, there were moments when Ms. Arias came close to telling me a different version of events. Think about it, all aspects of her case, were tied to her story of what happened on June 4, 2008 and she was planning on telling the world and most importantly her jury, a version of events that was not believable in any way. In my mind if she got up on the stand and told the "ninja story" she would be found guilty of First Degree Murder and she would be sentenced to death. Ms. Arias was acting as her own worst enemy and my job required that I make efforts to put a stop to it. The question was how was I going to accomplish this goal? How was I going to get out of this dilemma of defending a death penalty case where I was not sure what my client's version of events would be?

First, I surmised that Ms. Arias believed that people would accept the "ninja story" as the truth. By people, I mean I think she thought a jury whose members were not trained in the law and/or crime scene investigation would buy her story because she could convince them that it was true. Ms. Arias could not be convinced that these people would see this story as a complete fabrication. Thus, in order for her to change from this "ninja story" I had to convince her that "real people" would not believe this story. Being a public defender meant that I didn't have the money to hire a focus group to demonstrate what people would think of the "ninja story" so I had to come up with another way of doing things. I also had to do whatever I was going to do without disclosing confidential information before trial. I would need my client's permission to disclose confidential information and that wasn't going to happen because she really would not have wanted me to do what I was doing because she was convinced that she could sell the "ninja story." Good thing for me that I did not need Ms. Arias' permission to disclose evidence that was already in the public discourse. With these realities in mind I, with the help of my mitigation specialist, came up with what I thought was a pretty good plan. We decided to show a class of undergraduate students the entire CBS documentary and then give these students a questionnaire about the case. I had to go to the lengths of creating this questionnaire but I wanted to know; what they thought happened on June 4, 2008; did they believe Ms. Arias' "ninja story" things like that. So we showed the documentary to them on one day and I gave them the questionnaires on another day and after they had completed their questionnaires, I took some time to discuss capital cases with them and then we were off to read the answers these students had written on our questionnaires. After reviewing these questionnaires the defense team compiled some data related to the believability of the "ninja story," suffice it to say, nobody believed it. Shortly thereafter Ms. Arias told the story of self-defense that she told at trial. You may have noticed that in describing Ms. Arias' revised version of events I have been using the word "story." I do this to highlight the reality that I did not believe this version of events. As I mentioned above, in Chapter 47 I will discuss what I did believe but for the purposes of this chapter as it relates to the "ninja story" that story was now dead.

Would it have been helpful to her case for her to revise her story sooner? Yes. It most certainly would have. If she had revised her story sooner, say before meeting with Dr. Samuels, he would not have been wrongfully attacked on the change in stories as it relates to his trauma testing. I guess one could question my choice to have Ms. Arias evaluated at all before she changed her story. But the problem is, as I described earlier, I had no choice because there was always the possibility that Ms. Arias wouldn't change her story and if she didn't change her story and I had no evaluation of her I would have been ineffective as her counsel and she would get a new trial and/or sentencing proceeding.

Would it have been helpful if Ms. Arias changed her story to something that made more sense? Most certainly and this will be addressed in Chapter 47, but for now in this regard, I hope you can begin to see that I was trying to save Ms. Arias' life, yet at the same time she was trying to make it harder for me to do my job.

CHAPTER 21

THE MURDER WEAPONS

If you are even remotely familiar with this case, I strongly suspect that you are acutely aware that the murder weapons at issue were a gun and a knife. However, those who watched the trial and/or the coverage of the trial may know something that those who are only remotely familiar do not know, that these weapons were never entered into evidence. Of course, had the State found these weapons they would have likely entered them into evidence and furthermore would have been obligated to disclose them to the defense, in order to let us know that they had been recovered. Because they were never recovered (or so I believed), the questions that surrounded these weapons once trial began were simple and straightforward; where did these weapons come from? Where were these weapons now? Both of which were certainly fair questions, no doubt about it. However, to me, as I prepared for trial, the answers to these questions did not mean as much to me as you might think. It was not that I was not curious, it is just that the answers to these questions might not mean that much to my case. That may sound crazy but let me explain.

If the knife used to kill Mr. Alexander was the knife found in Mr. Alexander's dishwasher it was never identified as the murder weapon. If this knife was not the murder weapon, the knife at issue could still be lying somewhere in the desert, it could be in a landfill somewhere, heck it could be anywhere. You might think that as I prepared for trial it would be beneficial to know where this knife came from. I certainly did not see it that way. In fact, it was always my hope that a particular knife was never identified as the murder weapon, because that could only hurt Ms. Arias' case. By this I mean; what if the knife used was not one she obtained from Mr. Alexander's home? What if somehow it could be shown that Ms. Arias brought the knife with her to Mr. Alexander's home? That certainly would not help her claim that she acted in self-defense. So as I prepared for trial, as long as there was no evidence supporting the idea that Ms. Arias brought the knife to Mr. Alexander's home, I really did not care much about the knife. Why was it that as I prepared for trial I did not really care about the knife? It may sound crazy to you at first blush, but consider it further. If the knife were found what evidence would it contain that would be of interest? The handle of the knife would likely contain fingerprints associated with Ms. Arias. It is also possible that other prints associated with Mr. Alexander would also be found. That may sound significant but think for a minute; was there any legitimate dispute of the fact that Ms. Arias was the person who used this knife to stab Mr. Alexander? No, of course not, Ms. Arias admitted to being the person who committed these acts. Thus, finding these prints would come as no shock, however, even if Ms. Arias' prints were not found that would not serve as evidence that she did not stab Mr. Alexander, she admitted to doing that. Not finding her prints would only demonstrate that, for whatever reason (recovering prints can sometimes be difficult depending on the surface they are on things of that nature) the print technicians could not recover them, that is it. I guess someone could also pose the question, well what if Mr. Alexander's prints were on the knife, wouldn't that prove something? Well, yes it could prove something, but nothing of note. At best it would show that Mr. Alexander touched the knife earlier in the day or when he was fighting for his life. Would evidence of that nature help Ms. Arias' case that she acted in self-defense? No.

As for the gun, my thoughts on this issue may shock you as well in that this too was somewhat meaningless to me in terms of what I thought happened and what the evidence pointed to happening. It was one of those situations where for the sake of Ms. Arias' case I had hopes that no particular gun was ever identified as the murder weapon. Again you might think this is a crazy thing to say. Crazy because if it could be proven that the gun was not the gun taken from the home of my client's grandparents that it would support Ms. Arias' story. Yes, that was a possibility, but Sunny Arias' gun was an unregistered antique that was of the same caliber as the one used to kill Mr. Alexander. Thus, if a particular gun was identified as the murder weapon there would be no way to identify it for sure as the gun that was stolen in Yreka, except for the testimony of Ms. Arias' grandfather and by that time his memory was not good at all. Thus, in my mind, if he said that this was not his gun it would not carry much weight either because of his failing memory or his clear bias and thus this would not truly help Ms. Arias much at all. Likewise, I could not envision how it could ever be proven that the gun used belonged to Mr. Alexander. Given the evidence I had at the time, there would be no way to link a gun found discarded near the Grand Canyon and determined to be the murder weapon ever belonged to Mr. Alexander.

However, for the sake of argument let's say that it could somehow be proven that the gun used to shoot Mr. Alexander was his gun. No doubt about it such evidence would have bolstered Ms. Arias' story, however, Ms. Arias still had one big problem as it related to her story of self-defense. The problem was that she grabbed this gun, whomever it belonged to and shot Mr. Alexander in the face with it. Furthermore, depending on which sequencing of injuries one believes, Ms. Arias around that same time period stabbed him 27 times. Keeping in mind that Ms. Arias was claiming that when she engaged in these actions that she was acting in self-defense. In my mind, regardless of whose gun it was, she still went to great lengths to kill him as opposed to "protecting herself" as she claimed.

On the opposite end of the spectrum, I did have some concerns that the gun that once belonged to Ms. Arias' grandfather would be found and that it would later be tied to the casing found in Mr. Alexander's bathroom. Certainly while I still doubted Ms. Arias' grandfather's ability to truly remember the specific gun that was stolen from his home. However, at the same time, I strongly suspected that if it was recovered and the Yreka Police brought it back to him that he might identify it as his gun and if he did, his belief would have been treated as sacrosanct. Obviously, this would not help matters, because it would once again prove Ms. Arias a liar, but at the same time that was nothing new. It would just add another instance of her lying to the pile of lies she told. But that pile was big enough in my mind so I certainly was not disappointed that the gun never surfaced and I was certainly not going to go looking for it.

CHAPTER 22

Ms. Arias' Supposed Guilt Phase Witnesses

After the first trial was over Ms. Arias went on television and during an interview complained about how certain people could have testified that they had seen bruises on her arm and I chose not to call them as witnesses. Her complaint centered around the idea that I had simply chosen not to call witnesses who could lend support to her claim that Mr. Alexander was physically abusive with her. As it was convenient for Ms. Arias to do so, during this interview, even though she knew why these people were not called to the stand, she did not provide any explanation as to why I had chosen not to call these supposed witnesses. Instead she chose to portray herself as a victim of my poor choices. Do you believe any of Ms. Arias' claims about these supposed witnesses? Do you believe that Ms. Arias is a victim of my poor choices? You would be wise not to believe either of these propositions because they are not true. At the time she was saying these things about me I was not happy about it as I could not respond. I was still her lawyer and the case was not over yet. So certainly at the time I was both upset that she gave this particular interview because of the damage it did to her case but also because she was lying about me and I could not respond. However, as I sit here today I am very happy she made these claims in such a public forum because I can now respond without fear of disclosing privileged information. Why? Ms. Arias herself waived privilege on this issue when she gave this interview.

So I suspect that you are now wondering; who was Ms. Arias referring to when she spoke of these supposed witnesses? I also suspect that you are wondering; why did I choose not to call them? I guess the short answers to these questions would be that she really only had one actual witness who could offer decent testimony and that person came with too much baggage that it would make it look like he was lying even if he was telling the truth. The long answer follows below.

Unless she has created other witnesses in her mind, the list of supposed witnesses Ms. Arias spoke of in her interview would be as follows; Ms. Arias' mother Sandy Arias, Ms. Arias' former boyfriend Matt and two other men whose names I will keep to myself so as to keep them out of this mess. I am assuming they thank me for this bit of discretion.

Ms. Arias' former boyfriend Matt was the person who I referenced above as a potential "actual" witness. I say that Matt was an "actual" witness because he did claim to see bruising on Ms. Arias' arms, though he could not remember when. However, there were several problems with calling Matt to the stand. The most prominent problem would be the fact that, at least in the mind of the State, Matt had something to do with the letters. In fact, they were so sure of this that Detective Flores showed up at Matt's house in California one day to see if he could find evidence to this effect. Detective Flores did not find any such evidence but I believed that if Matt was called as a witness the State would be allowed to assert that Matt was willing to lie for Ms. Arias about seeing bruises because he cared for her so much that he was willing to help her create and/or distribute these letters. Such a dialogue would inevitably lead to a discussion about the letters themselves. In my mind, as I discussed in Chapter 16, any discussion about the letters would make Ms. Arias look like a crazy person who took elaborate steps to slander Mr. Alexander's character by creating these letters. Furthermore, it would make Matt look like he was lying about the bruising. Thus, the way I saw things, calling Matt to the stand would have resulted in a huge "net loss" for Ms. Arias. In my mind, for the reasons I discussed in Chapter 16, putting Matt on the stand would have put Ms. Arias one step closer to living on death row. That is why I never called Matt to the stand to talk about bruising. It was because, as I explain in Chapter 2, my ultimate job was to save Ms. Arias' life.

As it relates to my client's mother, Sandy Arias, I had several reasons for keeping her off the stand but the biggest was that she was so clearly lying about this issue, lying so poorly that it would have been laughable under other circumstances. Did this surprise me? Not in the least. Sandy Arias was more than willing to lie for her daughter, the only shock came when she did it so poorly on the day she tried to convince me that she saw bruising on Ms. Arias' arms. As you might guess, I do not remember the exact date and month that Sandy Arias tried to convince me that she had seen bruises on her daughter's arms. However, putting the date aside, I remember everything about Sandy's disclosure to me about seeing bruises on her daughter and the circumstances around it as clearly as I would if it happened yesterday. To set the stage for you, this happened before the former team left the case but after I had left the Public Defender's Office in February of 2011. I am certain of this because I met with Sandy during a weekend at my office because the Public Defender's Office was closed, making my office the only place to meet. The fact that this meeting took place over a weekend also explains why my salaried government employee teammates (soon to be former teammates) were not available to meet with Sandy. So yes, the attorney who did nothing for Ms. Arias (or so those who love her now claim) gave up part of his weekend to meet with Sandy Arias to talk about this supposed bruising and a few other things. Backing up a bit, it is important for you to know that a few weeks before my meeting with her mother, Ms. Arias (my client) advised me for the first time that her mother had seen this bruising and that I should talk to her about it when she came to town. Not to sound like a character in a gangster movie, but "I smelled a rat." However, as I have alluded to earlier, had I not followed up on this I could have been found ineffective down the road by an appellate court and Ms. Arias could have received a new trial because of my ineffectiveness. So, I did my due diligence and I came in on the weekend to talk to Sandy Arias about what she supposedly witnessed on her daughter's arm. So when Sandy arrived we talked in the reception area of my office, mainly because I did not want Sandy to see any of the personal effects I had in my office. Why? One, I did not like the woman at all. Why? For starters she accused me of being unethical because I wanted to leave the Public Defender's Office and start my own practice. However, it was more than that, she was very juvenile, rude and untrustworthy. Let me give you but one example of this type of behavior to illustrate my point. After her son Carl and his wife ran into myself and my wife in Las Vegas, Sandy referred to my wife as a "skinny blonde bitch" during a jail call with Ms. Arias. Why she would say such a thing I had no idea (quite a way to treat the wife of the man who is trying to save your daughter's life isn't it). Sandy had never met my wife and other than say hello to Carl and his wife, my wife did not do anything to cause such a statement to be made. I always assumed Sandy said this to Ms. Arias to curry favor with her, to prove to her daughter that she did not like me either. However, it still pissed me off and it served as a clear example of why I did not like Sandy Arias. I am sure that we can all agree that Sandy's behavior in this regard was at best, juvenile and stupid. As you might guess, I could have cared less what she thought of me or my wife for that matter, but it still did not mean that I had to like her. Furthermore, even though I did not care what she had to say about me, at the same time, I did not want to give Sandy more fodder to bond with her daughter by relaying her observations of my personal effects to her daughter. I did not want to provide Ms. Arias with more fodder from which to try to manipulate me. So there we sat in the reception area of my office, no personal effects to be seen and after I updated her on the case and answered whatever questions she had, I asked Sandy if she had ever seen bruising on Ms. Arias' arms. First thing I found funny about this is that I had to ask, the second thing that was funny was that when I asked Sandy it was like a thought bubble went on above her head reading "Oh yeah, I forgot to tell him about seeing bruises, Jodi wanted me to tell him that." Anyway, when I asked her if she saw bruises she said yes. I asked her to describe where on Jodi's arms was this bruising visible? Sandy could "not remember." When did she see these bruises? Sandy could "not remember." I asked Sandy a few more questions of a similar nature that she also could not answer. Her inability to answer these basic questions, questions that any mother should be able to answer if they saw bruising on their child, along with her body language when I was asking them made it very clear to me that she was not being truthful. It did not take me too long to figure that out. It was sadly obvious. I knew the jury would reach the same conclusion that I did so there was no way I was going to put her on the stand. Not only that, but putting Sandy Arias on the stand would serve as a direct invitation to Juan Martinez to play the recordings of my client talking to her mother and as I discussed in Chapter 19, these calls were awful. In these calls my client would yell at her mother, degrade her mother. These calls made my client sound like a monster and listening to them made me want to send my client to death row and I strongly, strongly oppose the death penalty. Surely, the jury's response would have been quite similar to mine and in this regard I had to keep in mind that my ultimate job was to save Ms. Arias' life.

The final unnamed persons that Ms. Arias claims saw bruising on her that I did not call as a witness is a guy I will refer to as "Frank." The claim by Ms. Arias was that she was at a Pre-Paid Legal meeting in Tempe, Arizona. That while at this meeting Ms. Arias spoke with "Frank" and another person whose name I will also keep out of this explanation. As the story moves on, the claim is that during this conversation both of these men noticed bruising on Ms. Arias' arm and that "Frank" made a joke about Mr. Alexander beating and/or abusing Ms. Arias. To be clear, Ms. Arias gave us the true names of these individuals and so my job was to follow up on what Ms. Arias was telling me, as ignoring Ms. Arias' claims was not an option. To follow up on Ms. Arias' claims, myself, my former Co-counsel and our investigator drove to the outskirts of the Phoenix area to the home of the man who stood next to "Frank" the "jokester" during this supposed meeting. He was not home so we put my card on his screen door and gave one to his neighbor, who told us that he was out of town for a few months which was not surprising as most people not tied to a traditional job do what they can to avoid Phoenix in the summertime. Even though he was out of the state he called me back right away, in fact he called before my cohorts and I had returned to our offices in Phoenix. I advised him why we were contacting him. He advised me that he was at a Pre-Paid Legal Conference with Ms.

Arias and "Frank" and that the conference was held in Tempe. I asked him if he had any conversations with Ms. Arias in which "Frank" was present. The answer was no, he did recall talking to Ms. Arias but not when "Frank" was present. Getting nowhere I asked him specifically if he recalled any sort of conversation in which a joke was made about Mr. Alexander beating Ms. Arias during a time when he and "Frank" were together with Ms. Arias. He told me that he recalled no such conversation. This man went on to tell me that "Frank" was on the other side of the room when he spoke to Ms. Arias and that he did not notice any bruising on Ms. Arias' arms so there was no joke of this nature exchanged between himself and Ms. Arias. Clearly, this man and Ms. Arias were telling completely different versions of events. In Ms. Arias' story, she this man and "Frank" were all together and a joke about Mr. Alexander beating her was told. In this man's version of events "Frank" was on the other side of the room and no such joke was told. Did that mean I could simply dismiss the whole thing and just attribute it to Ms. Arias being a liar? No, because the law ultimately requires that I investigate every plausible issue. Thus, the next step in the process was to contact "Frank" and see what, if anything, he would have to say about any encounters he might have had with Ms. Arias. Sadly, for us the real "Frank" had a common name and was not so easy to track down. We tried everything we could to find him and we never succeeded in finding him. We called all the numbers we could find related to those who could be the correct "Frank." We even made an inquiry about Pre-Paid Legal through his web page and we got no response. We either did not have the right guy or we did have the right guy and he wanted nothing to do with us and made sure he did not leave any trail from which we could find him. I am not sure which was the case, however, that really did not matter in the end because it was clear that he was not going to offer helpful testimony. All this being said, had we found him and had he agreed to speak with us, I never held any delusions that he would have been helpful to Ms. Arias' case, in fact, I really sensed that just the opposite was true.

Despite this reality it would seem that Ms. Arias remains either convinced that this person could set her free or that my failure to find him is reason enough to have her conviction overturned. Perhaps she thinks that both of these things are true because as I read between the lines of an interview done with Ms. Arias' privately retained investigator, the quest to find "Frank" goes on.

So there you have it, when Ms. Arias claims that we had witnesses that saw her bruising that were not called as witnesses on her behalf, unless she has created new witnesses in her mind, these people are the supposed witnesses to whom she was referring during her post –verdict interview. Of course as you can see these supposed witnesses would really be of no help to Ms. Arias' case. Probably not what her "fans" want to hear but this is the reality of the situation. "Facts are stubborn things."

CHAPTER 23

WITNESS INTERVIEWS WITH THE STATE'S GUILT PHASE WITNESSES

Obviously, I will talk about the witnesses who actually took the stand and what they said while they were up there in greater depth in my next book wherein I discuss the first trial. However, any discussion of the pretrial happenings that surrounded this case would be incomplete if I did not give you a sense about what goes on with the people who are potential witnesses before they take the stand.

To give you a bit of background, in Arizona the law requires that both parties disclose the people who they may call as witnesses in a case to the opposing side. The opposing side then has the opportunity to interview these people. As you might guess, for a defense attorney who is serving as lead counsel in a capital case, being fully prepared for trial means making sure that you or another person on your team speaks with all of these people before they take the stand. Why? Because, if you are a defense attorney in a capital case and you do not interview a particular witness who winds up taking the stand that is not a wise move, because you might very well be found ineffective down the road and the trial might very well need to be redone.

For the sake of clarity let me emphasize that the fact that an individual's name makes its way onto a disclosure statement does not mean that they will actually be called as a witness, but instead that they may be called to the stand by either side. Thus, really what both sides disclose is a list of potential witnesses and it is fair game for both sides to call these people to the stand during the trial.

Given the number of people that you saw called to the stand during the guilt phase, you might think that the State called everyone on their list(s). Well that would be wrong. In fact, if I were making a guess I would say that the State actually called about half of those on their list to the stand.   In saying this I must admit that as I am making this guestimate. I do not know exactly how many witnesses the State put on their initial witness list nor do I know exactly how many they added to that initial list as the years went on but the list was quite lengthy and many lived outside of Arizona. So adding to my "joy" about being "Trapped with Ms. Arias," adding to my joy of being assigned to and later stuck on this case was the fact that I had to travel to places I would not otherwise travel to conduct these interviews. Regardless of whether or not I made these trips as a Public Defender or as a private attorney being Ms. Arias' lawyer meant that I had to travel to places that I would prefer to never have been.

Yreka, California, Ms. Arias' hometown certainly tops the list of places that this case took me that I never had any interest in visiting.   For those of you who are not familiar with Yreka, it is a town in northern California near the southern border of Oregon. It sits right off of Interstate 5, an interstate highway which by in large runs from Canada to Mexico (via California, Oregon and Washington). I have driven on this Interstate many a time and it has many scenic locations along the way, but for my money, Yreka, California is not one of them. To me Yreka seemed like little more than a big truck stop and a sleazy one at that. It had a few restaurants, a few hotels and about 7,000 people, none of whom seemed the slightest bit happy to live there. In my mind, Yreka, California, was one of the worst places I have ever been to and I have been to some sad looking towns in my day and by sad I do mean sad. I have been to the prison town of Rawlings, Wyoming. Look it up and you will see that it is an awful little prison town in the middle of Wyoming where the wind never stops blowing. Yes, in my mind Rawlings, Wyoming was pretty awful but it had nothing on Yreka, California which, to date, is the worst town I have ever visited. To make matters worse, getting to Yreka is no easy task. One route would involve flying to Sacramento, California and then taking a small plane to Medford, Oregon. Once in Medford you would then still need to drive for an hour or so to Yreka. Or you can fly to Sacramento and drive for 4 hours to reach Yreka. Either way a long trip, but for a guy who had a bad experience in a small plane I wanted to drive from Sacramento. The good news in this regard was that it was a nice drive through scenic mountains and it did not take too much longer than if we had flown to Medford and driven for an hour. I still remember this four hour drive with my then team members. I remember my investigator and my mitigation specialist both complaining about how slow I drove (many people have complained about this over the years). For the record, slow to these ladies was the speed limit and I was driving on a windy mountainous road and I was driving a crappy rental car of some sort. But anyway, once we got there I think we could all sense the despair inherent in Yreka, California. I remember driving through the town and immediately feeling how horrible it was. Most of the hotels, especially the ones the county wanted to house us in, looked more like run down "no tell motels," the kind of places where prostitutes and those cheating on their spouse would go to do the deed. Fortunately, we had somehow convinced the county to spend a few extra bucks to put us in the only livable hotel, the local Holiday Inn. It was a good thing we were there too because the trip lasted several days as we had to do some work on our mitigation case as well and sleeping at a quasi- brothel would not have helped us get the work we needed to get done, done (more on that in Chapter 26).

As it relates to the interviews of the State's witnesses, all were law enforcement and all the cops worked for either the Yreka Police Department or the Siskiyou County Sheriff's Office. As for the witnesses themselves, they were all great people, the kind of people all of us would want to serve as police officers, they were objective fact witnesses. Having said this, it was also the case that these officers were unfamiliar with the procedure because such interviews were not commonplace in California so it took a bit of time for them to understand what exactly was occurring but once we got that out of the way everything went relatively smoothly. As for the interviews them-selves, two things stand out, the first was the location. What sufficed as the Sheriff's Office for Siskiyou County was not what you might expect. It was not even an actual brick and mortar building, it was closer to a manufactured home or what my grade school would call the "portable classrooms." The second thing that stands out to me about these interviews is that during one of the interviews my investigator asked one of the officers a question, but Mr. Martinez advised the officer not to answer. Why? Well based on his statements it seemed to me that in his mind, I was the only one allowed to ask questions. I vehemently disagreed with this sentiment thus I advised Mr. Martinez that she could definitely ask questions. He tried to argue reasonable accommodations; I advised him that we could get the judge involved (this was before Judge Stephens took over the case). Mr. Martinez then wanted the investigator to tell me her question and then have me ask it. Yes, that is what he suggested, it seemed very juvenile to me and gave me great insight into who he was as a person. It seemed to me that he was the type of person or at least the type of attorney who thought he was in control of the entire case. This was one of the first times that I recall of Mr. Martinez trying to bully me, but it was far from the last. This was one of the first times that he tried to control a situation when he had no right to do so. It certainly would not be the last. For those of you wondering, after I stood up to him at this interview, the officer answered my investigator's question.

Other interviews took place in the area that surrounds Salt Lake City, Utah another place I doubt that I would have otherwise visited were it not for being "Trapped with Ms. Arias." If you recall, after June 4, 2008, Ms. Arias drove to the suburbs of Salt Lake to meet Ryan Burns and a few other people so it made sense that we needed to talk to those people and a few others that Ms. Arias had contact with. Before talking about the substance of the interviews I feel compelled to talk a bit about my experience in Salt Lake City. I flew in on a Sunday, got a rental car and drove into the city. I chose a hotel in the heart of downtown Salt Lake City as this would provide me with a central location for all the interviews I would have to complete while I was there. After checking into the hotel I realized that I was hungry and low on cash (yes I realize a few of you are laughing at these comments). In order to resolve this situation my plan was to walk around the downtown area, find a cash machine and a restaurant. Not too difficult a task in most cities, but if you have ever been to Salt Lake City on a Sunday you know that finding anything open is a tall order. ATM's were behind locked bank doors and virtually nothing was open. It was a surreal experience. I remember talking to my wife on my cell phone while I was walking around downtown Salt Lake City and telling her that it appeared as if some sort of evacuation was in effect because here I was in the heart of this big city and I was practically alone on the streets. Certainly, I realized that the true reason for my solitude was because most of those who reside in Salt Lake City are of the Mormon faith and Sunday is a day reserved for family, but this did not make the experience any less surreal nor did it help me find food or money (keep laughing). Luckily for me, I stumbled across what I suspect was one of the few places where the non-Mormon residents of Salt Lake City can go on a Sunday if they want to get out of the house. The place even sold beer, a regular sinner's paradise by the standard in Salt Lake City, but I could have cared less. It was open and they had food (yes jokesters they still had food after I left as well). After eating I still had very little cash in my wallet but everything else was back on track for me and when I woke up Monday morning Salt Lake City was every bit as alive as any other American city. I found food and I found a functioning cash machine with no problem. Now before you start thinking that I am bashing the Salt Lake City area I am not. It is a beautiful city, certainly a better place to be than Yreka, California, but those of you who live there will have to admit it is a much different place on a Sunday.

As for the interviews that we did in the Salt Lake City area, I interviewed Officer Galetti who pulled Ms. Arias over because her license plate was upside down (as I will explain in the next book a true "red herring" during the trial). That was truly a brief interview, as I recall that interview took longer to drive to than it did to conduct. That being said I will readily admit that this had something to do with the fact that I got lost trying to find the right police station. As I recall Mr. Martinez got quite a kick out of the fact that I got lost. Back then we did not despise each other (or so it seemed) so he was laughing with me not at me. We also interviewed some civilian witnesses as well. Those that stick out most prominently are Leslie Udy and Ryan Burns. I think these individuals stand out to me because of the fact that it was obvious that neither one wanted to be there. Certainly this could be said for almost everyone involved but I took their reluctance to be there in a different way than I did with other witnesses. It seemed to me that they both understood the inherent sadness of the entire situation. Why? Perhaps it was because they both had known both Mr. Alexander and Ms. Arias well before this tragedy took place. Perhaps it was because at one point in time they were both fond of Ms. Arias and Mr. Alexander. Perhaps it was because they simply chose to see this tragedy as a tragedy and not a reason for unmitigated anger. Certainly, I am only speculating you would have to ask them yourselves, maybe somebody will someday. Moving onto the interviews themselves, as it relates to Ms. Udy, I found her to be a wonderful person, a person who seemed to me to be, as I alluded to earlier, somewhat overtaken by the sadness of this tragedy. Ms. Udy was someone who was not upset about having to sit with Ms. Arias' defense attorney but she was upset about having to reflect on the entire tragedy. To her, this was more about the fact that she lost two friends than about condemning either individual. In this regard I found her answers to be honest and forthright and not designed to support either side, only the truth. As for Mr. Burns, I think he realized that he was in a very awkward position. He had been contacted by the media and had done some interviews. He seemed keenly aware of the attention this case would receive once trial started and it seemed as if he was very concerned about how he would be portrayed. For this I could not blame him, he was married, he had a child and he was still involved in Legal Shield (the company formerly known as Pre-Paid Legal). Thus, whatever he would say could jeopardize his standing either at home with his wife or his business. Consider the position he was in. It was obvious that in 2007 and 2008 that he had a romantic and or sexual interest in Ms. Arias, a woman who was now accused of being a murderer. Testifying truthfully would mean that he would have to admit to kissing and/or making out with Ms. Arias. I doubt his wife would like that and I doubt it would play very well with his business associates. Beyond that wouldn't you be nervous about how the media would portray you if you made out with Ms. Arias within a day of her killing Mr. Alexander. Granted he had no idea that she had done this at the time, but I am sure that if you were in his shoes you would be nervous about these things too. I assumed that for these reasons, and perhaps others that I had not even considered, he might be more than a bit hostile towards me in the interview but he was not. I think he certainly tried hard not to say anything that could possibly be perceived as being to Ms. Arias' favor, but when pushed he admitted some favorable things. Overall, I found Mr. Burns to be a great guy, who got caught up in a bad situation and as I could empathize with that situation, I never held a grudge against Mr. Burns and to my knowledge he never held a grudge against me, something that cannot be said about all of the civilian witnesses.

Certainly, there were also many pre-trial interviews that took place locally. As you might guess, because most of the State witnesses worked for the Mesa Police Department most of the local interviews took place at their offices. There were interviews with the crime scene technicians, the fingerprint examiners and the officers who stood guard over the house. As you might guess, after Ms. Arias claimed that she acted in self-defense many of these interviews did not mean a lot and in this regard I will not bore you with these irrelevant details.

However, the interviews with Detective Flores and Melendez were very meaningful to the case so I suspect that the details will not bore you. I base my conclusion on the idea that if you would be bored by such things, you would not have purchased this book. Of course, I will talk about the testimony these men offered during trial in my next book, instead in this book I will talk about the things that were said before they took the stand.

I had never met Detective Flores until I interviewed him during my work on this case, however, that did not mean I did not have a sense of who he was before I met him. I had a sense of who he was because I had heard him on audiotape and I had watched him on videotape on several occasions. Specifically, I had seen videos of his interviews with Ms. Arias and I had seen him on videotape interviewing other civilian witnesses such as Chris and Sky Hughes. As you might guess, having videos of this nature was not uncommon, though in this case I certainly had more than I had in most cases, however what I had in this case that was so uncommon was hours of video in which the lead detective in the case was the subject of an interview. You see Detective Flores was also interviewed by the CBS program "48 Hours" and during these interviews he made some statements that might have seemed unimportant at the time but were very helpful to Ms. Arias now that some additional evidence had come to light. Specifically, I am talking about his statements that there was no evidence that Ms. Arias slashed Mr. Alexander's tires, that they did not know who sent an ominous e-mail to Mr. Alexander's former girlfriend Lisa Andrews and that there was clear evidence that the contact Ms. Arias and Mr. Alexander had was mutual.

Taken as a whole, from all these videos I was left with the impression that Detective Flores was a kind mild mannered man. That he was not an aggressive cop who got in people's faces, but instead the type who would simply let a person talk until the person had tied a noose around their own neck, so to speak. He also, especially during his interview with CBS, appeared to be very objective in that he was honest when he talked about the evidence related to the crime. All this being said, his reputation amongst defense attorneys was that he was not honest, which at the time surprised me, but I had yet to meet him.

When I met Detective Flores in person for the first time, I found him to be very likeable and professional. You might think that this would be the case with all officers but many just simply hate defense attorneys, all of us, because we dare question what they do. In contrast to the demeanor I saw on the various videotapes, once I started talking about the case and asking questions related to the newly obtained evidence, such as the text messages, it seemed to me that he became very evasive and further seemed suddenly incapable of providing straightforward answers to simple questions. While his evasiveness was surprising based on my observations of him, it is not uncommon for police officers who want to subvert defense attorneys from getting accurate answers typically they do not want to give objective answers to simple questions. I was very happy to have these interviews because I knew that Detective Flores could not deny making certain statements because he had made them on videotape.

As for Detective Melendez, if you recall he performed the forensic analysis on the camera and Mr. Alexander's laptop amongst other things. Thus his testimony would typically be pretty straightforward in that his job is to simply relay what he found on the computer and describe how he found it. During my interview with Detective Melendez, I learned that his qualifications to do this ultimately amounted to passing a quickie computer course that is offered to police officers, which is to say he really lacked the qualifications to do what he was doing for a living. By this I mean that he was not a true "forensic computer expert" who was qualified to do a complete forensic analysis of a computer. Instead, he basically knew how to run one program, EnCase. This is not to say that this program is not capable of obtaining a fair amount of data, instead it is to say that Detective Melendez did not seem capable of exploring further, he did not seem capable of running other programs or performing more complex tasks. Despite these limitations, when he wrote his report he wrote it as if he was truly a computer expert, however, when I interviewed him it seemed to me that, if I was to believe his answers, he could barely turn on the computer or find a web-page and that he did not truly inspect what was on the computer, he simply ran the program. When pressed, to his credit, in my opinion, Detective Melendez was great at being vague and it was truly a shame that he did not give an interview to CBS's "48 Hours", I would have loved to have him on videotape.

As a whole, my interviews with these men left me with the impression that they were not the impartial fact witnesses, which in theory is the role that police officers are supposed to serve during a case. Was I surprised by this? No, in my opinion, police officers rarely actually serve as impartial witnesses. However, to be clear, what I am talking about here is something more than the typical agenda driven police officer. In my opinion, these men simply wanted to serve whatever agenda Juan Martinez had at that moment. A fact I found disconcerting because I knew that the testimony of these two Detectives would be very important to the outcome of the case.

As you might guess Detectives Melendez and Flores were not the only government workers who in my opinion were placing the agenda of Juan Martinez above the truth. Chief amongst these people would be Dr. Kevin Horn. Dr. Horn was the county medical examiner who performed the autopsy on Mr. Alexander. If I recall correctly, I had interviewed Dr. Horn on one other occasion but I guess I had forgotten his demeanor. He appeared to me as being a very arrogant man who just expected to be believed because he was with the "good guys" and he was handsome and articulate. By this I mean he did not keep up on medical research, he seemed to know very little about how the brain functioned. The interview with Dr. Horn took place after Ms. Arias had claimed self-defense and articulated that she shot Mr. Alexander first. Remarkably, it was in this interview that Dr. Horn claimed, for the first time, that the gunshot was last. This had to be a coincidence right? It could not be the case that Juan Martinez told Dr. Horn about what Ms. Arias said about the order of wounds and that as a result of this conversation that Dr. Horn, in a strange coincidence, changed his mind about the sequence of events could it? That would be so hard to believe.

As you are likely aware, the State listed some civilian witnesses who lived in the Phoenix area as well. As you might guess, most of these people were people who had some sort of relationship with Mr. Alexander. Of all these interviews I think two of these interviews would be of interest to you, the interview myself and my former Co-counsel did with Deanna Reid and the interview I did with Mimi Hall in her mother's home.

When Ms. Reid was finally formally interviewed that interview took place in Phoenix at the Public Defender's Office in July of 2011. I say finally because it took so long to get Ms. Reid to agree to an interview and I say formally interviewed because this was not the first time I met Ms. Reid. The first time I met Ms. Reid it was fairly early on in the case, I cannot recall exactly when but I would guess in the summer of 2010. At that time Ms. Reid lived in Riverside with her parents and she was really a bit of a mystery to me at the time which is why I wanted to meet her. Why was she such a mystery to me in the early days of the case? Because it seemed that she played such a unique and undefined role in Mr. Alexander's life. To hear the Hughes talk, Ms. Reid was the love of Mr. Alexander's life but she was not attractive enough for Mr. Alexander to marry. Based on some of the evidence it also appeared as if Ms. Reid was engaged to Mr. Alexander when she went off to her mission, then when she came back he was engaged to someone else, yet Ms. Reid remained in Mr. Alexander's life. It appeared that they then dated again and still remained friends. It always seemed to me that Ms. Reid was Mr. Alexander's back up plan and I was not sure why she was okay with this, maybe she wasn't, hence my confusion, I was not sure how this woman would feel about Mr. Alexander. The one thing that I was pretty sure of is that she was not interested in talking to us. Looking back we now know that she had something to hide.

Knowing that Ms. Reid would not be excited about talking to us, we simply showed up at her house unannounced. That may not sound appropriate to you but it is not an uncommon technique for investigators on both sides of the fence to do business this way. When we arrived at the home Ms. Reid was not present, but her father was and it was our belief that he was not too fond of Mr. Alexander. When we spoke to him he certainly did not confirm that belief but he certainly did not hesitate to invite us into his home. Ms. Reid then came home to find us sitting in her living room talking to her father. We wound up talking at the dining room table and while Ms. Reid was polite I could certainly tell that she was being very cautious about what she said and I could certainly tell that she was not looking for an opportunity to speak ill of Mr. Alexander.

When this formal interview came to pass, we had much more evidence from which to base our questioning. We now had text messages, the sex tape and most importantly as it related to Ms. Reid, we had an e-mail that Mr. Alexander had written to the Hughes in which he talked about ruining her or words to that effect. We now had a better idea of who he was and had enough evidence from which to assume she had a sexual relationship with Mr. Alexander.

Because the bulk of this interview would relate to the romantic and/ or intimate relationship that Ms. Reid shared with Mr. Alexander, my Co-counsel and I thought it best for her to ask the bulk of the questions. To her credit my former Co-counsel asked these questions with tact, a tact that would later serve as Ms. Reid's excuse for not admitting that she had sexual relations with Mr. Alexander, but, tact nonetheless. For her part Deanna Reid denied that she knew of anyone else having sex with Mr. Alexander, apart from Ms. Arias at a time when she knew full well that she did in fact have sex with Mr. Alexander. It was quite obvious to me at the time that she did in fact have sex with Mr. Alexander at least once, what else could Mr. Alexander have meant when he mentioned ruining her? I got the sense at the time that she was not being truthful. At trial she later admitted that she did have sex with him, one time. So did she go into this interview knowing that she would lie if asked this question? Did Juan Martinez talk to her about how important it might be to cover up the sexual aspect of her relationship with Mr. Alexander? I certainly will never know the answer to that question but it was very obvious to me that Ms. Reid had told a great deal of untruths to keep Mr. Alexander's secrets during his lifetime and that she certainly was not going to stop doing so now after he was killed. In defense of Ms. Reid, she was not the only woman to cover for Mr. Alexander in this way but she seemingly was the one who had done it for the longest time and the one who had the most to lose as she had the most secrets about Mr. Alexander, secrets that she needed to keep because they would likely harm her reputation and/or status in the Mormon community as well.

For those of you who do not immediately recall who Ms. Hall is and what her role in this case was I will remind you that Ms. Hall was a friend of Mr. Alexander's whom Mr. Alexander had a romantic interest in. In fact, based on what Mr. Alexander had said during his electronic correspondence with his friends, it seemed that Mr. Alexander believed that Mimi Hall would someday be his wife. Sadly for Mr. Alexander she did not share his passion, she saw him as a friend. As a further reminder all of this was going on in the spring of 2008. Now, those of you who might not be so familiar with the case may be questioning why Ms. Hall was a witness in the case at all. The State called her to talk about what a gentleman Mr. Alexander was to her and to advise the jury how Mr. Alexander had spoken to her about how he had a "stalker." Though he did not name this stalker the State presumably wanted to use this evidence to argue that Ms. Arias was stalking Mr. Alexander.

As for Ms. Hall, before I met her I had every reason to believe that she was a proper Mormon girl. That she was a Mormon who followed the rules and presumed that everyone else did as well. I also got the sense that she was a shy person. I got this sense mainly because she wanted her interview to take place in her mother's home, with her mother present. I took this as a sign of shyness because while this would be understandable for a young girl, it seemed out of place for a woman in her twenties. When I met Ms. Hall in person the presumptions I had about her were confirmed. You might ask then why did this interview stand out to me amongst all the other civilian interviews I did in the case. The answer is simple, what Ms. Hall had to say solidified my opinion that Ms. Hall was the kind of girl that Mr. Alexander could be a gentlemen with because he had Ms. Arias to handle those things that a proper Mormon girl would never do. In my mind this served as pretty clear evidence that Mr. Alexander was living a double life, he was telling people that Ms. Arias was a stalker while she was serving as his sexual outlet, an outlet to satiate him while he sought out a proper wife. Just my opinion of course, but please tell me how I am wrong. "Facts are stubborn things."

CHAPTER 24

THE STATE'S INTERVIEWS WITH MS. ARIAS' ACTUAL GUILT PHASE WITNESSES

Just like the defense has the opportunity to interview the State's witnesses before trial, the State has the opportunity to interview the defense witnesses
before they take the stand. As there were no witnesses to the events of June
4, 2008 and because Ms. Arias was not claiming that she did not kill Mr.
Alexander on this day, the people who Ms. Arias would call would be those
who could speak to the way Mr. Alexander treated her, people who saw
them together. Certainly, a fair amount of people had seen them interact
but it was often not that accurate of a glimpse. Daniel Freeman and his
sister Desiree, however, had had the opportunity to see this relationship
in a different light than most have, so they would be called to share their
perspective. Because Ms. Arias was claiming to have some memory issues
related to the few minutes in time during which she killed Mr. Alexander,
Dr. Richard Samuels was to be called to explain this phenomenon as well
as the trauma that evidenced itself on Ms. Arias' psychological testing.
Finally, as it related to Ms. Arias' claim of domestic violence, an expert
on that topic was to be called as well. Combined, these people along with
Ms. Arias herself would all be providing pieces to the puzzle that would
help Ms. Willmott and I make the argument that Ms. Arias was acting in

self-defense. Of course as I explain in Chapter 50 there was more to it than this, I had a plan.

For their part, the State, in order to make their case against Ms. Arias, needed to prove that Ms. Arias did not act in self-defense. By in large then it would seem that the State's goal in these interviews would be to probe for something that would help attack Ms. Arias' claims of self-defense when trial began. To some degree that would mean that the State would be attacking the conclusions of our experts. I should say that is typically how it goes, but for Mr. Martinez, the tactics he employed during these interviews seemed to me to be designed to obtain information that he could later use to attack the experts, not just on their opinions but as people. What sort of tactics am I talking about? To begin with Mr. Martinez displayed a much different demeanor in the interviews than he did at trial. He was professional and very calm. He also listened to the person's answer so that he could probe for more information. The interviews themselves took hours, much longer than most prosecutors would take, however, I must admit it was interesting to watch him try to disguise the bombastic nature of the attack to come. It appeared to me that he thought he was getting away with something during these interviews. However, the way I saw it, his reputation preceded him in terms of his demeanor but to his credit over an interview that would last several hours, he would manage to trip a person up and use that later. In my mind, not what a prosecutor is supposed to do but this too was expected because of who we were dealing with.

One of the interviews took place with a well-qualified domestic violence expert. This expert had a Ph.D in psychology. This expert also had years of experience working in the field of domestic violence. She had both "real life experience" in helping those who have experienced domestic violence and academic experience as well. In sum, it was this expert's belief that Ms. Arias was a victim of domestic violence during her relationship with Mr. Alexander. To reach this conclusion this expert had reviewed an extensive amount of records and put Ms. Arias through a battery of psychological tests. (Yes, I realize that many a trial watchers believe that this is not true because there were no reports of domestic violence, meaning the police were not called or just because Ms. Arias is a liar. I will speak about this more in my next book, but for now let me just pose a rhetorical question to you – Why is it that you think you know better than experts in the field? As an added bonus during her interview this expert did not back down on her conclusions at all. Regardless of how much Mr. Martinez pushed, she would not give an inch, this certainly seemed to make him angry. However, that did not bother this expert having been in court with Mr. Martinez this expert knew his game and was not going to tolerate it. This expert would not back down from her assertions that Mr. Alexander had abused Ms. Arias. In fact it would seem that the more he probed the more resolute she became. It would have been interesting if this expert was able to take the stand, during the first trial. Not only would it have been great theatre but my gut tells me that the whole case would have been different.

When Mr. Martinez interviewed Dr. Samuels the interview was lengthy, one of the longest interviews I had ever experienced before I had a case with Juan Martinez. As a guy who has often been accused of being a workaholic I began to feel pretty good about myself in that Mr. Martinez always seemed to work many more hours than I did. In fact, I got the sense that he worked non-stop. One thing I will say about Mr. Martinez, in terms of the hours he put in for his salary, and only in those terms, the taxpayers were getting their money's worth. As for the substance of the interview itself I do not recall every detail, nor would it be interesting for me to listen to the recording of this interview and recount every detail for you. It would be tedious, trust me. I was there and it was tedious. So rather than putting us both through such an ordeal, I will recount the facts I do remember because those are also likely the most interesting. However, before I detail the interesting highlights of the interview, I want to back up a bit, as I should explain that apart from being a learned psychologist Richard Samuels is one of the kindest and most empathetic people I know. During his interview with Mr. Martinez it became apparent to me that Mr. Martinez was taking advantage of Dr. Samuels' kind disposition by trying to put words in his mouth. It seemed to me that Mr. Martinez was trying to use Dr. Samuels' desire to be accommodating to others against him. Mr. Martinez's clear goal was to get Dr. Samuels to say things that would undermine his position. For Mr. Martinez's purposes he was successful enough to later use this interview to attack Dr. Samuels, primarily on a personal level (of course my next book will cover this in greater detail). The other thing that stands out in my mind is one occasion that Dr. Samuels steadfastly held his ground against Mr. Martinez. In my mind the issue was a curious one for Mr. Martinez to push on but push he did. Recall if you will that Mr. Alexander, on the day of his death, had taken a picture of Ms. Arias' anus. Those of you who followed the trial closely enough likely know which photo I am talking about but for those of you who do not and for those of you who need some reminding as to what picture I am referencing, I am talking about the picture that Mr. Alexander took of Ms. Arias' anus from a very close range, not her butt, but her anus. In my mind this looked more like a picture that a proctologist might take, but be that as it may that is the picture I am referencing and I suspect if you want further clarity you can probably find it online. When Mr. Martinez asked Dr. Samuels about this photograph, Dr. Samuels expressed his opinion that because Mr. Alexander had taken a photograph of this nature, that Mr. Alexander could have had an anal fixation. To be clear, Dr. Samuels was not saying that Mr. Alexander did have such a fixation only that he could. Dr. Samuels further clarified that he could not diagnose Mr. Alexander in any way because he was now deceased. In my mind, the whole issue was meaningless in that Dr. Samuels was not going to testify to this belief and Mr. Alexander's comments on the sex tape along with the photograph he took seem to speak for themselves. However, for whatever reason, this angered Mr. Martinez and the two argued about this idea for several minutes.

Before completely moving past the subject of Dr. Samuels, while I will talk about his testimony and the reaction to it more extensively in my next book, I wanted to take a brief aside to say that the attacks on him were unwarranted and that it always amazed me how those who know little to nothing about the field of psychology would know more than a PhD in the field, much less one as highly decorated as Dr. Samuels.

As I describe in much greater detail in Chapter 37, when the prior domestic violence expert could not continue her work Alyce LaViolette, who was also an expert in domestic violence was brought onto the case as her replacement (I like Alyce as a person but this was not a good exchange for Ms. Arias). When Mr. Martinez interviewed Ms. LaViolette the interview took place in Ms. Willmott's office in a small uncomfortable conference room. Being in an uncomfortable place did not motivate Mr. Martinez to move the interview along at a rapid pace. Instead, this interview also took several hours. If memory serves, Mr. Martinez took much more time interviewing Ms. LaViolette than he did with the other experts. To be fair to Mr. Martinez, a fair amount of this time was spent with him asking questions about Ms. LaViolette's handwriting that I will concede was very hard to read. Furthermore, as Ms. LaViolette had not written a report, these notes were all he had to base his questions on. However, as far as substance went, Ms. LaViolette's conclusions were not subject to any legitimate challenge and Mr. Martinez seemed to be figuring this out as he progressed during the interview. By this I mean that a concrete fact could not be pulled out of the air that would prove Ms. LaViolette wrong. Instead, her conclusions were her beliefs based on her experience as a domestic violence counselor. At the same time it was obvious that what Ms. LaViolette believed, her professional conclusions were based on what Ms. Arias had told her and as we all know Ms. Arias had a history of lying. Undoubtedly we will talk about Ms. LaViolette and the conclusions she testified to in court more in my next book, however, before we completely move on from Ms. LaViolette in this chapter let me again ask a similar rhetorical question that I posed as it related to Dr. Samuels. What makes you, the trial watcher, so positive that Ms. LaViolette is wrong? What makes you, the trial watcher think that you know more about domestic violence than Ms. LaViolette?

In addition to Ms. Arias' experts she had two people, the aforementioned Dan and Desiree Freeman who were willing to speak to what they knew about the relationship. As it relates to the Freemans I want to be clear, the fact that Ms. Arias was calling them as witnesses did not mean that they in some way supported Ms. Arias and were against Mr. Alexander. Instead, they were willing to testify as to what they knew, as all citizens should, if they happened to be called as witnesses in any trial. Never did I get the sense that the Freemans desired to "bash" either Mr. Alexander or Ms. Arias but to tell what they knew. Given that they were members of the LDS faith I knew that doing so might be hard on them, so I admired them greatly for their willingness to share their observations. However, as this chapter deals with the interviews that Mr. Martinez did with Ms. Arias' witnesses, let me turn you back to the interviews themselves.

Because the Freeman's lived on the outskirts of town and making it into the downtown area would not be easy for them, the interviews took place in their parent's home. On a personal note I always loved visiting the Freeman's home because the entire family was so kind to everyone and they had a great dog. As for the interviews themselves the interview with Desiree seemed relatively brief and focused on the observations she had made when she spent time with Mr. Alexander and Ms. Arias, both when they were together and when they were apart. While Mr. Martinez certainly asked Mr. Freeman about the same sort of issues the interview with him also moved into questions about the LDS faith for whatever reasons he had Mr. Martinez seemed compelled to ask if Daniel had any romantic interest in Ms. Arias.

Based on his interviews it sure seemed to me that Mr. Martinez was convinced that the only people who were willing to testify for Ms. Arias were those who wanted to sleep with her.

SECTION 4

PREPARING FOR THE MITIGATION PHASE

The Mitigation Phase of a death penalty case is typically the most important phase of the case because the evidence presented in this phase often makes the difference between a life sentence and a death sentence. It is the point in the case where more often than not the jury learns the most about the defendant. It is the point in time where focus shifts from the crime itself to who the defendant is as a person. It is the point in time that the jury oftentimes hears things about the defendant they have not heard before. Of course, as I have often said in this book, Ms. Arias' case was far from typical. However, even though Ms. Arias' case was far from typical it did not mean that Ms. Arias had no mitigation, it just meant that her mitigation would likely come into evidence in a different way. To set the stage for this section, in Chapter 25, I will talk about what a "mitigation phase" typically involves so as to provide you a better understanding of what tends to occur in most cases. In Chapter 26, I will discuss "The Mitigation Investigation by Prior Counsel" so as to make you aware of what was done on this aspect of the case before I got the file. In Chapter 27, I will speak about what I did, in terms of finding mitigation once I got the file and I conclude this section with Chapter 28, wherein I talk about the State's attempt to counteract Ms. Arias' case for life.

CHAPTER 25

WHAT IS THE POINT OF THE SENTENCING PHASE AND MITIGATION?

Certainly, I have and will make references to mitigation throughout this whole book. I strongly suspect that this trend will continue in my next two books. Despite these other references I wanted to dedicate a distinct chapter to the subject of mitigation so that there is as much clarity about what constitutes mitigation as is possible. Why do I think that this is important? Because the idea of mitigation and how it is presented in the sentencing phase of a capital trial seems to aggravate so many people. Many people seem to think that it does not matter who the defendant is or what is wrong with them. These people tend to be of the mindset that if a person kills somebody, they should be killed, period. Others may just simply be so mad about what Ms. Arias had to say about Mr. Alexander that they do not believe that such factors should come into play for her. Certainly I understand all of these feelings. However, at the same time I am of the belief that mitigating factors are an important part of any death penalty system. In my mind, if we are going to impose the death penalty as a punishment we must allow juries to know who they are sentencing. I realize that as I say this many of you will disagree with me. To my credit the United States Supreme Court agrees with me and it is that court who determines what must be done to make a sentence of death lawful under our Constitution.

Many of you may not realize this but there was a point in time that the death penalty was not legal in this country. Why was it illegal? Because the United States Supreme Court determined that the imposition of such a sentence amounted to Cruel and Unusual Punishment. The Court, at that time, believed that a death sentence violated the 8th Amendment to our Constitution, which specifically prohibits Cruel and Unusual punishment. That changed in 1976, when the United States Supreme Court decided the case of Gregg v. Georgia. In sum, this case legalized the death penalty across the United States. Admittedly, this is an oversimplification of what the case says, but at the same time this is not a legal textbook either. With that same disclaimer in mind, let me again oversimplify the relevant legal precedent and say that since legalizing the death penalty the United State Supreme Court has said that in order for a sentence of death to be legal, a jury, not a judge, must make that determination. Furthermore, the law says that when the jury is making this determination they must consider everything about the person and the circumstances of the offense that is presented to them.

What this means from a practical standpoint is that an attorney and his or her team, in order to be effective counsel to their client, must gather all the information they can about their client and then decide which information to present to a jury. It also means that if they do not present some of this information to the jury and the defendant is sentenced to death, that sentence may very well get overturned if that attorney does not have a very good reason for not presenting that evidence. By the way, "I did not believe it" is not a sufficient answer.

As Ms. Arias' claims about Mr. Alexander raise such anger, to illustrate my point about the role mitigation plays in a death penalty case and what a lawyer must do to prepare for the sentencing phase, let me use another situation altogether, a hypothetical situation. In Chapter 41, I talk about the felony murder rule and to illustrate that rule I talk about "Jim" a hypothetical defendant who robbed a store clerk at gunpoint. In this example I describe the fact that during this robbery two people die. I further describe that Jim did not intend to kill either of these people (one dies of a heart attack and one is accidentally run over as Jim flees the scene in his car). Now let's say that Jim is now facing the death penalty for these two murders (in Chapter 41, I explain why Jim's actions are First Degree Murders). What must his lawyer do for Jim in terms of mitigation and what must the jury consider?

As for what the attorney must do, the quickest and simplest way to say it is that the attorney, with the help of his or her team, must do all they can to gather all the information they can about Jim. Once this information is collected then the lead attorney decides how best to tell the complete story of Jim's life to the jury. In practical terms this means that the defense team must investigate Jim's life from conception to the day he is being sentenced. Yes, I said conception. Why that far back? Because if Jim's mother drank or used drugs when she was pregnant with Jim that could have impacted how Jim's brain developed. Now again, you might not care about these things but this is the kind of information the law says jurors should hear before they choose between a life sentence and a sentence of death. In fact the law dictates that jurors must not only hear the evidence but give it meaningful consideration.

Again using "Jim" as my example, let's say that Jim's attorneys do their job and they obtain all the information they can about Jim's life and present it to the jury. To further my point let's put you on that jury. Yes you, all of you, even those of you who are saying to themselves something to the effect of "who cares about this stuff, he killed two people and he needs to be killed," can be on this hypothetical jury. Moving forward in this hypothetical, assume for me that as a juror you hear about how when Jim was five years old that his parents were killed in a car accident and that after that time he was raised by family members and spent some time in foster care. You also hear that at the age of 10 Jim claimed that he was molested while in foster care, though you are provided with no evidence to substantiate these claims. You learn that despite all these obstacles that Jim graduated high school and joined the army. As the story of Jim's life moves on, you learn that while in the army Jim was wounded by enemy fire and was diagnosed with post-traumatic stress disorder. You further learn that after being discharged from the hospital for his "war wounds" Jim became addicted to the pain pills that he was given to aid in his recovery. Finally, assume for me that you hear that Jim's sole motivation for committing this robbery was to get the money he needed to feed his pain pill addiction. Keeping in mind that he did not intend to kill anyone, the question now posed to you the jury becomes: Do you as a juror think that Jim should be sentenced to death? Some of you may think "yes" and some of you might think "no, of course not." However, regardless of your answer I suspect all of you on the "jury" think differently of Jim now after learning about his background. In a nutshell that is the point of mitigation and the mitigation phase of a capital trial. This phase is designed to help the jury understand who they are sentencing, not just what crime this person committed. The law in this country says that we must give consideration to these issues.

I hope that makes sense to you but with the hope of not belaboring the point I think one final point should be made about the role of mitigation in capital cases and the presentation of evidence in a "sentencing phase" of a capital trial. Point being, that sometimes these factors come out during the guilt phase of the trial and sometimes they do not. In the "Jim" hypothetical I discuss above, none of Jim's background is related to the offense in that the evidence concerning his background would not speak to Jim being guilty of a lesser crime than First Degree Murder. In contrast, in Ms. Arias' situation her entire relationship with Mr. Alexander was of the sort that it could lead to a finding that Ms. Arias was guilty of a lesser included offense (such as second degree murder and manslaughter) which is why, as I will discuss in greater detail in the next book that much of Ms. Arias' mitigation came out in the guilt phase of her trial.

CHAPTER 26

The Mitigation Investigation by Prior Counsel

As I described in the previous chapter, when an attorney is in the position in which they must defend a client's life, the rule in our country essentially is that the attorney, with the help of his or her team must investigate their client's life from conception to the day he or she is sentenced and must likewise, absent a good reason not to, present that evidence to the sentencing jury.

This means that Ms. Arias' prior counsel was also obligated to investigate these things on behalf of Ms. Arias. I know that this will aggravate some of you and that many of you do not want to hear this but, Ms. Arias, by law, was entitled to the same level of defense as anyone else accused of a capital crime. The fact that you may hate her does not change that reality. Furthermore, if she did not receive this level of defense and she was sentenced to death that sentence would almost undoubtedly be overturned and she would be in court again for another trial.

In this regard, Ms. Arias' previous attorney, being a diligent attorney, collected this information and had it documented in the form of memorandums that were written by Gwen, the woman who, at the time, was working as Ms. Arias' Mitigation Specialist. As a whole these interviews really did not paint a good picture of Ms. Arias, in fact, far from it. The Interviewees, most of whom were either Ms. Arias' friends or family, presumably people who loved her, did not say nice things about her. There were claims that

Ms. Arias had abused animals as a child. These people further described her as being a weird child who was violent with her mother as a teenager. Those who knew her from work or school described Ms. Arias in many different ways. To some she was highly sexual and acted as if she was "in heat," to others she was quiet and professional and/or a quiet and talented student.

So what was the truth? Was Ms. Arias just an otherwise normal shy girl? Was she an overly sexualized young woman? These interviews did not paint a clear picture. Despite the fact that the picture was not very clear, reading these interviews along with the other materials her previous lawyer obtained gave me a great deal of insight into who Ms. Arias was to particular people. Having this insight only bolstered my theory that Ms. Arias was a victim of sexual abuse as a child. Why? Because my experiences in defending those accused of sexual crimes, many of whom were also victims of sexual abuse, has taught me a few things. My experience has taught me that these victims turned offenders "learn" at far too young of an age that their value to the world is their sexuality. Put another way, they are oversexualized. More specifically, as it related to Ms. Arias, it seemed to me from reading these interviews that Ms. Arias was an otherwise quiet and reserved person, but at the same time was a person who would assert her sexuality when she wanted to be liked. Certainly in this respect reading the memorandums was valuable to me in that it bolstered my belief that Ms. Arias had been sexually abused as a child.

That being said, I certainly wished that it was only members of the defense team(s) that had access to these memos. In this regard you must understand that these memos could have remained confidential. Attorney-client privilege would protect them from the State getting a hold of them. In fact, the only way that the State could obtain these memos was if the choice was made by Ms. Arias' lawyer to disclose them to the State. In my opinion there were way too many harmful statements about Ms. Arias in these memorandums to make their disclosure to the State a wise move. I would have kept them confidential. However, that was just my thinking. My thinking did not enter into the picture before August of 2009, when I was assigned to the case.

By then it was too late as it related to this issue of disclosing these memos to the State, because by that time, they had already been turned over. Why did her former counsel do this? I do not know. Do I hold it against her or think it was stupid of her to do? No, that is not what I am saying. I am simply saying that I would not have done it. But, it was done and now it was my job to deal with it.

CHAPTER 27

MY MITIGATION INVESTIGATION

In Chapter 25, I have described in general the type of mitigation investigation that needs to be conducted in a death penalty case. In Chapter 26, I discussed what was uncovered by Ms. Arias' former counsel as it related to Ms. Arias' situation. In most death penalty cases such investigations likely uncover the need to present both civilian and expert witnesses. In a typical case the defendant will have many family members and/or close friends who wish to speak on their loved one's behalf and that is almost always helpful. However, as I have and will mention often in this book, Ms. Arias' case was far from the typical. Instead of having several people who were willing to speak on her behalf, I could find but one who could truly offer help. Her ex-boyfriend Darryl was the only one who I thought could truly help Ms. Arias. Many of you who find joy in hating Ms. Arias might find glee in what I am saying, but I would ask you to consider this reality in another way. Think about how Ms. Arias truly had so little support in her life before this crime was committed.

If you watched the first trial you knew that when it came time to present Ms. Arias' case for life during the sentencing phase, I chose not to call anyone, not even Darryl. Why did I choose this course? I will certainly explain this further in my second book, but for now let me just summarize my reasoning and say that I made this decision because I did not have enough good cards left to play by the end of the guilt phase of the trial. Was the media to blame for some of this? Yes certainly. We will talk about why in the next book. But, as it relates to the subject of this book, pretrial events, I certainly cannot blame the media for the fact that I did not even have one family member whom I could count on to help Ms. Arias make her case for life. The fact that I did not have any family members that could help was apparent to me back in 2010, when I, along with two other members of my team, went to Yreka, California, Ms. Arias' home town. I speak about this trip and what I thought about Yreka when I speak about the pretrial interviews in Chapter 23. However, for those of you who have forgotten let's just say that Yreka was not a place I enjoyed spending time. What I did not speak to in Chapter 23, was the portion of the trip that I spent with Ms. Arias' family trying to gather mitigating evidence. Thus I will address that issue presently.

At the time, I do not believe that any of us had actually met any of Ms. Arias' family. Perhaps some on the team had met Ms. Arias' mother Sandy, but I cannot recall with certainty. Regardless, once the interviews were over, off to the Arias house we went. The plan was for us to meet Ms. Arias' mother Sandy, Ms. Arias' father Bill, her brother Joey and her sister Angela. Our initial meeting took place in the kitchen and living room areas of the home. In that initial conversation we spoke a bit about mundane things and while this conversation was taking place I devoted a lot of energy to taking in the aura of the place. It may sound a little strange to you but if I am at a place where my client had been before they became my client, be it their home, work place or school, I like to get a sense of what the experience was like for them. It helps me get to know my client better on some level. I guess you could call it my attempt to walk a mile in my client's shoes, their mental "shoes" if you will.

As for the Arias home itself it was small for 5 people, it was furnished with old looking furniture and it was messy. Please do not take this as a condemnation of the home, I am simply telling you what I observed. Did my observations mean anything to me? Most certainly they did, but remember, I am more interested in getting a sense of the home's aura, the feel of the home. In that regard, I recall sensing a feeling of coldness and a sense of despair all at the same time. This might be hard for you to understand so let me try to explain by way of analogy. When I speak to the coldness of the home, the best analogy I can come up with is having the experience of walking into a newly constructed home that nobody has lived in. If you have done this you know that regardless of how nice the house is, it just does not feel the same as a home that is occupied by people who love each other. As it relates to the sense of despair in the home, the best analogy I can think of would be the polar opposite of a new unoccupied home. I would describe the sense of despair that I felt while standing in the Arias home as being akin to the feeling of being in an abandoned home, a home whose life blood had left. I hope that these analogies make sense because I think it is important for you to understand how the Arias home was both "cold" and at the same time filled with a sense of "despair." Put another way the Arias household did not feel like a home, in the true sense of the word, at least not to me.

As to the people who lived in this residence at the time, Sandy, Bill, Angela and Joey Arias. It was readily apparent that none of them took the time to clean any portion of the house. This was strange to me because if my child and/or sibling was facing the death penalty and I knew that the people who could save my child from that fate were coming to my home, I would make every effort to make the place comfortable for them, no such efforts were apparent to me. In fact, it really seemed as if it was a bother to them to have us there. It seemed to me that having us there messed up their daily routine. Did they say this directly? No, of course not, but they did not have to say it, their actions an attitude spoke volumes in this regard.

Once the initial pleasantries were over, I decided that I wanted to talk to the person that I thought was closest to my client, her sister Angela. Wanting to talk to her in a place where her parents could not hear her meant that Angela and I went outside into the yard to chat. She was certainly young at the time, maybe 16. However, she looked much younger than her age and spoke in a voice that made her sound much younger, almost childlike. Apart from deepening my suspicions that someone had sexually abused my client and her sister, I found another thing about her to be odd. You see, based on everything I knew about the situation at the time I expected Angela to be heartbroken over her sister's situation. I expected her to ask me several questions about what could happen. I expected her to be in tears, begging me to do everything I could to help her sister. Instead, what I got was a girl who seemed emotionally disconnected to the entire situation. Perhaps this was another sign of Angela's victimization but it seemed like more than that. It seemed to me that she did not care all that much about what was going on with her sister. Given that Angela has recently come out on Twitter and proudly pronounced her sobriety, perhaps she was high at the time we spoke I do not know, but there was certainly no sign that she was concerned for her sister. I found her attitude and the whole conversation to be strange.

After my strange conversation with Angela I thought that when I went back inside to speak to my client's parents, that they would ask dozens of questions and that I would hear a greater level of concern out of them. After all, we were talking about their daughter's life. Surprisingly, I did not really feel as if much concern was expressed at all. Instead of talking about his daughter, which was the point of the visit, for his part, Bill wanted to blame others for Mr. Alexander's death. Bill wanted to tell me about his theories on who killed Mr. Alexander. As you might guess, none of these theories involved his daughter committing the crime and as an added "bonus" none of his theories made sense. As for Sandy, she just seemed like she was being bothered by the whole visit. Silly me I would have thought that a mother of a child who was facing a trip to death row would drop everything to visit with her child's attorney. Not Sandy Arias. Instead, Sandy seemed irritated because, due to our visit, she had to take a few hours off work to come home to speak with us. After talking for a short time, she went back to work. I remember thinking that while I understood the need to put food on the table that her lack of concern was mind-blowing. Again, many of you may laugh at this but if you take a step back from your hatred of Ms. Arias and think about it. How sad was it for Ms. Arias that she had a family, her parents in particular, that seemingly did not care about her enough to help her legal team do their jobs.

After Sandy left, myself and my investigator went out to a storage shed that was in the backyard of the Arias home. That is not to say that we did not have company, the Arias family dog, Jewel, joined us while Bill remained inside. I mention Jewel at this juncture because not only was she the only family member to come out with me as we searched through this shed but because she also seemed to be the family member most interested in my visit. I got the sense that Jewel rarely got attention in this house and was thrilled to have somebody that loved dogs around to give her attention. The way I figured it, the Arias family probably got Jewel as a puppy, thought she was cute and got bored of her once she became a dog. Looking back perhaps, Bill and Sandy took the same approach to parenting their children, meaning they got bored of their kids after they got older. Hard to say for sure, but it sure makes sense to me. Returning you back to the shed, I ask you to picture me, the heavier shaved head version of me that I was at the time, looking through this small shed with a lab mix who wanted to play and my investigator nearby. When you paint this mental picture in addition to laughing, you might be asking yourself, why was Nurmi doing this? What was he looking for? My answer may not excite you in that I was not searching for one of the murder weapons or some other evidence that you have not heard about. Instead, my answer is that I was looking for nothing in particular. The reason I was looking for nothing in particular in this shed was because this is where the Arias family had put my client's stuff. Can you believe it? Her parents, the people that are supposed to love Jodi Arias unconditionally had moved on if you will. It seemed to me that they were pretty much done with her. It seemed to me as if they had "erased" their eldest daughter from their house. Again I realize that many of you might get a kick out of this fact, but think about it, she had not even been convicted yet by all accounts it seemed as if Ms. Arias' immediate family was done with her, which indicated to me that they did not care very much in the first place. If further proof of this fact was needed my client's eldest brother did not even make time to meet with us during our trip.

Those of you who followed the case closely and/or who were reading closely may have noticed that, as of yet, I did not talk about my conversation with Ms. Arias' youngest brother Joey. Ultimately I have not done so because it was of absolutely no importance to the case. I only mention it here to satisfy those who might be wondering about Joey.

Next stop on the "Arias family tour" was the home of Ms. Arias' grandparent's Caroline and Sunny. Caroline came across to me as a genuinely kind woman. Her house was a home. It was clean and while the furniture may have been old it was well-kept. It was the kind of place you would expect to belong to somebody's grandparents. As for Sunny, Ms. Arias' grandfather, he was a bit odd, but as he was elderly (as was Caroline) I simply paid little attention to his oddness. We talked about several things, the theft of the gun, the day Ms. Arias was arrested and they told us a great deal about Ms. Arias. To their credit, Caroline and Sunny seemed more concerned about Ms. Arias than her parents were. In an effort to address their concerns we spent a few hours talking to them and answering their questions. They were clearly warm and caring people however it was just as clear to me that their testimony would be clouded by their age and by their clear desire to help Ms. Arias. That may sound obvious but let me explain further. I am not saying simply that they wanted to help by sharing the information they had to offer. Instead what I am saying is that they wanted to help in the way Ms. Arias wanted them to help. They were clearly following her wishes. No finer example of this reality can be found than the fact that while I was there talking to my client's grandparents; guess who called? Ms. Arias. My client knew we were going to be there so what a shock (insert sarcasm here) to have her call. After speaking with her grandmother for a few minutes she wanted to talk to me. Weird right, (insert more sarcasm) she knew we would visit in a few days so; why would she want to talk to me? Now I guess in theory it is possible to call this a coincidence. However, I could hear Caroline's half of the conversation that she was having with my client and I too had a conversation with my client minutes later. Based on what I heard over the duration of this call, this was no coincidence. It was obvious to me that she wanted to control the conversation I was having with her grandparents. Ms. Arias also wanted to make sure that I spent time with her cat, Luna. Yes, you read that correctly, she was facing the death penalty and wanted to make sure that I, her lawyer, not her friend, pet her cat.

To me, more important than the cat, even more important than talking to Ms. Arias' grandparents was my opportunity to see Ms. Arias' room in person. I had seen pictures of her room before, but as I mentioned earlier, whenever I can do so, I try to walk in my client's "mental shoes." I could think of no better place to do this than in her room. The reasons for this should be obvious this was the last place she lived before she left on her trip to Mesa. It was the place she slept the night before she was arrested for murder. The room itself contained a twin bed. The walls were painted pink and one of the walls had a "dream board" pinned to it. Many of Ms. Arias' things were still in the room. As you might guess, this demonstrated to me that Caroline and Sunny were not as quick to erase my client from their lives as her parents were. More important though to me at the time was that having these things around made it easier for me to take in the aura of the place. As I stood in this room absorbing the aura, walking in my client's mental shoes as I call it, the sense I got from this room is that it seemed much too juvenile to be the room of a 30 year old woman. Perhaps the color played a role in this assessment but what really got me was the "dream board." Ms. Arias' dream board was filled with the type of things and experiences that one has to actually work to earn. To me, it seemed very juvenile for a woman in her 30's who could not even afford to rent her own place to have such delusional dreams. What made these dreams even more delusional in my mind was the fact that she still seemed to be holding onto them despite the fact that she killed Mr. Alexander. However, there was more to my assessment than this. As I stood in this room looking at this bed I began to think that this is where Ms. Arias was when she had phone sex with Mr. Alexander a few weeks before his death. I began to contemplate how this bed was where she would sit and converse with Mr. Alexander via online chats. This bed was where Ms. Arias might have been sitting when she looked out the window and gazed at the trees. It was strange and chilling being there because I also knew that this might have been the exact spot that Ms. Arias planned to kill Travis Alexander. She might very well have been sitting in this small pink room, looking out her window and planning a murder, truly chilling.

While certainly not as chilling as being in Ms. Arias' room I definitely had a bit of the chills after spending a few days meeting with Ms. Arias' family. When I considered calling them as witnesses I had to believe that the jury would see what I saw. That Ms. Arias' grandparents would simply say what she wanted them to say and that the jury would catch on to the fact that neither Ms. Arias' parents or her sister, supposedly her closest friend, seemed to care for her or be upset about the prospect of her being executed. As it related to my client's parents and her sister Angela, in my mind, the jury could have seen this in one of two ways. They might feel sorry for Ms. Arias because her immediate family did not seem to care about her, or they could see this reality as another reason to condemn her to death. Thus, I knew going into the trial that once we got to this phase of the trial that calling any of Ms. Arias' family would create a huge risk. Furthermore, as valuable as testimony like this could be, I also had to consider the fact that Bill and Sandy had given interviews with Detective Flores a few hours after Ms. Arias had been arrested. I have mentioned these interviews previously but for now it is sufficient for you to recall that the lowlights of these interviews include Sandy Arias asking Detective Flores how my client could kill someone and come home and act so normal and Bill Arias talking about his daughter being obsessed with Mr. Alexander. With all of this in mind, I decided that calling Bill and Sandy Arias would probably do more harm than good.

On the flight back to Phoenix, I remember that apart from wishing that I would never need to return to Yreka (one of my few wishes related to this case that actually came true), I was concerned about how I was going to break it to Ms. Arias that I saw very little chance that her family would be of much help. When I got back and finally sat down with Ms. Arias I realized that my client did not seem too surprised by my conclusions. It seemed as if she knew that when push came to shove her family really would be of no help. Perhaps she knew deep down on some level that they just did not care that much about her. At the time this certainly surprised me but it was not what truly amazed me upon my return.

The amazing part of my post Yreka meeting with Ms. Arias is that she was seriously upset that I had not pet her cat, Luna. You might think I am joking about this but I am not. Ms. Arias was not happy with me about the fact that I had not pet her cat. This was certainly a strange position for me to be in. In my many years of representing criminal defendants I have never had such an irrelevant conversation. I did not see her cat as important to the case. Furthermore, if I was in her shoes I do not think I would have been pestering my lawyer about this cat either. However, as the ABA guidelines suggest that the attorney attempt to build a relationship with their client and because, as I have said elsewhere about trust I had to suppress my inclination to tell her how it was not my job to pet her cat. I had to hold myself back from saying that I did not give a crap about her cat and that her cat was crazy. Instead, at that time, I had to justify my conduct so as to maintain the dialogue.

Certainly, I talk about other visits I had with Ms. Arias elsewhere in this book, but I wanted to share this story in particular as it relates to my visit to Yreka. As you might guess it still stands out as one of my strangest visits with Ms. Arias.

Finally, Ms. Arias, if you are reading this please be advised that I do not care about your cat.

CHAPTER 28

THE STATE'S SENTENCING PHASE WITNESS

Due to Ms. Arias' lack of criminal history and because for the most part she was well behaved while in custody, I believed that the State, absent the jail calls I discuss in Chapter 19, had very little to offer in the sentencing phase. That is to say they would have nothing new to add that they had not already presented in either the guilt phase, or the eligibility phase of the trial. Ultimately, it seemed to me that the State's case for death would, by in large be the crime itself. However, that did not mean that they were not going to try to negate the testimony of our experts who were intending to offer mitigating circumstances during this crucial phase of the trial. In this regard two experts were listed on the State's witness list, Dr. Jill Hayes and Dr. Janeen DeMarte. For reasons that I still do not understand, Mr. Martinez chose Dr. DeMarte as the expert that would evaluate Ms. Arias for the State. This choice did not make sense to me. Dr. Hayes seemed much more equipped to handle the task than Dr. DeMarte was at this point in her career. Dr. Hayes had more experience than Dr. DeMarte, she was a university professor who had experience testifying. Be that as it may, Mr. Martinez chose Dr. DeMarte so she was the one who was to receive the bulk of my attention.

When I researched Dr. DeMarte the first thing that stood out to me was the obvious fact that she had very little experience. Beyond the glaring reality of her inexperience, I recall looking at her web page and not being impressed. Dr. DeMarte did not strike me as being very accomplished. She had written nothing of note, meaning she was unpublished in academic journals (most who testify have been published in academic journals) and she had no true experience in the field of domestic violence. It was clear to me that the bulk of this woman's career had been spent doing evaluations for the county in which the only issue is whether or not the person is competent to stand trial and acting as a counselor for those who sought her out for therapy. Please do not get me wrong, I am not saying that there is anything wrong with doing this work. Instead, what I am saying is that it just did not seem to me that her background was such that she would have the ability to competently assess Ms. Arias. Put another way it seemed to me that Dr. DeMarte was in over her head. It seemed to me that what Mr. Martinez was asking her to do was akin to asking a pediatrician to perform heart surgery.

Once I read Dr. DeMarte's report I became of the opinion that the reason her inexperience did not create a problem for Mr. Martinez was because the goal did not seem to be to conduct an intellectually objective assessment of Ms. Arias. Instead, it seemed to me that Dr. DeMarte's goal was to simply create a diagnosis that would both fit with the State's theory of the case and could be sold to a jury. It further seemed to me as if once she figured out what diagnosis would fit best with the State's theory of the case, her plan was to then work backwards and search for and/or bend facts that would support the desired diagnosis. To this end, facts that did not support her chosen diagnosis were either ignored or assessed as untrue. Furthermore, rather than focusing on an actual psychological assessment Dr. DeMarte focused on behaviors that showed certain traits and then exaggerated their diagnostic value so as to create her so called diagnosis. In my mind she did this for two reasons, primarily because it was a great way to attack Ms. Arias and secondly because it was a great way to convince the jury that she was right, even when the science behind her indicated that she was wrong.

I base my assertions on several facts that I will discuss throughout this chapter and in the books that will follow this one. However, as the focus of this book is things that happened before trial began, I must emphasize that it seemed to me that Dr. DeMarte had this plan in mind well before she wrote her report and that it is highly likely that she had this plan in mind before she met Ms. Arias. As I cannot read minds this is only my opinion, but rest assured that it is not without foundation. Examples of this that come to mind are her willingness to misuse a test designed to assess domestic violence to draw her conclusions that no domestic violence existed in the relationship that Ms. Arias and Mr. Alexander shared. You did not hear about this test during the trial and in retrospect it may have been a mistake to keep it out of evidence. However, Dr. DeMarte did in fact "mold" a test that was supposed to be given to supposed domestic violence offenders (in this case that would have meant Mr. Alexander) and instead gave it to Mr. Alexander's brother. Yes, the same brother that thought that Mr. Alexander died a 30-year old virgin was her source. Furthermore, Dr. DeMarte was unwilling to acknowledge the fact that all of Ms. Arias' testing showed that Ms. Arias had clear symptoms of trauma. Dr. DeMarte was also unwilling to acknowledge that Mr. Alexander's choice to call Ms. Arias names like "whore," "slut," "three whole wonder" and a "corrupted carcass" was abusive. I always wondered what Dr. DeMarte would say if she was testifying in a case and the person who made those comments were the defendant and not the victim. My guess would be that she would say that a defendant's use of such terms was evidence of their abusive tendencies. I suspect I will never be able to confirm my suspicions but I feel rather confident that I am correct.

Had I had any doubts about the fact that Dr. DeMarte had a preconceived plan, reading her report eliminated all of them. In an effort to avoid a long complicated discussion about the specific tests used, the scoring of the tests and other complex issues, I have chosen to translate Dr. DeMarte's report into layman's terms. Using these terms my view of Dr. DeMarte's report is as follows. One key point of her "diagnosis" seemed to be that Ms. Arias was a liar and therefore everything she said was a lie. The exception to this rule were those things Ms. Arias said that helped Dr. DeMarte support her "diagnosis," statements of this nature were the truth. Dr. DeMarte's "diagnosis" went on to assert that Ms. Arias was a slut who jumped from man to man. Dr. DeMarte also asserted that Ms. Arias always had to have a boyfriend and that once she had a boyfriend she would alter her identity to conform to the wants of that boyfriend. In Dr. DeMarte's mind all of this proved that Ms. Arias had Borderline Personality Disorder. In asserting this diagnosis Dr. DeMarte did not seem to give any credence to the fact that the testing did not actually support her "diagnosis." Nor did it appear to me that Dr. DeMarte was interested in accounting for the facts that did not fit within the framework of her conclusions. Furthermore, the way I see it Dr. DeMarte simply summarily dismissed the suggestion that the behaviors that she used to formulate her "diagnosis" might be a product of Ms. Arias having low self-esteem or being a victim of a childhood trauma. It seemed to me that Dr. DeMarte was of the mindset that Ms. Arias was simply a slut who just happened to have borderline personality disorder. To me, this seemed like a strange position for a forensic expert to take as this position was not very scientific. Such a position was not supported by any of the evidence and to me it seemed downright sexist. As I say this, keep in mind, I surely did not like Ms. Arias at the time and that I could have cared less about her image. However, at the same time I did not believe that it was Dr. DeMarte's job to "slut shame" Ms. Arias and in my opinion that was exactly what Dr. DeMarte was doing. Perhaps Dr. Hayes was not chosen because she was not willing to use such tactics. That being said my job was not to communicate my distaste for Dr. DeMarte and/or her tactics to the jury, instead, my job was to assess how this testimony would play to a jury. To that end the key question I had to contemplate was; would Dr. DeMarte's testimony make it more likely that Ms. Arias received a death sentence?

Despite having the Arias case for years, I did not meet Dr. DeMarte in person, until shortly before the trial at the defense interview. Why? Generally speaking, the defense gets one chance to interview the State's witnesses. Thus, when one has a volatile case, a case where new evidence could arise at any moment, from a strategic standpoint it is often best to wait until closer to trial to conduct the interview. In my mind this not only negates the need to seek out a second interview but also eliminates the potential for the expert to change their mind about every answer they gave you. Therefore, a few weeks before trial Jennifer and I went to Dr. DeMarte's office for our defense interview. Given that Dr. DeMarte was going to be Jennifer's witness at trial it was her task to do the bulk of the interview. This was great for me because it left me in the position wherein I was able to spend a lot of time just listening to Dr. DeMarte's answers and observing her demeanor as she answered the questions. As I read her body language my initial thoughts were that she seemed to have a very cold disposition. Not cold when compared to the general public but cold for a therapist. Most therapists I know are kind and warm, they are the type of person whom people want to talk with, the type of person people want to befriend. I did not see these traits in Dr. DeMarte. What I did see in Dr. DeMarte was an arrogant disposition. She seemed to be of the mindset that nothing she did should ever be questioned, by anyone, let alone Jennifer Willmott. Dr. DeMarte seemed to despise Jennifer both on a personal level and because Jennifer was questioning her conclusions. It was fascinating watching these two in this setting because it was a setting in which Dr. DeMarte had no reason to display the amount of disdain and arrogance that she did during this interview. I began to wonder; what was Dr. DeMarte trying to prove? I pondered thoughts of this nature as I watched these two women converse. Specifically, I began to wonder if Dr. DeMarte was actually this arrogant of a person or if the arrogance she was displaying was specific to this situation (being questioned by a smart defense attorney who was asking difficult questions). As I continued watching Dr. DeMarte demeanor my leading theory became that she was not an arrogant person but rather that she was acting with arrogance in this situation because she was feeling insecure. Why was she so insecure? In my mind, it seemed as if she was insecure about her opinions and her ability to justify those opinions. It was as if Dr. DeMarte knew that the facts were not on her side. It further seemed that Dr. DeMarte knew that her "diagnosis" was, at best, on shaky ground. Perhaps it was during this interview that Dr. DeMarte was getting the sense, for the first time, that we knew this as well.

If I was to venture a guess, I would assume that prior to the interview neither Dr. DeMarte's "diagnosis" nor the supposed support behind her conclusions, had ever been challenged. It was certainly challenged at the interview and I suspected that this really surprised Dr. DeMarte. She did not seem to be expecting such a probing inquiry. The list of facts that were not on Dr. DeMarte's side was extensive. Perhaps the biggest problem she had was that there were insufficient indications of Ms. Arias having a personality disorder in her adolescence, which is a requirement of a diagnosis of Borderline Personality Disorder. Furthermore, none of the objective testing supported such a diagnosis. Additionally, many "facts" that Dr. DeMarte used to support her diagnosis simply were not accurate. For example, Ms. Arias did not jump from boyfriend to boyfriend as Dr. DeMarte had claimed in her report. Instead the facts were that several months of time passed between her breakup with Matt and the beginning of her relationship with Darryl. Dr. DeMarte also asserted that Ms. Arias altered her personality to fit the wants of her boyfriends. In support of this contention Dr. DeMarte provided at least two examples. The first claim being her assertion that Ms. Arias acted professionally and maturely when with Darryl. While technically true, Dr. DeMarte chose to ignore the fact that this professional and mature behavior related to Ms. Arias' demeanor during a job interview and at the work place, not when she was dating Darryl. The second example Dr. DeMarte would cite regarding this molding behavior is the idea that when she was with Matt she altered her life to live in a tent. In this regard, Dr. DeMarte chooses to forget two important facts. Matt and Ms. Arias were not in a relationship at this time. She also ignored the fact that they were living in a tent as roommates because it was the only employee housing they had available to them at the time. Thus, it seemed to me that Dr. DeMarte's conclusions were simply based on false premises that she chose to ignore certain facts in order to advance her conclusions and it further seemed to me Dr. DeMarte was of the mindset that nobody should question her about any of this.

Moving past the interview and shifting focus back to Dr. DeMarte's conclusions for a minute, I believe that I would not be doing my job as an author if I did not speak to some of the conclusions about my client that Dr. DeMarte made in her assessment. I must confess that whatever qualms I had with the objective and scientific nature of Dr. DeMarte's report, I have to concede that the description she gave of Ms. Arias and her behavior in some respects was incredibly accurate. As mentioned previously, the cynic in me thinks that Dr. DeMarte made these observations and worked backwards to prove her "diagnosis." That being said she was not wrong when she concluded that Ms. Arias did tend to idealize people and then later demean them if they tried to pull away. In fact, I describe my experiences with Ms. Arias acting this way towards me in Chapter 31. Dr. DeMarte was also correct when she concluded that Ms. Arias was extremely moody. I also had first -hand experience with this aspect of Ms. Arias' personality. At one moment I could be on the phone with Ms. Arias and she would be very angry with me, so angry that she would be screaming at me in a high pitched shriek. Perhaps she would even go so far as to hang up on me. After such conversations she would call back almost immediately, apologize and be friendly as if the screaming that occurred moments ago had not happened. Dr. DeMarte was also correct when she concluded that Ms. Arias did act very immaturely. Dr. DeMarte would describe this as acting like a teenager. Granted, I would quibble a bit with this statement as I would have said that dealing with Ms. Arias was like dealing with a really smart five year old. This may sound like a similar thing, but while teenagers tend to be narcissistic, they still have a greater level of empathy than your typical five year-old. The Ms. Arias I knew had very little true empathy. However, placing that distinction aside Dr. DeMarte did do a great job of describing the Ms. Arias I knew. My real problem was that this description was not a true psychological diagnosis.

I will talk more about Dr. DeMarte's testimony in my upcoming books, but, as I prepared for trial I always wondered if the State was concerned about what Dr. DeMarte's "diagnosis" would say about Mr. Alexander. Think about it, if Dr. DeMarte was correct and Ms. Arias adapts herself to the men in her life; what did that say about Mr. Alexander? If she acted like a "whore" or a "slut" or a "3 whole wonder" the logic of Dr. DeMarte's diagnosis would be that she became those things for Mr. Alexander. Her diagnosis would have to account for the fact that Mr. Alexander wanted her to be these things. It was in this logical reality that I saw the biggest flaw in Dr. DeMarte's report and conclusions, because it raised the question; would a jury kill the woman who killed her former boyfriend, the former boyfriend that was still using her for sex?

SECTION 5

I QUIT!

In this section I talk about my choice to leave the Office of the Public Defender. A move at the time, as I explain in Chapter 29, that I thought would rid me of Ms. Arias and her case. In Chapter 30, I explain just how wrong I was.

CHAPTER 29

I WANT OUT!

By the fall of 2010, I had been Ms. Arias lead attorney for over a year. As I described in previous sections, I had met Ms. Arias' family, investigated the case and I had spent a great deal of time with my client. I had done all the things that a lead attorney does when they have such a complex capital case. In fact, I would say that I had gone above and beyond what is expected for Ms. Arias, given the complexities of her case that I have described in previous chapters. The only personal benefit of having dedicated so much to the Arias case was that by the fall of 2010, I had a real good idea of what I had on my hands.

What I ultimately had on my hands was a woman who clearly had brutally killed her former boyfriend and who wanted to claim that he was an abusive pedophile. Her story went on to include assertions that on the day of his death this abusive pedophile tried to attack her and she was forced to defend herself. Equally clear to me was that Ms. Arias wanted to make these assertions in a high profile setting. Ms. Arias wanted to attack Mr. Alexander's reputation on a worldwide stage and she wanted me to aid her in this quest. Frankly, it seemed to me that making these attacks was more important to Ms. Arias than the outcome of her case.

As I outlined earlier I did not believe many of her accusations. However, because I couldn't definitively disprove them, if she wanted to take the stand and tell this story the law dictated that she had every right to do so.

Additionally, because she had this indisputable right, I was ethically bound to help Ms. Arias tell her story. Did I want to aid her in this quest? No. Did I think making these claims was wise from a strategic standpoint? No. Could I stop her from taking the stand and saying these things? No. Was I forced to build a trial strategy around these claims? The short answer would be yes.

In my mind a better defense would have been for her to say nothing and let me argue that she was guilty of manslaughter. It would have made sense to base the claims that she was guilty of manslaughter, instead of murder, on the chaotic nature of her relationship with Mr. Alexander. Ultimately, in my mind, the best defense would have been to argue that she just lost control after it became obvious to her that Mr. Alexander had used her for sex yet again. However, the constitutional rights due Ms. Arias in essence placed me in a position wherein I had to run with her story or at the very least, work around her story because she had every right to take the stand and tell her story. To paraphrase County Attorney Bill Montgomery, Ms. Arias was entitled to the defense she wanted. Furthermore, I think it is important to note that if I did not bring up Ms. Arias' assertions and she was sentenced to death, the question in post-conviction proceedings would become why I did not bring up her claims of abuse. An appellate court's answer to that would likely be that it was improper for me not to bring these things up and thus Ms. Arias would get a new trial.

So once again I was in a situation where what I thought did not matter in terms of strategy, under these unique circumstances what Ms. Arias desired would prevail. That did not mean that I did not have my own thoughts on this situation. In sum, I wanted no part of Ms. Arias' plan to attack Mr. Alexander. I did not want to assert Ms. Arias' defense, especially in a high profile setting. However, for the reasons mentioned above, the only way I could accomplish this was to leave my job at the Public Defender's Office. You see, I could not simply give the case to another attorney in the office. Nor could I find an ethical issue that would require my team to withdraw. Leaving the Public Defender's Office was the only realistic option. Back then working as a Public Defender was a job I really liked, though I must admit I was a bit tired of doing capital cases. I had done two capital trials in two years and the toll they took on my life was too high for my liking. So while I will admit that I had other reasons for wanting to leave this job behind, leaving Ms. Arias behind was a big motivating factor.

At the same time I did not want to give up on over 10 years at a job I liked over a client as clients come and go. That being said I really didn't like Ms. Arias at all. Beyond not liking Ms. Arias, without leaving the job, I could not alter the fact that Ms. Arias was not just another client. Ms. Arias was a capital client who was receiving the bulk of my attention during any given work day. In essence Ms. Arias was my job at that time. On top of this reality, as I said earlier I was tired of capital work in general. So during the fall of 2010, I decided to give thought to the idea of actually leaving the Office of the Public Defender. I did not want to rush into a decision this big therefore I decided that I would make a decision after the holidays.

After the holidays I had made my decision, I wanted out! I decided that I was going to leave the Office of the Public Defender. I was going to go into private practice. My plan was to defend DUI cases, sex cases and whatever else came through the door. So in January of 2011, I advised the Public Defender's Office that I was leaving. My plan was to stay on until February because we had a major hearing in Ms. Arias' case scheduled for that month. I planned on staying until this hearing was over because I did not believe that anyone else could be as prepared for the hearing as I was (as the saying goes, no good deed goes unpunished). Based on my resignation, the people who run the Public Defender's Office put plans in place for me to be replaced on the defense team after I was gone. In essence, my former Co-counsel would take the lead spot and a new Co-counsel would be named. Over the next few weeks then my job was to prepare for the hearing and help the newly assigned Co-counsel get up to speed on the case. All was going well, or so I thought.

With a plan in place to leave my job and Ms. Arias' case, as you might guess, I had to tell my client that I was leaving and about how her team would be reorganized. I recall driving to the jail unsure of how she would react to this news. I assumed that she would not be happy and I was correct to say the least. In fact it is more accurate to say that not only was Ms. Arias very unhappy with my plans but that in her mind this plan, the plan I had for my career, was not acceptable to her. Ms. Arias thought I should stay at the Office of the Public Defender until her case was complete. In essence she believed that I should put my aspirations to go into private practice aside and endure her trial just because she wanted me to, merely because it suited her interests. As you might guess, on the day I broke this news to her she thought that crying and assuming the role of a victim would help convince me to stay. When that did not work she would call on a daily basis to either explain why her new attorney was not right for her or to advise me of her latest theory as to why I should stay with the Public Defender's Office until her case was over. She simply would not accept my refusal to comply with her request. As time went on she became increasingly frustrated that she could not manipulate me into staying. At the same time I also sensed that some part of her could not believe that I would actually choose to leave her case. I sensed that there was a part of Ms. Arias that felt as if I should have seen being her lawyer as a privilege. Looking back I think this is where my real problems with Ms. Arias began, in that it was at this time she began to resent me for wanting to leave her case and because I did not see working on her case as a privilege. However, it also seemed that there was more to it than that. I sensed that she felt as if a friend had betrayed her.

So after weeks of trying to convince me to stay, the hearing that kept me at the Public Defender's Office until February was upon us and I still planned on leaving. At the end of the hearing Judge Duncan, who was presiding over the case at the time, asked me about scheduling our next hearing. I responded by advising her that scheduling would be up to my Co-counsel as she was assuming the role of lead counsel because I was leaving the Public Defender's Office. When I said this I certainly wished that I could have read Mr. Martinez's mind as I was really curious what he thought of all of this. As for Judge Duncan I did not need to read her mind. She openly shared her thoughts with me by asking me if I had filed a Motion to Withdraw. I told her that I had not because this was not something typically done when a person leaves the Public Defender's Office. Judge Duncan also asked if I had a "contract" meaning, had I agreed to defend indigent criminals for the county in exchange for a specified hourly rate of pay. After I replied that I did not have a contract Judge Duncan made it clear that what typically occurred in these situations did not matter to her and that if I did not want to accept the case at the contract rate she wanted me to file a Motion to Withdraw.

At the time I assumed that Judge Duncan just wanted to have her say and that after I filed my motion I would be out. Why? Because the Public Defender's Office already had someone assigned to the case, my leaving the case would not delay the trial and because things like this happened all the time. It was commonplace for an attorney to leave the Public Defender's Office and have their cases reassigned with that office. Such movement was almost exclusively viewed as an internal issue that was most properly dealt with within that office. It was for these reasons that I assumed that there would be no reason for her to order me to stay. However, for Ms. Arias this provided her with the opening she needed to keep me right where she wanted me.

CHAPTER 30

SPOILER ALERT I DID NOT GET OUT

After the hearing that I discussed in Chapter 29, was over I went back to my office and started working on my motion right away. I was not happy even contemplating having to keep Ms. Arias' case. However, as I wrote this motion, as I mentioned in the previous chapter, I simply assumed that Judge Duncan wanted the motion and that when she had it, her point would have been made and the motion would be granted. However naïve that might sound now, this was my mindset when I filed my first Motion to Withdraw from this case back in late February of 2011. Yes, this was the first Motion to Withdraw that I filed in this case. Silly me, I assumed that it would be the last motion of this type that I would file. In fact, I was so naïve that I thought that it would be the last motion I would file in this case, period. At the time I never would have thought that this motion would be one of several motions of this type that I would file over the course of the case or, for that matter, that I would be filing motions on the case over 4 years later. How wrong I was.

After I filed my motion I became concerned when it was not immediately granted. My concern grew when Judge Duncan wanted to hear oral argument on the motion. As best as I could recall the argument was held about a week after I had filed my motion. Not a long time but in some ways it was for me because I could not take on new business until I knew whether or not I would be allowed to withdraw from the Arias case. However, more importantly than business considerations was the fact that, I really, really wanted out. On a personal level I really wanted to be rid of Ms. Arias. My desire to get out increased each time I had to speak with Ms. Arias. I say "had to," because at the time she was still my client and ultimately speaking with her was something that I was required to do. However, because of my belief that I would ultimately get off the case, I wanted her to talk about her case with her new team and not me. Little did that matter in that she did not want to talk to me about her case. Instead her real desire was to convince me that I should keep her case. Having failed to convince me in prior conversations, Ms. Arias now took the tactic of trying to use every word Judge Duncan said to me at the previous hearing to her own advantage. Ms. Arias would assert that I should take the contract rate for her case and move forward as Judge Duncan had offered. She felt as if she had the right to ask me to put my own ambitions on hold to serve her ends. Why she felt she had that right to ask these things of me, I have no idea but she definitely felt as if she had the right to make such requests. As the days went on Ms. Arias grew increasingly frustrated with her inability to convince me that I should keep her case. None of her new tactics were working.

However, more than being frustrated, though she did not say so directly, it seemed to me that Ms. Arias was genuinely shocked and angered that I did not want to remain her lawyer. It seemed to me that Ms. Arias was genuinely shocked and angered that I wanted nothing to do with her. Think about it, prior to Judge Duncan talking about the possibility of my remaining on the case as a contract attorney it was just about me leaving the Office of the Public Defender. Now that I had the opportunity to both leave the Office of the Public Defender and still keep her case, in declining this opportunity, I was actually rejecting her case and her personally. I sensed that this made her very angry and perhaps even more determined to keep me.

No doubt about it when Ms. Arias wants something she does what she can to get it. To this end in her effort to keep me working as her attorney Ms. Arias wrote a very well written letter to the Judge detailing how important I was to her case, her future, things of this nature. Ms. Arias also asked her mother to write a letter to the Judge as well. Sandy Arias, always one inclined to do what my client demanded of her, did in fact write such a letter. In her letter Sandy explained to the Judge how unethical it was for me to leave the Public Defender's Office. Sandy's letter to Judge Duncan also included her belief that I should be forced to remain working at the Office of the Public Defender. Now, you might think I am kidding when I use the word forced, but I am not. In her letter Sandy asserted that I should be forced to work at the Office of the Public Defender until her daughter's case was done. Sandy Arias did not seem to care that slavery had been abolished in this country many years ago. If her daughter needed a slave, it was a slave she should have. In the mind of Sandy Arias I had my whole life to start my private practice and that I should be forced to hold off on doing so until her daughter's case was done. What I wanted to do with my own life was, at best, a secondary concern to Sandy Arias. To those who might suspect that I am exaggerating the gall that Sandy Arias displayed when she wrote this letter, I suspect that if you search hard enough the letter she wrote to Judge Duncan is online somewhere. If not, I am sure you can look to the comments she made on the day her daughter was sentenced to evidence the sorts of things she is willing to say for her daughter.

The night before this hearing I was filled with hope that this would be a quick and easy process that I would be off the case by lunchtime. My hopes were dashed the very moment I arrived in court, as once I arrived I immediately recognized that the hearing itself was looking like it was going to be quite the spectacle. Though he had no "dog in the fight" Juan Martinez was there for the State and I suspected he was certainly looking forward to watching this spectacle unfold. As you might guess, other members of the Public Defender's Office were there and so was the man who ran the contract program for Maricopa County. After a fair amount of bluster, ultimately nothing was resolved at the hearing itself. By this I mean in that there was no final ruling regarding my status on the case. Instead, I was to remain on the case for the time being and two lawyers were appointed to represent my client as it related to my Motion to Withdraw. For the curious, these lawyers were appointed because at this point in time Ms. Arias and I had adverse interests and/or positions related to my Motion to Withdraw. Ms. Arias wanted me to stay on the case and I was uninterested in representing Ms. Arias at all. Apart from not wanting to be her lawyer anymore, given the hourly rate the county was paying, it was readily apparent to me that I could make more money working a DUI case or other more standard criminal cases, which is what I wanted to do anyway. I said as much at the hearing and thus after this hearing my assigned task was to submit an affidavit about the hourly rate I wanted if I was not allowed to withdraw from the case. After the hearing was over we all went our separate ways for another week or so. When we came back to court I was adamant I still wanted off the case. I knew that representing Ms. Arias would be a full time job and that being her lawyer would mean that I would have little to no time to take on other clients. Taking on other clients is a key component of building a private practice, something I would have to forgo until the case was over. Ms. Arias, now aided by her two lawyers still decided to stand her ground and oppose my Motion to Withdraw. As for the other parties, like the State and the Public Defender's Office, since they did not really have a say in the outcome of the motion, the decision Judge Duncan had to make was between my interests and Ms. Arias' interests. In this regard, Ms. Arias prevailed. When Judge Duncan made her ruling I was still on the case, my first Motion to Withdraw had been denied. From what she said on the bench it seemed that Judge Duncan made this decision largely because the case was scheduled to go to trial in August of 2011, so my desire to build a practice would only be delayed by 10 months or so. I did not get out! I was now "Trapped with Ms. Arias."

As some of you might be skeptical, let me be clear. I did not want to remain on this case period. I knew that remaining on the case would damage my ability to start my own practice and quite possibly my whole career. However, since the day I was "Trapped with Ms. Arias," it was my clear wish the trial would begin as scheduled. I had the hope that if trial went as scheduled that by early in 2012, I would be rid of the case. I wanted to start my own practice and I was well aware of the fact that the longer things went on the longer I was to be "Trapped with Ms. Arias." Likewise I knew that the longer this case went on the more damage this case would cause to my career. You see, after Judge Duncan ruled that I had to remain on the case, I was stuck and Ms. Arias knew it. I think she knew it because as difficult as she might have been in the past, she was much more difficult after Judge Duncan's order of April 4, 2011. After this order was entered she had no reason not to be difficult. Realistically, I could not get away from her now and she was super pissed that I wanted to leave her to begin with. Leaving Ms. Arias is not something she takes kindly to and she expressed her anger in both passive aggressive ways and ways that were all out aggressive. While I wish I could discuss things more directly, I can tell you one story because when a client threatens an attorney it is no longer confidential.

A few days after Judge Duncan issued her ruling that kept me on the case, I went to visit Ms. Arias at the jail. I gave her my new business card again and when I did I made some off-hand remark about how I was starting my practice. In response, Ms. Arias informed me in no uncertain terms that she was going to speak about me in very unfavorable terms at the jail so that none of her fellow inmates would want to hire me. She wanted all my time. In her mind, pursuant to Judge Duncan's ruling, I was to be her personal lawyer and she was not willing to share me with other clients even if she had to lie about me to keep other clients away. Ms. Arias also strongly implied that if I did not act according to her wishes she would bad mouth me when things were over. Her threat to me in essence was that I needed to do as she desired, period.

Given my failure to comply, I am not shocked to see the bad mouthing of me she did after the first trial and I suspect more will be coming in due time. Regardless of what is to come, back in April of 2011, the golden handcuffs were firmly around my wrists.

SECTION 6

DEALING WITH MS. ARIAS

Once Judge Duncan ordered that I was to remain on the case, as the title of this book indicates, I was truly "Trapped with Ms. Arias." In this section I deal with what it was like dealing with Ms. Arias before trial began but certainly with a focus on those things that occurred after April 4, 2011, the day Judge Duncan issued her order. The day the trap was set. In Chapter 31, I talk about "The Immediate Consequences of Being Ms. Arias' "Personal Lawyer."" In Chapter 32, I discuss what it was like to visit Ms. Arias in the jail. In Chapter 33, "The Naked Pictures" I discuss Ms. Arias' issues with the pictures she posed for. In Chapter 34, "Viva Las Vegas" I discuss a trip the team had to take to Las Vegas. I end this section with Chapter 35, "This is your Brain on Jodi," wherein I discuss the affect that Ms. Arias can have on a person's brain.

CHAPTER 31

THE IMMEDIATE CONSEQUENCES OF BEING MS. ARIAS' "PERSONAL LAWYER"

When I left the Public Defender's Office I never would have imagined that I would be in the position I was in after Judge Duncan issued her ruling. Before I could do anything I now had to make space in my office for about thirty or so file boxes of evidence. That might not sound like a big deal to you but I did not choose my office space with the needs of this case in mind. Furthermore, I had to contemplate how best to serve as the lead of a defense team who were no longer simply down the hall. I had to contemplate how I would handle this case when I no longer had first hand daily access to my team and the infrastructure of the Public Defender's Office. This might not seem like a big deal to you but think about it, after leaving the Office of the Public Defender, I had to deal with this case in a much different way. For example, I went from having a full time secretary that was experienced dealing with capital cases who was being paid by the county, to a part time secretary who knew nothing about capital cases who was being paid by me.

To be clear, these are not complaints, instead what I am attempting to do is provide you with insight into the logistical realities that I had to deal with after my first Motion to Withdraw was denied by the court. Could I deal with these things? Yes. I had a great team and we would simply figure it out. However, I must admit that there was one logistical reality that I did not consider, one logistical reality that I was not prepared for to some degree. A reality that was so inconsequential to me that at the time I had not given it any thought. However, this was a huge deal for Ms. Arias. Her phone calls.

Prior to April 4th, 2011, I had not contemplated all that would be involved in taking her legal calls if I was forced to remain on the case. I really never thought that this would be an issue. Since she was my client and I was her court appointed lawyer I assumed that she could simply make legal calls to me and that I would not get billed for them. However, as it turned out, because I was not a "contract attorney" I was not set up to take free legal calls from the jail. Legal calls being those that are not recorded. Furthermore, as I was not a "contract attorney" I was certainly not eligible to receive these calls for free. As I discuss elsewhere, the jail charges nearly everyone who receives/accepts an inmate's phone call.

It did not take long for me to get to the point where I could take legal calls from the jails (in fact that did occur before April 4, 2011) but not being charged for them that was a different matter. When I first got into private practice and became Ms. Arias' lawyer one of the first things I became acutely aware of is that every time I accepted her calls. I had to pay to speak with the client. Ironic isn't it that I had to pay to talk to the client that I did not want to represent. Under normal circumstances, I will grant you this was not a big deal. I could just simply pay the bill. However as I have often said, there were few things about representing Ms. Arias that were normal. Why was this issue such a big deal as it related to the job I had to perform for Ms. Arias? Because it meant that not all of her phone calls to my office would be answered. It meant that if I was not available to personally take her call that either my secretary or our answering service would simply not accept her calls. In practical terms, not accepting Ms. Arias' calls meant hanging up on her so that I would not be charged for them. Even though I explained this to Ms. Arias, she did not like how I was running my business. She did not like to be hung up on. I assume that she felt as if she should be treated different than other clients. It seemed to me as if in her mind she was "special" and that because she was special she should be able to leave her meaningless messages with whoever was answering the phone simply because she did not like for her calls to be rejected. The fact that I did not alter my practice to conform to her wishes really seemed to upset her. It seemed to me that in her mind she was the boss and I should be doing as she said. Now keep in mind that during this time period she could still call other members of her defense team and talk to one of them and/or leave a message. All of them had secretaries who were available to accept their calls and take a message if need be. Furthermore, if she wanted to leave me a message these people could also e-mail me a confidential message, whereas if she left this message with someone from the answering service I would have less control over where her message would wind up. This seemed like a smart approach to me but this approach did not satisfy Ms. Arias. She seemed to feel as if she deserved unfettered access to me, her "personal lawyer."

To some extent I guess I could understand her frustration if these calls were made to discuss important issues in her case, but when I was available and had to take her calls these calls typically had nothing to do with her case. It was not uncommon for Ms. Arias to call me and ask where another team member was or what that person was doing. I typically had no idea because I no longer worked down the hall from them. I had no idea what other cases they were working on or if they happened to be off on a particular day. When I explained this reality to Ms. Arias, such explanations fell on deaf ears and the pattern continued.

Being Ms. Arias' "personal lawyer" meant more than her attempting to dictate my office policy on phone calls. Being Ms. Arias' personal lawyer meant that she felt as if she had the right to comment on all aspects of my practice in a way that your supervisor might discuss your job performance with you. Ms. Arias would comment on the time I arrived at the office, as if she was my boss asking why I was late for work. She would comment on the time I would leave the office as well in the same way a boss might ensure his or her employees were not leaving early. Ms. Arias seemed to be of the mindset that as her "personal lawyer" I needed to clear my daily schedule with her and that if I wanted to take a vacation she needed to approve of that as well. Lest you think I am kidding, I recall telling her that I was going to be out of the office a certain amount of days and Ms. Arias responded by saying that she understood the need for vacations but that the time I was away was too long. I took my vacation anyway and no, I did not cut it short. Sadly for Ms. Arias, I was the boss of my law practice and frankly I did not care what she thought about the hours I chose to work or the vacations I took.

CHAPTER 32

Jail Visits with Ms. Arias

I recall that back when Jennifer and Maria joined the team one of the first things I told them was that when they visit Ms. Arias in the jail they should plan on the visit lasting about two hours. As visits of such length were unheard of, even when working on a death penalty case, they did not seem to believe me. In fact this might have been the first time that they thought I was out of my mind. Certainly this would not be the last time they felt this way but definitely one of the first. My sanity aside, I knew what they did not know that Ms. Arias not only craved attention but demanded it. I knew that Ms. Arias needed attention almost to the degree that humans need air to breathe. It did not take them long to figure this out and realize that I was right regarding the length of these visits and Ms. Arias' need for attention.

Apart from the length of the visits I suspect that you the reader are interested in what it was like to go to the county jail and visit with the infamous Ms. Arias. Well to begin with you need to understand that to me she was not the "infamous Ms. Arias" she was just another client. Now I am sure Ms. Arias wanted me to see her as a "special client" but to me she was just another client.

Ordinary client or not, the visits themselves occurred at the same place, the county jail. As you might guess, the county jail is not a fun place to hang out. Even if you do not live there, even if you know you will only be there for a few hours as a visitor, it is a place where most people would rather not find themselves. Even if you actually wanted to see the inmate you were visiting, you will never really enjoy your trip to the Estrella Jail. Why? Well to begin with the Estrella jail, Maricopa County's only jail for women, is not exactly in the best part of town. Not only that, but after driving through this seedy part of town, your reward is to enter an old musty building. In addition to being old and musty the building itself is tan, drab and lifeless. The Estrella Jail is the type of place that those of you who want to be "tough on crime" would love.

Once you enter this building you are immediately confronted with the reality that nobody wants to be there. Those trying to visit loved ones are unhappy because they have to wait in this awful building and remove almost everything from their pockets before they enter the visiting room. Those who work there tend to be unhappy because they face a constant barrage of anger from those who want to visit their loved ones. Now you might think once an attorney gets into the actual visitation area that they would be happy about getting that far along in the process. Yes, it is nice to get closer to the visit you need to make, but the visitation area itself can be one of the most depressing points in the journey. Why? It is depressing not because I will be talking to my client soon, but because of all the other inmates that are sitting around at the visitation tables either talking to their attorneys or loved ones. I always found it sad to see table after table of women, many times very young women, most of whom are no more than twenty-five years old some of whom were crying because they did not like the news their lawyer was breaking to them. Certainly, I was used to scenes such as this, I had delivered unwanted news to many female inmates but that still did not make it a pleasant thing to witness. However, what I truly never got past as a human being, was watching these young women who were sitting there talking to their parents or their children, all of whom were typically in tears. I always found scenes such as this to be heartbreaking. To be clear, I am not saying that I am feeling sorry for all of the inmates, though some may be worthy of a degree of sympathy, most have earned their time behind bars. Instead, the bulk of my sorrow always went to the inmate's loved ones who did nothing wrong. Think about how sad it must be for a parent to be forced to visit their daughter at a jail. Or worse for a young child to have to visit their mother at jail, not a promising start to a young life and seeing such visits always bummed me out.

As far as visiting Ms. Arias herself, we did not sit at one of the tables like most of those having legal visits. Instead, due to Ms. Arias' classification we had to visit in a special room reserved for "high security inmates" and Ms. Arias had to be escorted in by at least one guard, oftentimes two. Typically that would mean that I would sit and wait for Ms. Arias to arrive to the visitation room while all these tragic scenes were going on behind me.

To give you a sense of the visitation rooms, each room had two doors. The door on the "visitors' side" of the room led to freedom. The door on the "inmates' side" of the room led to the bowels of the jail. The room was divided into two identical portions by a cinderblock wall that housed a wire screen that served as a window of sorts. Below this window was a slot through which legal paperwork could be exchanged. Bolted to the wall was a metal shelf or desk that paperwork could be placed on. As you might guess, the seating in these rooms was far from comfortable. Each side of the room had a hard metal stool in it. The stool was bolted to the ground and the seat was not more than twelve inches around. Not something that anyone would want to sit on for a long time. The good news, for the attorney anyway, is that if you were lucky you might get a cheap plastic lawn chair to sit on. Hardly comfortable but better than a metal stool.

So it is in a room such as this that I would sit and wait for Ms. Arias. Sometimes the wait was five minutes other times longer but I could always tell when Ms. Arias was coming down the hall, as I could hear the sound of several feet shuffling down the hallway as well as the sound of the chains they placed around Ms. Arias' ankles hitting the floor as she walked toward the room. In addition to the chains around her ankles, typically her hands were also chained to a belt. Given Ms. Arias' stature, the precautions always looked ridiculous, especially when she had two or three guards around her, but given her crime, I understood the precautions.

Once Ms. Arias arrived in the room, typically at least one hand was un-cuffed and it was time to talk. After getting past the initial few minutes of listening to Ms. Arias complain about the guards that brought her to the room, it was finally time to have a legal visit. By now I hope you can see that a legal visit with Ms. Arias meant sitting in one of these awful little rooms and talking to her about whatever the subject at hand was on that particular day for at least two hours. As you might guess, I never really enjoyed having to make these visits but I was ultimately ethically bound to make such visits on a regular basis. When I worked for the Public Defender's Office the expectation was that we were to visit our clients once a week. So, yes, I met with Ms. Arias in this manner, at least once a week, when I worked for that office, apart from the time period that I was in trial on another death penalty case.

That is correct, during my tenure as Ms. Arias' lead counsel I only went to trial on one other capital case. I only mention this event because it was such a big deal to Ms. Arias. When I was in trial on this other case the visits occurred less frequently, perhaps once or twice a month. In the past all of my clients have understood that when I was busy trying to save another client's life that I would not be able to visit them so frequently. These clients seemed to be understanding of the situation because they knew that when their time for trial came, they would not want someone else taking their attorney's time. As silly as it may sound in some ways this was a sign of respect that these clients were paying both to me and my other clients. Either this reality did not make sense to Ms. Arias or she just did not care for it because she felt as if she deserved special treatment. In this regard, it would not surprise me if she felt as if time should be taken away from another client's case so that her needs could be addressed. However, regardless of the reasons she certainly let it be known that she was unhappy about the fact that I was not seeing her at least once a week. She would call to complain to me about this before court or at the end of the day. She may even have called my supervisor about the issue, I am not sure but there is no doubt that regardless of the circumstances Ms. Arias wanted and/or demanded my attention.

The ironic part was that when I was in private practice, I did not have to play by the rules of the Public Defender's Office and I did not have to visit her once a week and beyond that if she was ever unhappy with the frequency of my visits she had nobody to complain to about me. That being said after I went out on my own, I typically saw her once a week just to avoid the added drama that would come with my failure to do so. Now, if you think that these weekly visits might be enough attention for Ms. Arias, you would be wrong. Ms. Arias craved attention. She cannot seem to get enough of it. Thus, these visits were on top of the constant phone conversations I would have with her on an almost daily basis. So yes, on top of talking to Ms. Arias for at least a half an hour on most days, we also had these weekly visits. Sometimes these weekly visits included another team member but, as best as I can recall, it was more often than not I went alone because I, as lead counsel, was the one that had the obligation to make these visits. That is not to say that these other team members were not talking to Ms. Arias on the phone and/or visiting her. In fact, they too were spending a fair amount of time with her as well. My point here is to illustrate for you how much of my attention she demanded from me, on top of all the other attention she was getting from others on her team.

In reading this, a reasonable question for you to have is; why after these daily phone calls would a visit with Ms. Arias take at least 2 hours? I know it sounds crazy but they usually took that long and ultimately the short answer goes back to Ms. Arias' need for attention. If I had it my way I would have updated her on the case, discussed any motions I had filed etcetera and then I would have been out of there in 30 to 45 minutes. So then what was this extra time spent discussing? As you might guess, some of this time would be spent by Ms. Arias trying to convince me to file or not file a certain motion, things of that nature. Certainly, these conversations were annoying but at least these conversations fell into the realm of legitimate attorney client conversation.

The same cannot be said for other occasions. On some days Ms. Arias, presumably driven by her need for attention wanted to talk about things unrelated to her case. For example, Ms. Arias liked to talk about her cat, what was happening in her pod, whatever the latest drama with her Mom happened to be, how she did not have enough money to order what she wanted on commissary, the painful list goes on and on. Now you might legitimately ask; why did you listen to Ms. Arias talk about all these irrelevant topics? You might think that listening to Ms. Arias talk about this stuff is silly or ridiculous because these things have nothing to do with the case. You would be right but it is not that simple. The answer to the question relates to the fact that Ms. Arias was facing the death penalty and when someone is facing the death penalty dialoging with your client in this way is often a wise move so that they will be more open to other, more relevant discussions, at other times. Thus, because she was facing death the best course of practice was to listen in hopes that this will lead to building a trusting relationship and/ or the type of relationship in which Ms. Arias would feel comfortable sharing details of her life with me. As you might be able to discern this was part of the "trap" I was stuck in. Had Ms. Arias not been facing death I could have ignored all this stuff that I really did not care to listen to, but listen I did for the most part. That is not to say that I did not have my limits. I remember one discussion I had with Ms. Arias that related to her sexual escapades with Mr. Alexander. Certainly a relevant topic given the facts of the case, but as a corollary to this discussion, for whatever reason (probably because she was a victim of sexual abuse as a child) Ms. Arias decided that she wanted to inform me of the current state of her vaginal grooming. In doing this, she went too far as, fortunately for me, the ABA guidelines do not require you to listen to that kind of stuff.

In addition to cutting off inappropriate comments from their client, the fact that a lawyer should listen to their client's appropriate personal issues does not mean that they are obligated to endure their client's attempts to manipulate them. I certainly could not always endure these two plus hour visits in which Ms. Arias' sole goal was to manipulate me into acting in accordance with her wishes. In this regard, I remember one visit in which I had decided that enough was enough. I cannot remember the exact situation that was at issue, if I recall correctly, the conflict I was having with Ms. Arias at the time related to filing a certain motion. We had discussed the motion over the week and I had explained to Ms. Arias why I was filing this motion. She was not happy about it and had tried to talk me out of filing it. Well, come the day of the visit, I delivered the motion to her, she wanted me to withdraw the motion, I would not do it and Ms. Arias started to cry and ultimately pitch a fit. She put her head down on the table, and cried loudly. Ms. Arias droned on like a child who was not getting her way and she kept going while I just sat there. As I sat there I certainly gained a great deal of insight into how Ms. Arias was able to prevail over her parents as a child. She would cry and cry. She would have a tantrum until her demands were met. I could tell that she thought that if she kept this tantrum going that I would eventually relent to her demands. During her fit I told her that if she wanted to discuss other issues in her case, she could pull her head up, stop crying and speak to me like an adult. I gave her a few minutes to pull it together and as you might guess she kept going with this tantrum. When the clock "ran out" so to speak I got up to leave and as I suspected she would do, Ms. Arias let out an even louder cry. To use a football analogy it was her "Hail Mary." It did not work, I left. Days after I left I remember Ms. Arias calling me and vigorously scolding me for walking out. To this I had much to say, but I could not respond in the way I wanted to because I was trapped. I was still her lawyer and I was obligated to act professionally. Beyond this reality I knew that I would still have to deal with her in the future so I listened to this without offering my true feelings in response. As today is a different day, in my final book, I plan to include a letter directed at Ms. Arias. In this letter I will offer my response to this and many other issues so she and all of you have the opportunity to hear exactly how I feel. Spoiler alert "nine out of ten days" was the "PG" version of how I really feel.

CHAPTER 33

THE NAKED PICTURES

You might think that an attorney who has handled as many sex cases as I have would have seen nude images of my client's before. Sadly for me, if you think that you would be right. However, cases that involved photographs of this nature were still the exception, not the rule. In fact, I believe that over the several years that I handled cases of this nature the evidence I received only contained photos of this type on two, maybe three occasions. Now I have had clients that wanted me to assist them in exposing themselves to the jury via photographs. Photographs, which would in their mind, if shown to the jury would prove their innocence. However, as the saying goes, that is a story for another day. As the current story relates to Ms. Arias and her alone, I think that it is sufficient to say that I have never had a murder case in which nude pictures were part of the evidence collected in the case. I guess this is just another example of how Ms. Arias' case was unique.

As for the photos themselves, when I reviewed the file and read the police report I assumed that these nude pictures would be part of the evidence that I would need to review. So in this regard, I guess my shock had to be much less significant than the shock that Detectives Melendez and Flores had when they discovered these pictures for the first time. That is not to say that I was not shocked when I saw them for the first time. The police reports mentioned some "nude images." Those of you who saw these pictures know that such a description, while true, is in many ways an understatement. A better description of most of these pictures would be that they were pornographic. The mild pictures were the pictures of Ms. Arias lying naked on the bed with her hair in pig tails or braids looking miserable, looking like a blow up doll or a "real doll" who just happened to be human. The pictures of Mr. Alexander nude, flashing the peace sign looking as if he was having the time of his life were also relatively mild. Then there were other more graphic photographs. Photographs that somehow seemed beyond pornographic in that they were so graphic that they took the objectification typically associated with pornography to a new level. For those of you who do not recall the images that I am referring to, I am talking about the pictures that Mr. Alexander took of Ms. Arias' vagina and anus. The pictures that he either took at a very close range or used a zoom feature to get up close and personal.

Undoubtedly, finding these pictures meant a great deal to the Mesa Police Department during their initial investigation because these photographs demonstrated that Ms. Arias was at Mr. Alexander's home on June 4, 2008. These photographs made her the prime suspect in their investigation. Ironically, these photographs were just as important to me as I sought to make my case for life. Why? Because it was undisputed that Mr. Alexander took the photographs. It was also beyond legitimate dispute that Mr. Alexander chose to take graphic objectifying pictures of Ms. Arias. Why was this important? Because these pictures demonstrated the fact that Mr. Alexander was really into Ms. Arias in a sexual way. That despite the religious convictions he asserted to the world, he wanted to not only take nude photographs of Ms. Arias, but graphic pictures of her vagina and her anus.

As you read this you might be wondering why I am sharing these thoughts in this section of the book rather than in sections in which I talk about the evidence. The answer lies in the fact that these photographs, beyond their role as evidence, were a big deal to Ms. Arias. They were a source of contention between us. These pictures played a big role in how I had to deal with Ms. Arias. Hence in this chapter, rather than talk about these pictures strictly as evidence, I will talk about them in terms of the issues they caused down the road with Ms. Arias.

Consistent with the strategy that I outline in Chapter 50, these pictures, along with the sex tape (that I describe in Chapter 17), played a huge role in my trial strategy and they played a huge role in my plan to save my client's life. They played such a key role because they demonstrated Mr. Alexander's desires in a way that could not be contradicted. As it relates to the pictures, that meant showing them to the jury, it meant showing them in the exact way that they were taken. I did not want the jury to see them covered up nor blurred because had the graphic nature of these pictures been tempered in any way, so too would their value as evidence. Ms. Arias may have realized this but she did not care. As I will likely mention several times over the course of my writings, image was important to Ms. Arias. It seemed to me that she cared more about her public image than her life. In contrast, as you read in Chapter 2, I did not care about her image. I had a job to do. If I were to venture a guess, I would guess that she would rather be on death row right now with these pictures having remained as private as possible than be serving a life sentence while knowing that the world has seen her vagina.

On what do I base my opinion? Well, when Ms. Arias realized that I was planning on showing the pictures to the jury she was not happy to say the least. Many a visit, many a phone call surrounded her articulating her desire that I not show these pictures. As was her habit, Ms. Arias' plan of attack was to whine, cry and nag until she got her way. As was her typical pattern, if she did not like the answer I gave her, meaning that I was still going to show the pictures to the jury, she would just keep talking seemingly with the intention of trying to wear down my resolve. If the option of hanging up on her at these times was a legitimate option, I would have done so. Instead, I simply listened to her whining, crying and nagging for hours on end. It was torturous. While I have never asked for your sympathy before, though I am tempted to do so now, I will refrain. Instead, all I ask of you is that you imagine yourself listening to Ms. Arias whine relentlessly about how the gallery in the courtroom and/or the whole world was going to see her vagina. I ask you to further imagine that her choice to call and whine about such things interrupted your work on a motion or something else that actually was important to the case. Or even better, imagine having to listen to this whining at the end of a long day when all you really want to do is go home and spend time with your family. As my recently departed friend Mark used to say, "Painful!"

Please, do not get me wrong, I could understand the embarrassment that any woman might have if her vagina was going to be displayed on the internet for the entire world to see. However, this was a unique situation. In this situation the woman attached to the vagina was an admitted killer and the pictures that she voluntarily posed for, were evidence that helped support her claims about her relationship with the victim and what happened on the day of the killing. As her lawyer I did not give a rip if this helpful evidence was testimonial, forensic or nude photos of my client, I needed every piece of evidence I could get. Furthermore, if that evidence came at the expense of my client's public image, then so be it. I was not concerned about the damage that displaying these images to the public might have on her image it is not as if her image was otherwise pristine, she had killed someone, my job was to save her life not her image.

Despite my position I must admit, I relented to some degree. The torture was too much. I finally relented to filing a motion with the court to restrict access on the monitors. I cannot recall what the exact title of my motion was but the best title would have been "Can we not throw my client's vagina up on the courtroom monitors." A true high point in my legal career (please note the sarcasm). At least after the motion was denied it shut Ms. Arias up for a while, at least as it related to the displaying of her nude photos at trial (more on that in book 2).

Of course, as you might guess, the nude photos were also a source of concern for me before the trial as I did not want them to be published anywhere before the trial began. I always had a bit of a concern that some county employee who was not getting paid very well would sell them to some tabloid or news outlet. This was a concern because I felt as if the photos would be quite impactful as evidence and I wanted the impact of seeing these photos to happen at trial, not in some magazine or on some show like TMZ, even though I love that show (on a brief side note I consider Harvey Levin to be a bit of a hero because he has one of the best careers a lawyer could have in terms of the fact that he makes the "big bucks" and seemingly has very little stress). Furthermore, I did not want to be in a position where I had to ask potential jurors which nude photos of my client they have seen and where they had seen them.

On this point the issue of pretrial secrecy of these photographs, Ms. Arias and I agreed. She was always very concerned about who would see these pictures. The strange part though was that she never seemed concerned if I saw them, which really, really, really completely creeped me out after someone pointed out to me, I was the most significant male relationship in her life. I took that to mean that in her sick twisted mind, Ms. Arias saw me as her boyfriend. Putting two and two together, this meant that Ms. Arias did not care if I saw her naked because she viewed me as her boyfriend. Sadly, the fact that your client creeps you out is not reason to file a motion to withdraw, trust me I filed many of those motions in this case and "she creeps me out" is not a viable legal motion. Trust me, if it was, I would have filed it.

CHAPTER 34

VIVA LAS VEGAS

As you read my books you will come to understand that Ms. Arias had a very self-destructive streak. To this point in this book we have not talked about this issue much, at least not directly anyway. In this Chapter I will begin to confront this issue and tell you the tale of the steps that I had to take in order to combat my client's self-destructive tendencies. As you might guess, this battle raged throughout the entire course of my representation of Ms. Arias but since this is a book about those things that happened before trial I will limit myself to those things that happened before trial. Furthermore, as this is a book of limited length, I will simply draw your attention to some of Ms. Arias' most prominent self-destructive acts. First on the list were the various stories that she told Detective Flores. As you likely know she followed that up by giving interviews with CBS in which she relayed the same nonsensical "ninja story" and in perhaps what is the stupidest thing I have ever seen a defendant do, Ms. Arias gave an interview to Inside Edition wherein she said that no jury would convict her.

By way of reminder, for those of you who may have forgotten, these things all occurred before I was assigned to the case and thus, I could do nothing about them. However, once I got the case, my duty to save my client's life meant that I needed to do everything I could to prevent my client from acting in self-destructive ways. Not an easy task when it came to Ms. Arias because even at these early stages of the case, part of the "fun" of being her lawyer was trying to prevent her from doing something self-destructive that might hurt her when trial began.

Given the strength of Ms. Arias' self-destructive tendencies I knew she would not listen to my advice about how the things she does before trial might harm her when we were in trial. In this regard, I was particularly concerned about those self-destructive acts that I would not know about until the State presented them to the court at trial. Without going into too much detail I had every reason to believe that my client was trying to do self-destructive things behind my back. As you might guess, trying to prevent these things from occurring created a large amount of extra work for me and sometimes even an ethical dilemma or two. Now I realize many out there believe that ethics mean nothing to me. However, those who say this are not really accounting for the ethical rules I have to follow as an attorney. Thus, to be clear, when I speak about ethical dilemmas, I am talking about following the rules of ethics that a lawyer must follow not any personal ethical dilemmas.

As it relates to these rules, the issue that often confronted me was how much effort, if any, did I need to expend trying to prevent my client from acting in self-destructive ways? Was I obligated to try to stop her from being self-destructive if I could? If so; could I act in a covert manner against my client's self-destructive ways? I had the questions, what I needed was the answers. Thus, for the first time in my career I called the Arizona Bar's "Ethics Hotline." For those who do not know the "Ethics Hotline" is a number which attorneys can call to obtain advice from the bar when they are facing ethical dilemmas that they cannot resolve on their own. After speaking to the Bar, I learned that the reality of my situation was that I could and should act covertly, even if my client would not appreciate my actions. In sum, the Bar's position was that if I felt those covert actions would save her life then I should act. Saving her life was, in essence, the ethical duty I owed Ms. Arias, even if I had to act covertly and/or upset her in the process.

At this point you might be beginning to wonder after reading all this somewhat technical buildup; why this chapter about the ethical dilemmas I was facing is titled Viva Las Vegas? One obvious answer would be that representing

Ms. Arias and trying to prevent her from acting in a self-destructive manner drove me nuts and because of this I would often daydream about running off to Vegas for a 3 or 4 day escape from reality. While representing Ms. Arias did lead to such thoughts on a regular basis that is not what I am talking about when I reference Vegas in this Chapter. Instead, what I am talking about is a very specific situation that forced myself and a few other members of the defense team into a position where we had to travel to Las Vegas. Now trust me, when I say forced, I am not complaining about having to fly to Las Vegas, I love Las Vegas but it somehow seemed wrong for me to be going there to work. So why did we need to go to Las Vegas?

From listening to Ms. Arias' jail calls I became very suspicious that Ms. Arias, with the help of another individual, a person who lived in Las Vegas, was hiding evidence from me. I did not know for sure if this was evidence that would help Ms. Arias' case or hurt her case, but either way, I wanted to know what it was. In reading this you might be asking yourself; how could Nurmi believe that the evidence his client was hiding could have been helpful to her? There is no doubt about it, that is a great question, but it is also a question based on logic, a question that is based on rational thought. Keep in mind that Ms. Arias was self-destructive and was also a person who cared more about her image than her case. If you think about it this way, I suspect you will then see that my concerns made sense. You see, based on my dealings with Ms. Arias I firmly believed that if there was evidence out there that would have helped her case but at the same time would be extremely humiliating to Ms. Arias personally she would hide it from me because she valued her image more than her freedom or her life. As crazy as it sounds, image was everything to Ms. Arias.

Now you might be wondering; why did this require you to travel to Las Vegas? Why could you not just call the person or something like that? The best answer I can give you is that the diverse interests that Ms. Arias and I had created somewhat of an unspoken battleground and when it came to fighting this battle I knew that if Ms. Arias was trying to hide something from me, as you might guess, I could not just let her know I was going to try to figure out what she was doing behind my back. In this regard, you might also begin to see how I could not just simply call the person at issue and expect them to talk to me and hand over any evidence they might have. Instead, I knew that Ms. Arias' "helper" would simply check with her before doing anything as these people were basically under Ms. Arias' control. Thus, if Ms. Arias knew what I was up to she could easily put a stop to my efforts. (On a related side note I used to joke with my fellow team members, those I had before the shakeup, that if Ms. Arias ever walked out of the jail that there would be twenty guys waiting and holding flowers thinking that they were her one true love or that she would reward them for their efforts). So what this all meant was that the only way to do this was to do it behind the back of Ms. Arias and without the person we wanted to talk with knowing that we were coming for a visit.

It was for these reasons that Jennifer, Bud and I went off to Las Vegas on a covert mission. We knew where our target lived but we did not know where he worked. Once we got into town we went to this man's apartment or condominium, I forget which it was. Fitting with the stereotype, he lived with his mother and I am assuming that we scared her a bit when we knocked on the door. In fact, she would not open the door, which was fair enough as I was a big guy with a shaved head (I guess putting sweet little Jennifer in front was not enough to overcome that reality). As she would not open the door, we left my card on her screen door and left. This whole ordeal must have been quite alarming to this guy's mother because he called me later that same afternoon. We talked and he really seemed intent on unburdening himself of all things Jodi Arias. Given his attitude, I assumed that his mom gave him quite a bit of grief. In my mind I could almost hear her yelling at him for talking to some girl who was in jail for murder and getting himself mixed up in this mess. He wanted to meet the next morning so he could get some stuff together. While I would have preferred to meet with him that night so as to not give him a chance to change his mind, rather than push the issue, I let him set the terms of the meeting. The meeting was to take place the next morning at a coffee shop at the MGM Grand.

That evening Jennifer and I went out for drinks and had a nice time. We talked about the case and got to know each other a bit better. The more I knew of Jennifer the more I liked her. We were becoming more than co-workers, we were becoming friends. Knowing Ms. Arias, I knew that this would upset her because if Jennifer and I became friends it would make it harder for her to pit us against each other (more on this issue in future books). As the night went on Jennifer continued to impress me with her drinking skills. In saying this, I will admit that I am not a big drinker. I will readily confess that I am a bit of a lightweight, so I might be easily impressed, however, given that she is about five feet tall at best(I think she claims to be 5'1"), I stood impressed that night. I was also impressed the next morning when she appeared at the coffee shop no worse for wear.

While Jennifer, Bud and I waited at the coffee shop, I waited with the concern that Ms. Arias' "fan" might have a change of heart and decide not to show up or that if he did show up he would tell us that he had talked to Ms. Arias and we could "pound sand." Fortunately, for the three of us, my fears were unfounded when this man arrived at the coffee shop. Perhaps it was out of fear of his mother's wrath or his own embarrassment but this man gave up everything he had related to Ms. Arias. Beyond that he even kept his promise to send me even more stuff in the mail. Why? I am assuming that he did this because he was scared. Maybe he was scared of his mother but I sensed that it was something more than that. Up until the point in time that two attorneys and their investigator showed up at his door he was simply talking to a girl in jail that he thought was attractive. However, when we showed up at his mom's door it was no longer just fun and games, things became real to him. This was no longer just some bizarre sexual fantasy that only existed in his head. It seemed to me that when we showed up at his door it became something different to him. Ms. Arias became a real person with a real case, a real case that this man clearly wanted no part of, period. The result of all of this was that yes, Ms. Arias was hiding something from me but it really was nothing of importance to her case.

In a relatively unrelated side note, since you have come to me seeking the behind the scenes story of what happened before the trial, I feel that it is my duty to give it to you. Thus, I thought it would be appropriate in the "Viva Las Vegas" chapter to talk about another occasion when I found myself in Las Vegas with my then friend Jennifer. Certainly, I will concede that other than the fact that both events took place in Las Vegas, this story has nothing to do with the story I just told. Having said this, I think the story is an important one because my relationship with my teammates will become an issue down the road as this story moves forward. Thus, I thought it might be of interest to you to see how much damage Ms. Arias needed to do to these relationships in order to cause the sort of divide she needed in order to get the control she wanted. How is that for a cliffhanger for future books?

Admittedly, I cannot recall exactly when in the chain of events this occurred but I know that it occurred sometime after Jennifer had joined the team. Regardless of when it occurred, on this particular weekend it just so happened that Jennifer and I were both traveling to Las Vegas with our spouses. So we had talked about the four of us doing something together, maybe meeting for dinner, something like that. So on one particular morning I get a text or a call from Jennifer, I cannot remember which for sure, she and her husband were out on the strip at one of the discount ticket places. She wanted to know if my wife and I wanted to go to the "Air Supply" concert with them, a double date of sorts. I got a laugh out of that because I had no idea they were still together. You see, while I am not a huge fan of the band I thought they were okay, but they were playing at the hotel my wife and I were staying at so we decided; why not? I remember at some point in time making a half-hearted pact with Jennifer that we would not tell anyone that we did this simply because "Air Supply" tends to be one of those bands that people enjoy but nobody will openly admit to liking (the place was packed by the way). On the night in question I remember that Jennifer and her husband showed up late and instead of a proper dinner it was off to the food court for a quick meal before the concert. Undoubtedly, this might seem like an extraordinary amount of detail and I would agree with you were it not for one important detail. You see a casino food court is not exactly fine dining and while we were eating some kid was walking around not looking so good and you guessed it, he puked all over the place just a few feet behind us. The real kicker was that the vomit was completely pink. I assumed the kid just had strawberry ice cream for dessert, but regardless of what made his vomit pink, the experience was the sort of thing that friends joke about down the road and Jennifer and I did for a while.

CHAPTER 35

THIS IS YOUR BRAIN ON JODI

Please forgive my digression from my usual practice of referring to my former client as Ms. Arias. I did so because I could not think of a better way of describing the effect that dealing with Ms. Arias can have on a person than the old anti-drug campaign, "This is your Brain on Drugs." For those of you not familiar with what I am talking about this was part of Ronald Regan's "War on Drugs." In the commercial you see a person holding an egg, the camera focuses on the egg and an announcer says, "this is your brain" the person then cracks the egg into a hot frying pan. You can then hear the egg begin to sizzle and you hear the words "this is your brain on drugs" For those of you who want to see it, I just searched for it and various versions of this add are online. Okay, now that we all understand the commercial I am referencing let me explain the need for my digression.

Using this commercial as my backdrop, dealing with Ms. Arias in terms of what she can do to your brain would go beyond merely placing my brain into the frying pan. The reality I experienced was much worse than that. I would describe the experience more like this. Take the egg but do not crack it, smash that egg into the pan, shell and all. Now the egg cannot just sit there and fry as that would not be enough to encapsulate the effect. Instead, to fully get a visual of what Ms. Arias did to my brain you would have to find some fecal matter, throw it into the pan, add a chopped up dead rat and scramble the whole mess up. Once completely cooked this concoction would then approximate the effect that Ms. Arias would have on my brain.

I wish that I could go into greater detail about my conversations with Ms. Arias as these details would clearly demonstrate my point. However, as our discussions are confidential, I am limited in that regard. What I can tell you is that there is no doubt about the fact that every time I left the jail after visiting Ms. Arias in person, I was exhausted. After these visits my brain was mush and it truly took a while to clear my head. The same could also be said about my telephonic conversations with her as even 15 minutes or so on the phone with her could make my brain feel like it was the "stuff" in the frying pan.

Even though I cannot talk about the substance of my conversations with Ms. Arias and why taking part in these conversations drove me so insane, I can certainly speculate about a theory about Ms. Arias that I heard a pundit offer to the audience of a national television program. I hope that the person who offered this theory will please understand the fact that I cannot recall their name with certainty. I hope that this person will understand that I saw them offer this theory about Ms. Arias while I was deeply involved in the case so I am not positive who to credit with this theory. That being said, whoever did offer this theory deserves a lot of credit as I believe their theory is highly insightful. As best as I can recall and putting the theory in its most basic terms the theory was that Ms. Arias had abilities like those of a cult leader. That Ms. Arias possessed a unique ability to convince people to follow her. That Ms. Arias had the unique ability to convince people that she was telling the truth, without actual proof, simply because she was the person saying it.

This theory rang true to me because I had certainly had similar thoughts about my client's abilities. In fact, I had seen the manifestation of this myself personally in the form of Ms. Arias' friend Donovan as well as many others who would by in large do as Ms. Arias requested. However, I saw no clearer indication of "The Cult of Jodi" than what I saw in a report that was broadcast on the local news before trial began. To be clear I am referencing a news report that was done about Ms. Arias' confinement. In way of further clarification, during this report, this reporter gets back into Ms. Arias' pod and while there, he tries to speak to Ms. Arias. As he was unsuccessful in his attempt to speak with Ms. Arias on this occasion he spoke instead to several women who were Ms. Arias' "pod mates" at the time. These "pod mates" almost universally supported Ms. Arias and the camera showed us several women lining up in support of her. Some of these women were even holding signs with slogans like "Free Jodi" written on them and if I recall correctly a few of them asserted Ms. Arias' innocence. In my mind that certainly demonstrated the power of Ms. Arias as a cult leader as these women were demonstrating a form of allegiance to Ms. Arias. That power can still be seen today by looking at a web page that asserts the innocence of Ms. Arias. Yes, even several months after the trial Ms. Arias' followers are still drinking the Kool-Aid. She is that good.

CHAPTER 36

9 Out of 10 Days

In Chapter 18, I talk about how as I prepared for trial I learned more about Mr. Alexander and I shared a few of my thoughts about him. As I authored that section I thought about including a chapter about what I had learned about Ms. Arias as I prepared for trial. As I contemplated doing so I came to the conclusion that rather than include such a chapter in that section, I would reserve comment on that issue for a later portion of the book. I came to the conclusion that I would instead lay all of this information "on the line" when I felt it was appropriate to comment on the one sentence of my closing that seemed to set cable news and social media "on fire." As the title of this chapter indicates, I am talking about the comment I made during my guilt phase closing argument, that now famous line in which I describe the fact that I did not like Ms. Arias 9 out of 10 days. My thinking was that, as talking about this comment was not really optional talking about the sentiment behind this comment would provide you with enough understanding of what I learned about Ms. Arias as I prepared for trial.

Please understand, as my next book relates to the trial itself, I am not going to deal with why I made this comment during my closing argument in this book. For that you will simply have to wait. However, that is not to say that I will not answer the burning question that this statement ignited; is it true that you really did not like Ms. Arias nine out of 10 days? The short answer is yes. In my mind my answer should not shock anyone, certainly not anyone who has read this book. However, based on what I have read on various social media outlets many people believe that because I was Ms. Arias' lawyer that I believed her story. Similarly many people seem to share the opinion that because I was her lawyer I supported her actions and that I liked her as a person. On this point make no mistake, none of those things are true. Frankly, I am not sure why people believe this to be the case. Think about it, as an initial matter, I did not ask to be her lawyer. I was appointed to her case while working as a Deputy Public Defender. Furthermore, after I left that job, I did so with the hope of leaving Ms. Arias' case behind. Instead of being able to leave the case behind I was forced by court order to remain on the case. So you will have to forgive me but I do not understand why anyone could conclude, based on these facts, that I liked Ms. Arias or believed in her story. In fact, as I explain elsewhere in the book I did not believe her claims of self-defense, I did not support what she did on June 4, 2008, and as I will explain in this chapter I did not like Ms. Arias.

Before I talk in greater detail about liking or not liking Ms. Arias I should throw in one disclaimer. When I represent capital defendants I do not tend to become friends with my clients or have feelings for them beyond the fact that they are my clients. I take the position that by-in-large that my role is to be my client's attorney, not their friend. Why not? If they are a capital client the odds are real high that they killed somebody and I tend to exclude killers from my peer group. So to me I do not really tend to "like" my clients in the sense that the word is most commonly used. Having said all this let me say that I am human and emotions can come into play. You see, in a capital case I spend a lot of time with my clients so over time I do tend to like some of their more likeable qualities or I feel highly sympathetic for their situation and/or personal histories, so in that regard it can be said that I do "like" some clients.

Yes, even with this highly narrowed version of the word like, I still did not and do not like Ms. Arias. Let me repeat myself since some of you seem so convinced otherwise. I did not and I do not like Ms. Arias. Everyone understand that now? Why don't I like Ms. Arias? Well, because of confidentiality I can only explain some of the many reasons. So please understand that the reasons I am articulating are the "tip of the iceberg." It is my hope that the reasons I can share are enough from which you can get a good sense of the reasons as to why I did not and do not like Ms. Arias.

Let me begin with the reality that Ms. Arias was perfectly content to risk ruining my career by forcing me into a position where I would have to help her make these assertions against Mr. Alexander. As I describe elsewhere in this book, this is not how I wanted to defend the case. If I had my way the accusations she made against Mr. Alexander would never have come to light during the trial. However, what I wanted or the damage that doing this would do to me did not matter to her. Beyond that, she was smart enough to know that I would have to go with her defense if I could not prove her wrong. Heck, if she had any question about these issues she had Pre-Paid Legal lawyers on standby to answer her questions on these issues. I suspect in her mind she thought that it was my privilege to represent her and/or that I believed in her because we were friends. She was wrong. She seemingly was failing to realize that I was more than willing to leave a job I liked to get away from her. When I tried to get away from her then she wanted to be nice and beg me to stay. When I was trying to get away Ms. Arias wanted to act like we were friends. She wanted to try to manipulate me into keeping the case. She wanted me to drink the Kool-Aid. Ms. Arias wanted me to join the "Cult of Jodi." After that did not work she tried to manipulate the court into forcing me to keep the case. When she succeeded in this regard, she thought I should be thrilled with the outcome. She certainly was thrilled as she thought she had her own "personal attorney." Instead of being thrilled with the outcome I was not happy. I was both resentful for the things that were said to keep me on the case and I was also displeased because I had other plans that were crushed. My plan was to go into private practice with a dear friend of mine who had been encouraging me for years to join her in private practice. I was excited to begin this new adventure. This woman, who also happened to author the Foreword to this book, is like a sister to me. We had some great plans, all of which were crapped on by Ms. Arias' ability to manipulate the court into forcing me to stay on as counsel. My relative dislike of Ms. Arias began to grow after I failed to get off her case, the already poor way she treated me only worsened. After I failed in my attempt to withdraw in the spring of 2011, she knew that I could not get away and decided that she could treat me any way she wanted because of this reality. As I recount in Chapter 30, one of the first things Ms. Arias did when I was officially "trapped" was to in essence threaten my business. For those of you who may have skipped over that chapter or who have forgotten, let me advise you that a few days after I was "trapped" Ms. Arias informed me that she was going to bad-mouth me in the jail so that no other female inmates would hire me. She then went on to imply that if I did not play ball with her that the bad-mouthing would continue after trial was over. We saw a bit of that after the first trial. I am sure we will see more of it in the future, but as it relates to back then my dislike was growing. After this initial threat things really did not get better. Ms. Arias was of the mindset that I should be working in the office when she wanted me there. In her mind, I was her attorney and she was the boss. I recall laughing to myself when she realized that she could do nothing when I did not comply with her demands. As you might guess, my not complying with Ms. Arias was a constant source of frustration for her and putting up with her only reinforced my dislike of her. So yes, I did not like Ms. Arias 9 out of 10 days and in many ways that was a bit of an understatement because it was more accurate to say that I disliked and/or despised her 9 out of 10 days.

Having read this chapter, which I will concede reads more like a rant (please forgive me but it felt good), I bet there is one more question you might have right now that deserves an answer. That question being; what about the tenth day? Did you really like her one out of ten days? No, I did not like Ms. Arias one out of ten days, at all. The tenth day simply accounted for the days I did not have to deal with her or think about her case. On those days I did not pay her any mind. If I did not have days like those where I did not think of Ms. Arias, trust me, it would have been 10 out of 10.

Before this rant began I said that this chapter served as a bit of an explanation as to what I learned about Ms. Arias as I prepared for trial. At this point that should be obvious in that I have described many of Ms.

Arias' characteristics but to be clear, I learned that in addition to being self-destructive, Ms. Arias was a highly manipulative individual who had abilities akin to a cult leader. The list could go on and on, however, I believe that my point can be made rather simply as I prepared for trial, I realized that I was dealing with a very disturbed woman.

SECTION 7

ROSTER SHAKE-UP

So by this point in the book you know that I was assigned the case when I was a member of the Office of the Public Defender. You have likely also come to understand that though I served as lead counsel on the case I was truly just a part of a team of people that also worked at the Office of the Public Defender. To this point in the book, I have not spoken much about these people. Please do not take this as a sign of disrespect when in fact just the opposite is true. I have avoided discussing my original teammates because, in this book, I am only speaking for myself. I do not feel entitled to speak for these people. They may disagree with some of the opinions I have shared. As a further sign of the respect that I have for these people, in Chapter 38, I will talk about what a devastating blow it was to me that I lost my original team-mates before trial began. In Chapter 37, I talk about how Ms. Arias' situation was further altered by the loss of her original domestic violence expert. Finally, I will end this section with Chapter 39, when I talk about how I went about building a new team, the team that all of you have come to know.

CHAPTER 37

Others Want Out, Some Make it, Some do not and Alyce Comes to Wonderland

A few weeks after Judge Duncan issued her order that I was to remain on the case as lead counsel, the Public Defender's Office decided they had a problem with a non-employee, aka me, being in charge of their employees. In this regard it is important to note that my cohorts on the defense team were not the ones with the problem. Instead, it was the administration of the Public Defender's Office that had the problem. In essence, these administrators decided that because I had left the office and they did not have control over me they did not want to play with me anymore. Despite finding humor in the insecurities behind their motion, I would have been more than fine with these administrators getting their way if I was the one to get off the case. However, as they were trying to strip me of my teammates, I had to file yet another Motion to Withdraw. The main assertion of this motion was that because of the Public Defender's Office antics I could not effectively serve as lead counsel to Ms. Arias. I based my assertion on the fact that due to the Public Defender's Office's antics I was leading a team that would not follow my directions because they were being directed by their bosses not to follow my instructions. Again let me remind you that this had nothing to do with my teammates themselves. We were all working fine together, in fact we were all friends. In this regard, I could tell that this motion put them in an awkward position. They had no problem working with me but I am almost positive none of them would have shed crocodile tears over being removed from the case.

So as you might guess, all this posturing meant that it was time for another court hearing. Administrators with the Public Defender's Office made their pitch claiming that it was not about me, but their system. After verifying that there was no actual problem with my conduct and confirming that I was not ordering these people to do inappropriate things, this motion was denied. The Public Defender's Office remained involved in the case. The only down side for me about this was the fact that once Judge Duncan ruled in this fashion, it made my Motion to Withdraw moot. As for the other members of the team, I'm sure this ruling did not make them very happy either. Combined, these rulings meant that we were stuck in the "poop soup" together. Despite their angst, the way I saw it, if I could not get out of this soup with them, I wanted them in there with me. They are all great people and they were excellent teammates. I wish I had them throughout the case, but more on that later.

Around this same time one of the experts working on Ms. Arias' behalf became ill. In fact, this expert became so ill that this person was not available to testify during Ms. Arias' upcoming trial. This expert was then ultimately allowed to withdraw from the case. In this regard some of you might be thinking; so what? Well in my future books I will talk about what a huge loss this was for Ms. Arias' case. However, as your "so what" might relate to the idea of Ms. Arias needing an expert of this type at all. To that end, if you consider the law I have talked about previously in this book you would understand why this was a big deal on an essential level. That is to say that Ms. Arias' case could not go forward without such an expert. For those of you who have forgotten what I have said about the law at issue and for those of you who skipped over this aspect of the book, let me just advise you that under the law a defendant in a capital case has the unrestrained right to not only defend themselves against the charges but to defend their life by presenting mitigating factors to their jury. To be clear, these rights are absolute. If a capital defendant went to trial without such evidence and the experts to support this evidence any conviction and/or sentence of death would likely be overturned. As the expert that could not continue on the case was going to speak to Ms. Arias' claims that she was a victim of domestic violence, I needed to find a new expert in this field.

At this time, this was not as easy of a task as you might want to believe. I realize many followers of the trial believe that there are unscrupulous experts with doctorate degrees just sitting around looking for some attorney to pay them big money. That these experts will say whatever a defense attorney thinks needs to be said if the price is right. That is not the case. Instead, it can often take quite a while to find the right expert. However, in this case, because of the court's timeframe, I had to find the right expert and one who could be ready for trial by November of 2011.

So after all of the dust settled as it related to the issue of Ms. Arias' domestic violence expert, the bottom line was that myself and my team, my original team, had to find the right expert and we needed to find them fast. This meant phone calls, phone conferences, team meetings, discussions with experts in related fields and even a road trip or two so that we could interview potential experts in person.

Finally, we found Alyce LaViolette. As many of you may know, Alyce worked primarily as a counselor for those involved in domestically violent relationships and as a domestic violence expert in various settings. One thing that struck me right away is that Ms. LaViolette did not have a doctorate degree. Using an expert who did not have a PhD was unusual and a bit risky. However, as she was one of the few experts willing to give it a go, out of a modicum of desperation, I was willing to consider using her. To this end, I sent her some material and we talked on the phone a few times. After these conversations I was impressed with her. Alyce was both very knowledgeable on the subject matter of domestic violence and quite likable as well. Thus, in considering using her as an expert witness, I had to weigh these positive aspects of Ms. LaViolette against the reality that she did not have a PhD. Having said this, I must concede that after these conversations Ms. LaViolette was not sold on taking the case either. Before she would agree to take the case she wanted to meet Ms. Arias and then we would talk from there about whether or not she was willing to participate in the case. Fair enough, in fact I thought it was quite wise of her to take this position which only served to impress me further.

Soon thereafter, Ms. LaViolette came to town to meet Ms. Arias and meet with the team. When she arrived, the first stop was the Estrella jail to meet Ms. Arias. To her credit Ms. LaViolette did not rush into anything. In fact, she spent the greater part of the day talking to Ms. Arias. So instead of the entire team meeting with Ms. LaViolette in the afternoon as was originally planned, the plan became that she, myself and the Mitigation Specialist would meet over dinner to discuss whether or not Ms. LaViolette would become our expert. I certainly had hopes this would be the case because there were not many other takers. I remember walking into the restaurant and seeing the Mitigation Specialist and the woman I would come to know as Alyce LaViolette. I greeted Ms. LaViolette with a hug and she said "Okay, I'm in." So with that, we now had our domestic violence expert and after a few more hours discussing things at dinner we also had a plan as to how it would be best to move forward considering the November trial date. As you might guess there will be more on Alyce later. However, as I drove home that night, after a very long day, I felt satisfied that at the very least things were back on track. Sadly, that feeling was short lived.

CHAPTER 38

I Lose my Team

With Ms. LaViolette in place and the Office of the Public Defender's issue having been resolved a few months prior, I got to the point that I thought we were going to get this case into a courtroom. I thought we might actually begin trial in November of 2011. Apart from the fact that I would be in trial over the holidays I was very excited. The thought of being rid of Ms. Arias by the summer of 2012 and being able to move on with my life was exciting. Though I had hoped to be rid of her much earlier in 2012, being done with the case in time for the summer vacation season sounded exhilarating to me. Unfortunately, for me, it did not take long for my exhilaration to turn to anguish.

My anguish began when I learned that the Office of the Public Defender determined that they had a conflict of interest and that they could no longer be involved in representing Ms. Arias because of this conflict. To explain further, lawyers are governed by a code of conduct that sometimes limits who they can represent. For example if an attorney knows something about a witness because that witness was a former client, they may not be able to represent their current client because that would mean disclosing confidential information about the former client to your current client. Conflicts like this can arise all the time with the Public Defender's Office and certainly this is an oversimplified way of describing one potential type of conflict. There are many more types of conflicts but I use this example because it is one of the more common types. As it related to the Arias case this conflict likely arose because something of this nature was discovered about a newly listed witness or that something was discovered related to an old witness that would not allow the Public Defender's Office to be involved in the case from an ethical standpoint. I wish I could tell you what this conflict was, but I do not know. What is even more of a bummer to me is the fact that had I known at the time what this conflict was, I might have had reason to withdraw as well.

Sadly, when I attended the hearing on the issue, I did not have the chance to learn what the asserted conflict related to and/or why this assert-ed conflict made withdrawal of the Office of the Public Defender the only option. Instead, the administration of the Office of the Public Defender simply met privately with the judge in chambers and presumably advised the court of their conflict and/or explained their reasoning as to why their office had to withdraw. Whatever they had to say, apparently, their con-flict and/or their reasoning were good enough to satisfy the Judge who, at the time, would have been very hesitant to delay the trial by granting their request, granted their request as soon as she returned to the bench. The Office of the Public Defender was off the case and thus, so were my original teammates. Was this ruling a shock to me? No, I saw the writing on the wall. That did not mean that I did not walk into court that day with some hope that somehow I could keep my current team. Now that all hope was dashed, it was time for me to deal with the consequences of this ruling. As for Ms. Arias I suspected that she was not surprised by the ruling either. In fact, I do not even think she was unhappy about the ruling. Ms. Arias could not seem to manipulate any of the people she was losing so I suspect that in her mind she at least now had a chance to manipulate her new team members. Thus, when I considered the consequences of this ruling, the likelihood that Ms. Arias would attempt to manipulate her new team was at the top of the list. This did not make me happy but my unhappiness in this regard did not provide me with a basis to argue against letting the Public Defender's Office withdraw from the case, nor did it provide me with a basis to ask if I could leave with them.

If there was any good news to come out of this hearing, from my perspective, it was that I would not be in trial over the 2011 holiday season. The bad news was that I had no idea when this case was going to get to trial. I had no idea when I would make my way out of this trap. To me this state of affairs was a huge blow on two different levels. The first being that I was going to be on the case for a much longer period of time because the rules in Arizona are clear that Ms. Arias' case could not proceed to trial until she had a complete defense team (see Chapter 3) in place. As it now stood, I was the only one on the team and creating the rest of the team did not just mean finding people to fill out the roster. The new members of the team also needed time to get up to speed on the case. Due to this reality there was no way for me to avoid the fact that I would be Ms. Arias' lawyer for many more months. My sentence had gotten much longer. The golden handcuffs were not coming off anytime soon. A big blow indeed but in my mind the bigger blow was the fact that for however many more months I would have the case, I would be working on the case without the team who I had worked with for about two years. In this regard, I felt that I was screwed. Screwed not only because I really cared for these people and they would no longer be helping me on a daily basis but also because they had a great deal of knowledge about the case. I knew that I could not replace the knowledge of my former teammates, ever. They had a history with Ms. Arias and feelings about her (let's just say they were not positive) that could never simply be transferred to others. This was a devastating blow at the time but as devastating as it was at the time, I had no idea how huge the impact this change would be moving forward.

So, after this ruling was made, there I was, alone. Not only was I "Trapped with Ms. Arias" but I was her only lawyer. I was the only member of her defense team. I could almost sense the delight that my old team members were experiencing when this ruling was made. They were out. To their credit, they subdued their glee to some extent for my benefit. I knew that they had genuine pity for me because I was still trapped. In addition to noticing the subdued glee my former teammates were experiencing, my thoughts began to turn back to my own dilemma. I knew that not only was I trapped alone with Ms. Arias, but my responsibilities were suddenly much more extensive. I now had so much more work to do than was the case before this ruling was made. Now that this ruling was done business, in addition to continuing to develop the case with Alyce LaViolette, I had to bring a whole new team on board. I had to educate them on Ms. Arias' case and more importantly about Ms. Arias as a person. The latter being of the most importance because frankly I knew that I had to do it quickly before Ms. Arias was able to figure out how she could manipulate them.

As all these thoughts were swirling in my head Judge Stephens brought up the fact that I now had to build a new team and do so rather quickly.

CHAPTER 39

BUILDING A NEW TEAM

A key component of building a team was figuring out where these people were going to come from. In theory all qualified attorneys in Maricopa County were one potential source. Another potential more defined source would be the "county contract list." (I suspect it has a more formal name but that is what most of us call it). To clarify the "county contract list" is a list of Capital Attorneys, Investigators and Mitigation Specialists that is maintained by Maricopa County. For further clarification, the names on these lists are people who have agreed to do work for the county at a certain hourly rate and visa-versa. The discussion I had with Judge Stephens at the previously mentioned hearing, about my need to build a new defense team for Ms. Arias, left me with the impression that instead of looking for any qualified attorney, I had to find my new Co-counsel and the rest of my new defense team from this "county contract list." If memory serves, I think that Judge Stephens gave me about a week to find these people.

Demonstrative of how she treated me as her personal lawyer, it was my understanding that Ms. Arias had a list of attorneys from which she wanted me to pick my new Co-counsel. I found it funny that she thought she knew better than I did who would be good for her case. Not surprising because she fancied herself as being so smart, way smarter than her lead counsel anyway, but funny nonetheless. The good news is that she never presented me with such a list. If she had it would have caused more conflict when I ignored her list. At this point in time, I could have cared less about what she thought about who my Co-counsel should be. I needed someone I could work with. The only value that this list could ever have had to me is that it would be fun to look back and see if Jennifer Willmott's name would have been on Ms. Arias' list. Of course, I had more than a new Co-counsel to select I also needed to find a new Mitigation Specialist and a new Investigator.

As it related to finding these individuals, I was in somewhat of a weird position in that I was not asking them to do too much or so I thought at the time. Back then, in my mind, most of the work had already been done. Furthermore, my theories on how it would be best to proceed at trial were also fairly well established in that I had contemplated and/or discussed virtually every fact from every angle possible with my former teammates. That is not to say that I was not open to new thoughts. However, when I thought about forming a new team, I thought about this reality. I realized that it might be hard for some people to accept my thinking because as they learned about the case they might have their own theories of the case and/or what evidence to present to the jury. I realized that they might feel frustrated when I explained to them that the former team already considered their thoughts and in essence, dismissed them. I knew that my new teammates might feel rejected or disrespected because of this situation so I was looking for new team members who could understand where we were at with things and accept the strategy that had been mapped out without too many problems. This is a lot to request of people. I knew that this could cause problems down the road in terms of how members of the team would get along with each other and/or how they would view me. At the same time I also figured that if I had people who were experienced and loyal enough that I had a chance to hold everything together until the trial was over (in my future books you will see this issue play out). This being said, let's face it I really had no other choice. I did not have the option of going it alone, nor would it have been realistic to do so anyway. So, with all this in mind, it was my job to find a new team and find them quickly. To that end I turned to the "county contract list."

As Co-counsel would ultimately be my closest confidant, finding the right person was my priority. Additionally, as my chosen Co-counsel they would also be in a position to interact and sometimes direct the rest of the team if I was not available to do so. For this reason, I wanted my new Co-counsel to have a say in who would make up the rest of the team. Thus, my plan was to find new Co-counsel first and then once I had him or her in place, together we would choose the rest of the team. As I had been at the Public Defender's Office for almost my whole career, I knew few names on the "county contract list" well enough to make an accurate assessment of who would be a good fit. That being said, I knew that I wanted someone who was experienced in capital cases, someone who would contribute their own thoughts but at the same time follow my direction, someone who would work hard and someone who Ms. Arias would like enough that she would not waste my time complaining about them. My first choice was and is an awesome lawyer. She is someone that I admire greatly. This woman had more experience with capital cases than I had. I assumed Ms. Arias would not like her but she brought so much to the table that I sure wanted her. Unfortunately for me, she was busy with another case and my timeframe was tight. My second choice was also a smart lawyer. She had tried at least a few capital cases and was not the type I would expect to cause problems. However, like my first choice, she too was busy. I then called Jennifer Willmott. Why? I had worked with her many years ago and I viewed her as smart, easy to get along with and extremely hard working. She lacked the capital trial experience I would have liked, which was why she was my third choice, but I assumed Ms. Arias would like her well enough (little did I know how much until later on) and that she would not "go rouge." Looking back, in many ways I wish that I never would have called Jennifer and not for the reasons you think. Instead, I wish that I would have never made that call because when I made that call, at the very least we shared a pleasant acquaintanceship if not a somewhat distant friendship. However, now, I believe that what we went through together created a level of distaste for each other and I realize that such distaste would not exist if I had not made that call. However, above any other reason stands the fact that when I called Jennifer about joining me in this case and she accepted, her life was forever altered and seemingly for the worse. Granted, somebody had to do it but Jennifer (I should say that I am calling Ms. Willmott by her first name because she would often point out that I would call her Ms. Willmott when I was upset with her and I don't want her to think I am presently) would never have said yes had she known what was to come. For example, she was threatened, her children were threatened. Truly ugly things were being said about her all over social media. I wish she never would have had to endure these things and though she must have thought it a thousand times, never once did she complain about being on the case, nor, to her credit did she ever admit that she wished she would have simply hung up on me that day.

Certainly, I will speak about Jennifer more as my writings move forward but given I have no publisher and I can say what I want and I want those of you who choose to bully or threaten Jennifer to understand who you are attacking. I want you to know that you are attacking a woman, who while not perfect, is an outstanding wife and mother, a woman who with the help of her husband has raised three wonderful children, a woman who somehow manages to do all this while running a successful law firm. She is someone who you would want your daughter to be like when they grow up. She is someone with whom, if the stars ever so align, that I would be proud to once again call my friend.

After Jennifer agreed to be my Co-counsel, we then discussed who would be good choices to fill out the team. In terms of choosing a Mitigation Specialist, I knew only one name on the "county contract list." Thus, I was ultimately in a position where I would have to rely on my Co-counsel for advice. Jennifer's suggestion was Maria DeLaRosa. Jennifer advised me that Ms. DeLaRosa (whom I will refer to as Maria going forward for the same reasons as I do with Jennifer) had done a lot of capital cases and was really great with the clients. Sometime thereafter I spoke with Maria on the phone and then we met in person. I found her to be smart, intelligent and to be a very compassionate person. So after we met it was decided that Maria would serve as Ms. Arias' Mitigation Specialist.

Before moving forward to the rest of the team, like I did with Jennifer, let me say a few words about Maria to all those who choose to cyberbully her. In future books I will reference choices Maria made that I was not happy with. I will discuss the things I wish she would not have done and the things I wish she would not have said. However, like with Jennifer, those who bully Maria should know that she is a smart, kindhearted woman, a woman of faith with a good sense of humor. She may not be perfect, none of us are. However, even though imperfect, she is someone who is worthy of your respect, not your disdain.

The final member of the team was Bud. Bud was to serve as the Investigator. At the time he came onto the case there was not much of a role for him because most of the investigation was complete, but ultimately he wound up doing a lot of work that I will speak about in subsequent books. Bud also ended up meaning a lot to me on a personal level. He became a huge asset to me because we shared the same outlook on Ms. Arias. I will speak of Bud in future books but for those of you who do not know, he passed away towards the end of the second trial. It was a heartbreaking blow to the entire defense team. It was also just another example of the devastation that surrounded the State of Arizona v. Jodi Arias.

So there you have it, Ms. Arias had her new team and when the time came Ms. Willmott and I appeared before Judge Stephens so that she could make all the required orders. It was at this time that Ms. Arias met Ms. Willmott for the first time. Ironically, it did not seem as if Ms. Arias liked Jennifer when the two first met. Ironic because of how much that would change over time.

SECTION 8

PRETRIAL ISSUES

Given all the things that I have written about so far in this book, you might be thinking that there could not possibly be any other pretrial issues to discuss. Certainly the amount of drama that I have talked about to this point would be more than enough for any case, but this was no normal case. This was the State of Arizona v. Jodi Ann Arias. There was much more to this case than what was typical, so much more than I have already described. So much in fact I could probably go on for pages and pages describing all sorts of details. However, as I suspect that many of you would not want to read all of these mind numbing details, I decided to stick to the highlights. Keeping in mind my inability to create a perfect chronology I will be talking about these highlights in the most organized fashion I can think of. In Chapter 40, I will discuss Ms. Arias' first experience going "Pro-Per." In Chapter 41, "Felony Murder?" I will attempt to educate you on the felony murder rule and the issue that surrounded the application of that rule to Ms. Arias' case. In Chapter 42, I will discuss the efforts that were made to settle this case before trial began in 2013. In Chapter 43, I will talk about dealing with the media before trial. Since I was unable to curtail the media during the first trial, in Chapter 44 "We Gotta Get Outta Town or Shut the Jury Down" I discuss the other steps I had to take. Finally, as there is so much hullabaloo related to "The So-Called Delays" that occurred before trial began I will address these delays in Chapter 45.

CHAPTER 40

Ms. Arias Goes "Pro-Per"

Due to attorney-client privilege I cannot share the details of the discussions I had with Ms. Arias relating to her choice to act as her own counsel. For these same reasons, I cannot share what I know about her decision to go "Pro-Per" but that does not mean that I cannot share with you some things related to these issues that you may not know about. To that end, back in August of 2011, before most of the world knew much about Ms. Arias, a hearing took place regarding the admissibility of "The Letters" as I refer to them in Chapter 16. So as to clear up any confusion, because both parties ultimately shifted from their original position, at this hearing, the State was seeking to keep "The Letters" out of evidence during the trial. Likewise the defense, with Ms. Arias acting as her own counsel, also had a different position in that the original assertion by the defense was that we had wanted "The Letters" to come into evidence.

Having said all of this presently, before moving forward I ask you to recall that as I made reference to in Chapter 16, in my mind, the viability of these letters as evidence supporting Ms. Arias' claims was almost non-existent after three by five cards and pens were found in Ms. Arias' cell. To refresh your memory, these were not just any 3 by 5 cards, they were cards with someone's attempt to simulate Mr. Alexander's handwriting on them, or so the State's expert would say. For these reasons, had I been the attorney, I would have walked into this hearing and withdrawn my desire to admit the letters. Once I did so the State's motion would have been grant-ed. At that time, this would have been a victory for the State. However, at that time, I saw it differently. My perspective on "The Letters" was that they would be harmful to Ms. Arias if they were introduced at trial. An idea it would seem Mr. Martinez came to years later (more on that in subsequent books). Under my plan, the letters would have been precluded from evi-dence in about 5 minutes and the issue would have been resolved. I did not have that opportunity on this day.

Instead, Ms. Arias became her own lawyer. In the legal world we call this going "Pro-Per." For those of you who are not familiar with what this means and/or why this can happen, let me try to explain it in the simplest way I know how to. As it relates to this issue, the Sixth Amendment to the United States Constitution says that everyone accused of a serious crime is entitled to a lawyer. Ultimately, this mandate means that you are entitled to counsel even if you cannot afford an attorney and that you can even act as your own counsel if you so desire. To clarify further, the right to act as your own coun-sel is absolute (at least the first time it is done). That is correct, all an accused has to do is stand up and say "I want to be my own lawyer" and the Judge, who is duty bound to follow the law, after a brief advisement that amounts to "words of warning" must allow the defendant to represent themselves. Thus, rather than having the issue resolved in 5 minutes, the hearing went on for some time. Most of this time was spent discussing Ms. Arias' desire to represent herself. When I left that day Ms. Arias was "lead counsel" and my Co-counsel and I were assigned to serve as "advisory counsel," meaning our job was to advise Ms. Arias during the hearing if she sought our advice. This also meant that Ms. Arias' job was to act as her own attorney in all respects. It was her job to call witnesses, cross examine witnesses and argue her posi-tion all the things that an attorney might do for their client she now had to do for herself.

The next setting was to be the evidentiary portion of the hearing. The State was going to call a handwriting analyst who worked for the Department of Public Safety. This man had analyzed the 3 by 5 cards, the handwrit-ing found in magazines belonging to Ms. Arias that were confiscated by jail staff and he examined the letters that had purportedly been written by Mr. Alexander and sent to Ms. Arias. He testified that, in his opinion, the words written on the 3 by 5 cards found in Ms. Arias' cell were someone's attempt to simulate Mr. Alexander's handwriting. He testified that it was probable that Ms. Arias wrote the messages in these magazines and that Ms. Arias' expert could not reach the conclusions she did about who authored the letters. For those of you who do not recall what I said in Chapter 16, the defense expert was of the opinion that it was "highly probable" that Mr. Alexander authored these letters. To further refresh your memory, the designation of "highly probable" is the greatest level of certainty in the field of handwriting analysis. With that reminder in mind, it was the opinion of the State's expert that Ms. Arias' expert was wrong when she concluded that it was "highly probable" that Mr. Alexander wrote these letters. Instead, the State's expert was of the opinion that using such a designation was improper. He was of the opinion that the rating of "highly probable" could not be applied when the hand writing comparison was being done from a photocopy.

In support of her quest to have "The Letters" admitted Ms. Arias called two witnesses. The defense handwriting expert I had retained and a woman named Heather. Heather had, for a time, lived in the same pod as Ms. Arias in the county jail. At the time of her testimony Heather no longer lived at the jail with Ms. Arias. By this time Heather had moved on, not on with her life, but to prison. First up was Heather. Ms. Arias asked Heather some questions trying to prove the point that Heather had written these things in the magazines. None of Heather's testimony or Ms. Arias' questions really made any sense to me. Furthermore, I did not believe a word that Heather was saying. For those of you might be thinking I was obliged to do something about this testimony that I perceived to be false I should point out that I had no such obligation. In fact, it is more accurate to say that I was obligated to keep my mouth shut so as to not interfere with my client's ability to represent herself. To explain further, I was not the attorney nor was I the person judging the testimony. That task resided with the Judge. Furthermore, the worst thing an attorney can do in that situation is anything that could be seen as interfering with their client's actions. When Ms. Arias finished asking Heather questions it was Mr. Martinez's turn. Those who watched the trials know how Mr. Martinez tends to act when cross examining someone. Imagine something like that only unrestrained by the objections of an experienced attorney. As for the substance of the cross examination, Heather continued to claim that she wrote these messages in the magazines. Her testimony on cross was every bit as unbelievable as it had been on direct, to be fair, maybe even more unbelievable. The substance of this testimony really did not matter to me. I knew in the end that the letters would be precluded and that this was just a long and tedious way of getting to the place I would have had the case weeks prior to this hearing. Having little interest in the substance allowed me to place more attention on Ms. Arias and I must say it really freaked me out a bit. Why? Because, Ms. Arias seemed so proud and happy with this girl's testimony, she seemed to be relishing in the fact that this girl was willing to lie for her. The look on her face was what I might imagine on a cult leader as they watch members of their flock kill themselves on command.

After Heather was done with her testimony Ms. Arias called the defense's handwriting expert to the stand. On direct examination Ms. Arias asked this expert some questions about what she had done to that point. Eventually the questioning uncovered the reality that this expert might be able to alter her conclusions if she had time to examine the new materials that had recently become available. This would have been a perfect point for Ms. Arias to ask for a continuance so that her expert would have time to do this examination. I think all of us in that room thought that this would be the next words out of her mouth. Instead, for whatever reason, Ms. Arias shocked us all and said something nonsensical about driving a ship that she did not know how to steer and then announced her desire to resign as counsel. Ms. Arias no longer wished to play and the nonsense was about to come to an end.

The Judge was more than eager to grant this request but before she did I had something to say. When I stood up I sensed that the Judge was not thrilled about my desire to speak. I strongly suspect that in her mind she was not looking for anyone to say anything that would interfere with Ms. Arias' desire to resign. However, I was way more knowledgeable on an important subject than the Judge was, that subject being Ms. Arias. I knew

Ms. Arias way better than she did and because of this knowledge I had other concerns. Certainly, I shared the opinion that the sooner Ms. Arias resigned from serving as her own counsel the better. However, I was also concerned about my ability to represent Ms. Arias if she was simply allowed to represent herself when she felt like it and have myself and my then Co-counsel take over when she did not want to play anymore. I feared this because this would mean every time that she disagreed with my legal strategy; she would simply ask to represent herself, screw up her case and give the case back to us to deal with whatever damage she had done. I wanted to do what I could to avoid this happening in the future (as time would tell my concerns were clearly justified). To this end and while fully anticipating that Ms. Arias would decide to stop playing lawyer at some point during or directly after this hearing, I researched the law surrounding self-representation. That research uncovered a clear legal reality. While Ms. Arias had an absolute right to represent herself upon her initial request, once she began acting as her own counsel, if she ever resigned from that position and once again accepted counsel any subsequent requests she made to represent herself were not entitled to the sort of automatic approval that her initial request enjoyed. On this point, the law was clear. When a defendant makes a "second request" to represent himself or herself, the court has the absolute discretion and/or ability to deny a defendant's second request to go "pro per" for whatever reason. An option a Judge would not have available when a "first request" is made.

It was for these reasons that before Ms. Arias resigned that I requested that the court advise Ms. Arias of this legal reality. I wanted there to be no issues down the road. I wanted the record to be clear on this issue. So I referenced the case law and the relevant portions of these cases that I needed to place on the record so as to secure my position down the road. After I was done, the court asked Ms. Arias to acknowledge that she understood this reality, which she did. In case you are wondering, my first act when I returned to serving as lead counsel (still a job I did not want) was to withdraw my intent to admit the letters and that put an end to "The Letters" for the time being.

In theory this should also have put an end to Ms. Arias' opportunities to go "Pro-Per." For as the case law I just discussed indicated, if Ms. Arias wanted to go "Pro-Per" again a Judge would have complete discretion to deny the request for whatever reason he or she chose. Thus, I assumed that when the inevitable happened and Ms. Arias would once again request to work as her own lawyer, the Judge would simply deny her request. At least I was half-right.

CHAPTER 41

FELONY MURDER?

At the close of the first trial the jury was asked to determine if Ms. Arias was guilty of First Degree Murder or a lesser offense such as manslaughter. I suspect most of you already knew this but how many of you knew that when asked to determine if Ms. Arias was guilty of First Degree Murder that the jury could find her guilty of that crime in one of two ways, either premeditated murder or felony murder. I suspect that less of you knew that and I suspect that even less of you know what felony murder is and the role it played in this case. In this chapter I will attempt to explain felony murder to you in rather simple terms in hopes that you can get a better understanding of the issues that surrounded the State's choice to charge Ms. Arias with the crime of First Degree Murder under the felony murder rule.

In Arizona, as is the case in a lot of States, the crime of First Degree Murder can be committed in one of two ways. The most common is premeditated murder. The kind of murder that a person plans to commit then does so by killing another human being. The other way that First Degree Murder can be charged is via what is often referred to as the felony murder rule. The felony murder rule basically allows the State to charge a person with First Degree Murder when they kill a person when they are in the course of committing another serious crime or when they are fleeing the scene of that crime. If this explanation leaves you confused perhaps some examples would clarify this crime for you. Let's say that "Jim", our hypothetical criminal, goes into a convenience store with a gun in his coat pocket. Jim's plan is to rob the place. Jim wants to take all the money in the cash register and get in his car and drive away without any problems. Jim is not planning on shooting anyone. In fact, there are no bullets in his gun. When Jim gets up to the counter he puts his plan into action and he points the gun at the clerk and demands all the money in the register. When Jim does this the clerk freaks out, gets scared and has a heart attack. Much to Jim's surprise the clerk drops dead right there on the floor. As I said moments ago, Jim did not intend for this to happen and it really freaks him out so he forgets about the money and runs to his car to drive away. Jim wants to get out of the area so quickly that, he is driving very fast and erratically. Not only that but because Jim is still freaked out by the death of the store clerk, he is paying so little attention to his driving he does not see the woman walking across the street and he thus runs her over and kills this poor woman. So did Jim commit felony murder? Yes he did. In fact he committed felony murder twice in this little scenario. Once when the clerk died of a heart attack and again when he ran over the woman walking across the street. That is right, even though Jim did not intend to kill any-one he could be charged with two counts of Frist Degree Murder in most states, but certainly in Arizona. I might add that for those of you who are asking yourself this question, yes, Jim could receive the death penalty in Arizona for killing either of these people even though he never intended to kill either of them.

As it relates to Ms. Arias' situation you might be asking yourself, what does this rule have to do with what happened between Mr. Alexander and Ms. Arias on June 4, 2008? I had the same question. In my mind, based on the facts of the case, either Ms. Arias arrived at Mr. Alexander's home plan-ning to kill him or she did not. I think we can all agree that this was the ground on which the battle of what happened would be fought. However, the State, perhaps out of a concern that they could not prove premeditated First Degree Murder, also charged Ms. Arias with this same crime via the felony murder rule. As this made no sense to me I challenged this alternative way of charging First Degree Murder.

The first thing I did to challenge this charge was to request that the State disclose what the underlying crime was. As I alluded to in my simplistic explanation of the felony murder rule, there has to be an underlying felony crime that a person is committing when the death occurs. When Ms. Arias was charged in this manner the State did not specify what the underlying crime was and since I could not attack the charge without knowing what that claim was, I moved the court to make the State provide this information. The State, as you might guess, protested even though it is a pretty basic principle that in the United States that persons charged with a crime are entitled to know of the charges against them. Fortunately, the court saw it my way and ordered the State to disclose the underlying crime. I sensed that Mr. Martinez was truly not happy about this because now he had to come up with something. He decided to assert that the underlying crime was burglary and the underlying offenses related to burglary. For those of you who do not know what that means, let me try to explain, I say try because it boggles my mind how this would work. The crime of Burglary, as it would relate to this case involves entering or remaining in a residential structure with the intent of committing a felony therein. So once this disclosure was made it appeared to me that the State was arguing that Ms. Arias committed the crime of burglary when she pointed a gun at Mr. Alexander with the intent to kill him and that during her attempt to facilitate this murder she actually committed the murder she intended to commit. Follow that? No? Well neither do I. However, based on what I could discern under the State's theory any murder that occurred indoors (because of the different types of burglary) could be charged as felony murder, even when the goal of the killer was to commit the crime of murder in the first place. Does that make sense to you? It certainly did not to me so I challenged charging Ms. Arias in this manner.

When I challenged these charges, the State's responding argument was exactly what I suspected, that the underlying felony related to murder and because she committed the murder that she could be charged with felony murder. Again this made no sense and I argued such to no avail and the charge stood.

You might be asking yourself why this issue was such a big deal for either side. Well it was a big deal for two reasons. The first being, that it gave the State two ways to get a First Degree Murder conviction when, in my mind at least, only one should have been available to them. Second and more importantly it was a way for the State to eliminate the lesser included offenses of second degree murder and manslaughter, crimes for which Ms. Arias could not be sentenced to death. It was a very big deal.

CHAPTER 42

TRYING TO SETTLE

Any resolution of a capital case short of trial inherently means that your client is not going to be executed. As I describe in Chapter 2, when a capital attorney's client is not going to be executed, that constitutes a win for that attorney. Ultimately it is also a win for the client whether they see it that way or not. Thus in my mind, the best kind of capital case is a capital case that does not go to trial. In addition to the inherent win involved in a settlement the other component of coming to a resolution before trial means that the attorneys and others who are working on the case do not have to go through all that is involved in taking a capital case to trial. As you might guess not having to go through a trial constitutes a huge win on a personal level for the legal team involved.

Avoiding a capital trial might not sound like a big deal to some but I suspect those who do not think it is a big deal have not had to try a capital case before. Having tried two capital cases before Ms. Arias' trial began in 2013, I unfortunately knew all too well what trying a capital case would mean on a personal level both to myself and the entire defense team. It means long hours almost every day of the week. Working several hours each weekend was also commonplace. As you might guess, working all these hours means that you say "I am sorry" to your spouse quite often. Why? Because working these long hours also means that you cannot make it to that matinee that you wanted to go to on a Saturday afternoon or that mid-week dinner plans have to be cancelled because you had to prepare for the next day of trial. The other sad reality is that when you are in the throes of a capital case, even when you have some down time, even when you have the time to catch a matinee or go out to dinner that does not mean that you will not be thinking about the case. Based on my experience, when the gravity of the legal case that you are dealing with is so serious it is almost impossible not to think about it constantly. Not a great way to live in my book because there is almost no true "down time" for several months.

Having detailed how having to try a capital case affects me, I am not asking you to feel sorry for me or any other capital attorney. Instead I just want you to understand the realities of the situation from the capital attorney's perspective. Because when you look at it through this lens you may see why I wanted to avoid the Arias trial so badly. My experience told me that this was going to be another tough trial to say the least. That being in trial in this case would likely bring about more of the same in terms of the way it negatively impacted my personal life. Beyond that given the high profile nature of the case I feared that the impact that this case would have would be much greater than a typical death penalty case. I feared that this case would require more apologies than the normal case. I feared that this case would creep into my mind when I did not want it to be in my head at all. Additionally, I sensed that the Arias trial might take longer to try than most cases, so in this regard the negative impact would likely exist for a longer period of time. It was for these reasons that avoiding trial was a huge goal of mine.

Fortunately for me, the good news was that doing everything I can do to settle the case is consistent with the role of lead counsel in a capital case. In fact, the rules in place in Arizona specifically dictate that lead counsel is to seek out a resolution short of death for their client (even if it is not the client's main goal) which makes sense because a life sentence is always the number one goal of a capital defense attorney. Sadly for all of us defense attorneys settling a case is not something that we can do on our own. Instead, settling a case requires both the State and the client themselves to agree on a resolution. In many ways this puts the defense attorney in the position where he or she is negotiating between the State and the client. In the Arias case that meant, for the most part dealing with Juan Martinez whose reputation was such that resolving a case by a plea was not typically an option. For her part, Ms. Arias thought that accepting guilt for the crime of second degree murder was doing the world a favor. The way I saw things, my only hope in this situation rested in the theory that the decision to offer a plea ultimately did not rest with Juan Martinez, but with the County Attorney, Bill Montgomery. Did this provide me with much hope of actually reaching a settlement? No. The rumors were to the effect that Mr. Montgomery felt intimidated by Juan Martinez. Admittedly, I had no idea if this rumor was true or not but I did know that when this case was charged Mr. Martinez was able to convince Mr. Montgomery that this was a crime for which a sentence of death was justified in the first place, which was quite the feat given the circumstances of the offense that they knew at the time they filed the "death notice." Given all this, despite all the favorable evidence we had obtained since I was assigned to the case, I still had very little hope of resolving the case short of trial. Nevertheless, for the sake of my ethical duty and my own desire to resolve this case as quickly and quietly as possible I had to give even the slim prospect of resolution maximum effort. I did not want to try this case. I wanted it to go away!

In my mind, my best shot to resolve the case was to lay a few of my cards out on the table. This was not my typical way of doing things which made me uncomfortable but I knew that I would need to take some risks if I had any chance to settle the case. My thinking was that if I disclosed some information to the State that I was not otherwise obligated to disclose, that Mr. Montgomery might then share my vision that it would be best for all involved if the case went away quickly and quietly. Now before all of you "tough on crime" types get all upset about me holding onto secrets or being a "sleazy defense attorney" you might want to review the 5th and 6th Amendments to the Constitution as they provide the authority for defense attorneys to hold back certain information. As it relates to the Arias case specifically, things that Ms. Arias said about the crime to her experts were things I could have hid from the State under the rules in Arizona. I chose not to keep things hidden or interfere with Dr. DeMarte asking similar questions. Why? I wanted Mr. Montgomery to know exactly where this case was going. To be clear, this was not an attempt to intimidate him or threaten him with the reality but to make sure he understood where this case was going to go so he could decide if he really wanted to travel down this road. I wanted him to know that Ms. Arias was going to claim that her victim was an abusive pedophile against whom she had to defend herself. I wanted him to realize how out of control this case could get. It was my thinking that if he saw how crazy this case was going to get that he might be more inclined to seek a resolution that avoided such a debacle from ever occurring. A resolution by plea agreement would also finalize the case since a person gives up their right to an appeal when they enter into a plea. If the right plea could have been negotiated things would have ended quickly and quietly. Obviously, we did not settle the case and well...

CHAPTER 43

DEALING WITH THE MEDIA BEFORE TRIAL

Those of you who followed the trial closely were likely well aware that I was not always thrilled with how the media conducted themselves during the trial. Many seem to attribute this to the idea that I have some sort of disdain for all media outlets. That is not true. My issue with the media always related to the idea that anyone accused of a crime deserved a fair trial. Not a trial tainted by the media. In my mind, certain media outlets can infringe upon those rights by the manner in which they cover a trial because, in essence, they demonize the accused and all of those around them before that person's guilt is established. As Ms. Arias' lawyer, it became my duty to try to either eliminate or limit in any way I could the possibility that the media would infringe upon her right to a fair trial by demonizing her in this manner. Before trial, that meant contesting any attempts by the media to cover the trial in ways that could affect the outcome of the trial. To be clear, I did not care about any characterization of Ms. Arias that would not affect the trial. I was more than willing to let her public image suffer if this would increase the odds of saving her life. My concern was that she got a fair trial.

Furthermore, my concerns did not center around social media. Unless potential jurors were viewing it I could have cared less about what people were saying about Ms. Arias on social media. Remember, I did not care about her image, only that she got a fair trial. In this regard, I also did not care about what was being said during webcasts because such webcasts would likely not affect the trial itself. I also had few concerns about the local news coverage of the trial as well. That might shock you to hear this but if the jury did not watch the local news I basically had no concerns about what the local news reporter was saying as they reported outside the courthouse about the events of the day.

Instead, my concerns revolved around the sort of bombastic coverage that could be seen on cable television. You likely have seen such broadcasts, the type where trials are treated as blood sports. Broadcasts during which trials are characterized as battles between good and evil, where the accused and those who might speak on his or her behalf are vilified as being evil wherein the prosecutor can do no wrong because he or she is on the side of the good and the righteous. In my mind, those networks and commentators serve as "anti-constitutional terrorists." Why do I use such harsh words? Because these networks and/or the commentators they employ show no respect for our constitution and preach fear and intimidation against those who wish to exercise their constitutional rights. In saying this, I realize that I am opening a big "can of worms" about the role that certain types of media outlets can play in trials. I will deal with those worms in my final book, but for now I want to focus on my concerns about how these types of media outlets concerned me before trial began and how I attempted to combat the potential that these outlets could have on Ms. Arias' trial.

However, before delving into this issue deeper I want to briefly take on those who say that I had no business contesting such things because Ms. Arias chose to take part in interviews before trial. In fact, this argument was made during trial. The only problem is that such an argument, while supported by the common sense of a grade school playground, it is not legally valid. No defendant can waive his or her constitutional rights by being stupid. Yes, it certainly was stupid for Ms. Arias to speak to the media before trial began but under the law her stupidity in this regard did not give the media the right to exploit her trial to the point that it became unfair.

Having made my point regarding my ability to contest the involvement of the media, as briefly as possible I want to now return your attention to the subject of the chapter, my attempts to deal with the media before trial began so as to lessen the effect that the media could have on the trial once it started. To that end, let me take you back in time to 2009 when I first got the file so that you can get a sense of the media coverage that existed at that time. Back then the most extensive coverage could be found on the CBS program "48 Hours." If you recall, these interviews took place in 2008, one when she was in California and one after she arrived in Arizona. Additionally, when she first arrived in Arizona, Ms. Arias also gave an interview to Inside Edition in which she famously said one of the stupidest things a criminal defendant can say in an interview when she said, "no jury will convict me." (I hate to "toot my own horn" but I have to say to those who criticize my skills as a lawyer; I kept her off death row even after she dared her jury to convict her. I think about that. I would say that was some pretty clever lawyering to pull that off). Putting the stupidity of partaking in these interviews aside, these interviews and the programs associated with them constitutes the extent of the pre-trial publicity when I got the case. In fact, there really was not much media attention related to the case for several months. The inattention persisted until we got closer to trial.

I began to sense how big of a circus this case was going to be when we got closer to trial and I started getting calls from various news outlets who sought to establish some sort of relationship with me. These people wanted to take me out to dinner just to "chat." I am sure they hoped dinner and drinks would lead to a slip of the tongue or some morsel they could use on their next broadcast. However, I was well aware that the real goal of these meetings was to establish some sort of relationship with me so I would feel obligated to interview with them when the trial was over. Knowing their end game made it easy for me to say "no" to these invitations. The only invitation that ever intrigued me came from the British Broadcasting Company (BBC). Based on the contact I received it seems that the BBC wanted to follow me around with cameras throughout the trial process. It seemed that they wanted to create a documentary of sorts in which they could tell the tale of the death penalty process through my perspective or at least telling the tale in a way that the trials and tribulations of the defense attorney are expressed to the viewer. This intrigued me because I thought it might provide the viewer with an interesting insight into what it is like to defend a person throughout an entire death penalty case. The thought crossed my mind that seeing such a documentary might actually change a few minds on the subject of the death penalty. However, the realities of having a camera crew following me everywhere sounded awful to me. I lived a low-key life and I wanted it to stay that way as much as possible. I had no desire to be a reality television personality.

I had the power to say no to the BBC however, I did not have the same control over the trial. I was not in control of whether or not Ms. Arias' trial would be broadcast to millions worldwide. That decision would be up to the courts. The media knew this as well and knew that they would have to get the court's permission to broadcast the trial live. In this regard the media, primarily CNN, must have seen the potential for huge profit because they were more than willing to pay what I believe to be a very expensive law firm what I assumed was a large amount of money in order to win the right to film the trial and livestream it on the internet. In this regard the media has no other interest but profit. Conversely, I could care less how much money was at stake. I feared that should the court allow this coverage that those who broadcast the sort of bombastic coverage that I referenced earlier would create a frenzy that would lead to witnesses being harassed and jurors being exposed to harmful pretrial coverage. Putting the legalese aside, this became a battle between Ms. Arias' right to have a fair trial and the media's right to report the news (I suspect that if you are interested in reading these motions in their entirety they can be found online). Certainly, I will confront these issues in greater detail when I look back on all of the trials in my final book. However, as it relates to the arguments made before trial in there most basic form, the media's argument was "we can do what we want" and my argument became "not if it interferes with my client's right to a fair trial." I argued that witnesses could be threatened and jurors could be exposed to pretrial publicity. The media and State basically responded that all my arguments were speculative, that I was guessing. While technically true, that is one of the most illogical arguments of them all because we always speculate based on known facts that is what we do in the law. Reflecting back, the bottom line of all of this was that I was right in my so-called speculation but nonetheless, the media won the right to broadcast the trial and of course they do not have to care about whatever damage they might do to the trial process because they are not a party to the trial, they only seek to profit from it.

As I alluded to earlier, I will discuss the issue of the media's involvement in trials and how media can turn them into reality television much more in my final book but for now let me say that I would be stunned if the media's actions during this case do not make their way into Ms. Arias' appeal.

CHAPTER 44

WE GOTTA GET OUTTA TOWN OR SHUT THE JURY DOWN

During the Arias trial it seemed as if every motion I filed would be analyzed for hours either by news organizations and/or social media. The thirst for information seemed to be endless. Despite this thirst, two of the most important motions I filed in this case received very little media attention. Perhaps these motions were not discussed because they portrayed the media in a bad light or perhaps they were not "sexy" enough to drive ratings. Whatever the reason, I thought these motions might be of interest to you because the subject of these motions really speak to the seriousness of the case and could have changed the dynamics of the entire trial. I am speaking of my requests to change venue and to sequester the jury. I realize they do not sound "sexy" but please stick with me.

For those of you who are unfamiliar with the terms "venue" and "sequester" please let me explain. Venue relates to the location of the trial, in what county or city the case trial takes place. So a change of venue motion is a request to move the trial to another city or county. Sequester means to close off. For lack of a better way of saying it, a motion to sequester is a request made by a party to a case to hide the jury away from the rest of the world. A party to a case makes a motion of this nature when they feel as if the jury might be exposed to extraneous information that could cause the trial to be unfair to their side. With this understanding you might now be asking yourself; why did I file these motions in Ms. Arias' case?

Most importantly it would have been negligent of me, on a professional level, not to do so. Why? Because if the jury pool of Maricopa County was prejudiced to any degree by pretrial publicity and/or the jury was exposed to publicity during the trial and I ignored the issue before trial began, Ms. Arias' conviction could be overturned and the trial could begin anew. Having said this, as it related to each specific motion there were good reasons for both.

As it relates to the venue motion, the citizens of Maricopa County were exposed to more pretrial publicity about the case than those who lived elsewhere in Arizona. Thus, it logically follows that potential jurors who live in Maricopa County might be biased against Ms. Arias to such a degree that she might not be able to receive a fair trial in Maricopa County. Thereby necessitating that the trial needed to be moved elsewhere in Arizona so that the trial she received is fair. Even though I knew that I needed to file such a motion I also knew that there was almost no chance my motion would be granted. Change of venue motions are rarely granted, heck, they are rarely filed. However, as I have often said, the Arias case was atypical in so many ways. Now you might think that I would be disappointed for this motion to be denied, but just the opposite is true, at least on a personal level. Why? Because if the motion was granted that would mean that I would have to live in whatever town the trial took place in for the duration of the trial. Likewise, I was well aware that the same would be true for every other participant in the trial as well and I certainly did not wish this fate on anyone involved in the case. You could imagine that this would be a nightmare for all the trial participants and the families of both parties to have to do this, not to mention the money that would be spent on all the hotel rooms and other expenses. I suspect that you are now beginning to get an idea of why such motions are rarely granted, as granting them creates huge personal and financial burdens to all involved. However, in my view the right to a fair trial is sacred in this country, which is why the law allows for such measures in extreme situations. Thus, my attitude was that if it had to be done, it had to be done. If I had to live in "who knows where Arizona" for six months in order for Ms. Arias to receive a fair trial then so be it, the Constitution means that much to me.

As it relates to my motion to sequester the jury, the concern was that once trial began a juror could be exposed to extraneous information, by this I mean information they do not learn in the courtroom. The reason this can become an issue is that for a trial to be fair to both parties a juror cannot render their verdict even to the slightest degree on information that they learn outside of the courtroom. A motion to sequester the jury is primarily designed to limit the jury's exposure to extraneous information by sealing them off from potential sources of extraneous information. In practical terms this means sealing jurors off from media, social media and oftentimes friends and family who might talk to them about the case.

When I filed this motion I did not believe that it would be granted. Why did I think it would be denied? Because if this motion was granted it would mean that we would not only be asking prospective jurors to give up several months of their professional lives to serve on a jury but we would also be asking them to give up several months of time with their loved ones so that they could serve on a jury. Not a request to be taken lightly for sure and the granting of such a request would also result in a great financial cost to the county. Even though I understood all of this, I certainly thought my motion to sequester should have been granted. I say this because given the gravity of the case and the amount of publicity that would infest the case once trial began. The way I viewed it, the potential for the jury to be exposed to extraneous information or opinions was too high. In my mind such exposure could be grounds for a mistrial and/or provide fertile ground for the conviction to be overturned on appeal. If I was in the Judge's shoes I would have granted this motion. However, for the reasons mentioned above, I could certainly understand why Judge Stephens did not grant this motion.

CHAPTER 45

THE SO-CALLED DELAYS

When I look at social media one of the common themes that seems to consistently resurface is the assertion that there were too many delays in the case. Furthermore, those who assert this theory seem to believe that I caused these delays intentionally because I wanted to drag things out so I could make more money or for some other absurd reason. My response to these claims may never be fully received but in this chapter I will discuss why the delays that occurred before the first trial were all necessary under the circumstances.

The first big delay occurred when the Office of the Legal Defender discovered a conflict in the late summer of 2009, a few months before the case was scheduled to go to trial. If you recall, I received the case in August of 2009, so the presiding judge knew that Ms. Washington and myself could not give Ms. Arias a proper trial with only two months to prepare. Instead, we were given over a year or so to review everything that had previously been done and decide what else needed to be done in order to be ready for trial.

When that year or so rolled around the next problem became a scheduling issue between the parties and the courts. As you might guess, the Arias case was not the only capital case in the system. Mr. Martinez had other capital cases, so too did our Judge. Ms. Washington and I also had a capital case in front of another judge. Since that case was older that case received priority and that case went to trial first so that took us off the Arias case for a while. As I have mentioned elsewhere in the book, when this trial was over, we still had unresolved issues that needed to be resolved before the Arias case could go to trial. Resolving these issues would take time and on top of all of this judges rotate to different assignments so you cannot just walk in and just try a capital case. Judges have to make room in their calendars, which is oftentimes, not a simple process. Once the dust on these issues settled we had a trial date set in August of 2011. The same trial date that served as the reason that I was not allowed off the case in February of 2011.

So why was it that in August of 2011, neither the State nor the Defense were offering our respective opening statements to a jury? No, it was not because I made my first attempt to get away from Ms. Arias in February of 2011. It was because, as I described in Chapter 37, in the summer of 2011, the domestic violence expert who was working on Ms. Arias' case became ill and was no longer going to be available to testify on Ms. Arias' behalf. Now again some of you might be thinking so what, there is no evidence of Ms. Arias being a victim of domestic violence so why bother? Well, as I have alluded to elsewhere, the law does not see it that way and it is the job of a defense attorney to tell the client's story unless they know it to be untrue. Thus, when Ms. Arias' domestic violence expert was unable to move forward the trial had to be delayed so that another suitable expert could be found and be prepared for trial. Judge Stephens gave us until November of 2011, to achieve this goal.

Trial did not take place in November of 2011, because later that summer or early fall is when the Office of the Public Defender moved to withdraw because of the conflict I discussed in Chapter 38. When they were successful in their request that meant further delay because my new Co-counsel would have to get up to speed and be ready for trial or Ms. Arias would not have had effective assistance of counsel. Beyond that, once Ms. Willmott and Ms. De La Rosa became involved their schedules had to be accounted for by the court. Unfortunately, this meant further delay because around this same time Ms. Willmott was involved in a manslaughter trial that was rather lengthy.

The result of all this is that we were heading towards a trial date near the 2012 holiday season. Because I did not want my holiday season ruined I had hoped we would pick a jury in January of 2013, but Judge Stephens wanted the trial to get underway despite the difficulties inherent in picking a jury during the holiday season. So we spent our holidays picking a jury.

So there you have it, you now know the story of these supposed delays, the reasons why the trial did not start until January 2, 2013. Like them or not, these are the reasons why the trap that I had hoped to get out of in 2011 or 2012, still held me captive.

Certainly, even after having heard these reasons many of you may still believe that all the delays were somehow orchestrated by me or were unnecessary. Rather than argue with you or defend myself from attacks that are baseless, let me conclude this chapter by reminding you that the law related to capital cases is such that if Ms. Arias was forced to proceed to trial without having had these issues resolved and she was sentenced to death it is almost a certainty that Ms. Arias would receive a new trial. Is that what you would like?

SECTION 9

What Did I Have on My Hands ?

So far in this book we have covered a lot of ground. Of course for a few years covering this ground was a huge part of my professional life and thus this case also came to dominate my thoughts over these same years as well. In this section I share my thoughts with you. I will share my thoughts about what I had on my hands. Specifically, in Chapter 46, I discuss my assessment on what I had on my hands from an evidentiary standpoint. In Chapter 47, I discuss what I believed (as opposed to what I believe now) happened on June 1, 2008 and I end this section with Chapter 48, where I share my belief of "What I believed the State Would Argue."

CHAPTER 46

So now what?

As the plan of selecting a jury in November of 2012, looked more and more like it was going to actually happen as scheduled. In the early fall of 2012, I was hit with the reality that this case was going to trial. Avoiding this reality via plea agreement was no longer an option. The case was not going to settle, nor was it going to get continued again. It was a bit of a double edged sword for me as you might guess. On the one hand I wanted to be rid of the whole mess, which meant I had to do the trial. On the other hand I did not want to go to trial on this case. Once this reality hit me the question became; so now what? What was I to make of all the evidence and all of the happenings of this case?

The one thing that was certain was that I had a ton of evidence. In fact, I used to joke that Ms. Arias' case was like handling 5 death penalty cases at once because of the amount of evidence involved. To give you a frame of reference, most death penalty cases might have roughly six file boxes full of evidence. Ms. Arias' case involved about thirty in addition to the countless hours of videos and audios. As trial approached I had to figure out what I had and what I was going to present to the jury. The best way to describe this step in the process to you would be that this is my time to take a "mental inventory" of what I had to work with before I decide on a trial strategy. Rather than review every piece of evidence with you, let me instead give you the general idea of the reality that I saw before me in the fall of 2012.

Though perhaps technically true, rather than being a "former girlfriend" of Mr. Alexander's, as many had been led to believe, Ms. Arias was still involved in a relationship with Mr. Alexander. At the time the two likely would have labeled this relationship a friendship. In fact, they might have objected to being labeled as boyfriend and girlfriend. However, it sure seemed to me that they sure acted like a couple. They were having a sexual relationship. They would travel together, use each other's cars. They would talk or communicate in some fashion if not every day then darn close to it. Of course we know that not all of these communications were platonic. What label would you place on this relationship?

Now when I say they acted as a couple, please do not mistake what I am saying. I'm not saying that this was some sort of healthy loving relationship, far from it as sometimes they treated each other horribly. The reality I saw back in the fall of 2012, was that this relationship, whatever label you want to put on it, was clearly toxic. Furthermore, that the sexual aspect of it made it more than a friendship and also likely added to the toxicity of the relationship. In my mind, there was a connection between these two that was hard to put a label on and that the evidence might make explaining this relationship even more difficult.

The evidence also demonstrated that whatever label anyone would put on this relationship, the true nature of the relationship was really only something that the two of them knew. To some degree I suppose this could be said about anyone's relationship but the way I saw it, what was going on here was more than a matter of privacy. Think about it for a minute. Your friends and loved ones may not know what goes on behind closed doors between you and your significant other, but they likely know who that person is and that a particular person is your significant other. In contrast, to those in Mr. Alexander's world the two were friends at most and at the least Ms. Arias was a "crazy stalker ex-girlfriend." Those who thought Ms. Arias was the crazy ex-girlfriend thought this because of what Mr. Alexander had told them. Likewise, those who thought these two were just friends believed that because of what Mr. Alexander had told them. Back in 2012, the other thing that was apparent is that it seems that neither Mr. Alexander nor Ms. Arias had told anyone about the full extent of their relationship. However, it seemed to me that at least one of them took active steps to divert attention from the true nature of their relationship.

When I considered the evidence before me, in order to make an objective assessment of the situation, I had to consider if Ms. Arias was truly the crazy ex-girlfriend who would not leave Mr. Alexander alone despite his desire that she do so. I suppose one could argue that Ms. Arias proved herself to be the crazy ex-girlfriend by slashing Mr. Alexander's tires and/or sending his former girlfriend Lisa a cryptic e-mail. However, as Detective Flores conceded during his interview with CBS, there was no evidence that Ms. Arias actually did these things. Incidentally, that remains true today. Beyond this reality was the fact that if Mr. Alexander truly believed that Ms. Arias had done these things why was he still involved with her at all, let alone sexually?

The text messages and other electronic communications demonstrated to me that Ms. Arias was intensely loyal to Mr. Alexander. They demonstrated that Ms. Arias would take his verbal grenades over and over again, yet she never let them deter her from the relationship. Furthermore, no matter what Mr. Alexander would say to Ms. Arias it never seemed to diminish the love she seemingly had for him. Conversely, however angry Mr. Alexander may have been with Ms. Arias it also never seemed to diminish Mr. Alexander's desire to maintain his relationship with her. Think about it, he would call Ms. Arias horrible names but he never acted like he wanted the relationship to end. He never took steps to permanently cease contact. He never sought out a restraining order against this woman. Instead, he continued to communicate with Ms. Arias and have sex with her. Thus, in my mind, he either truly cared for this woman or he was using her for sex, there was no other explanation. "Facts are stubborn things."

The sex tape told me that these two had a sexual relationship that was intense to say the least. It also seemed to me that the fact that this sexual relationship was forbidden by the dictates of their religion only added to its intensity. Based on what I had heard on the sex tape and what I had seen in the nude pictures, this sexual relationship was something that some might consider kinky and/or wild. It seemed to me as if there was no way one could claim that this forbidden sexual behavior was something that they truly regretted because there seemed nothing tame about their sex life. The sex tape also made me consider the fact that Mr. Alexander might have had a sexual interest in children because in this tape he compared Ms. Arias' orgasm to that of a 12 year old girl. He also talked about corking the pot of a 12 year old girl. It never made any sense to me why he would say such things if he did not have such an interest. With my experiences as a sex crimes attorney and my knowledge of his background I felt that if he had such an attraction he had likely been a victim of sexual abuse as a child. Could I conclude any of this definitively? No, but the evidence pointed in that direction.

As it related to what exactly happened on June 4, 2008, if you recall, in Chapter 8, I talked about my initial thoughts on the crime scene. The question I then had to contemplate in the fall of 2012 was; did any of the evidence I had obtained and reviewed since I made that initial assessment change my view of how Mr. Alexander was killed? The answer was a resounding no. I still believe that the crime scene was fueled by passion that the evidence pointed to the reality that a brutal struggle took place that day that ended in one lover having killed the other.

Upon reading this you might be asking yourself; how can Nurmi be saying such a thing, given that after his initial review of the file Ms. Arias had changed her story? While it is true that Ms. Arias changed her story, I would challenge you to come up with a single piece of evidence that I should have viewed differently once this change occurred. Certainly, I will get into Ms. Arias' trial testimony more deeply in other books but for the purposes of this book and the challenge I just made to you, let me just refresh your recollection to some degree.

In her testimony Ms. Arias stated that she was on her way from southern California to Utah when she finally decided to give into Mr. Alexander's request and come visit him in Mesa. Ms. Arias went on to describe how she arrived at his home around 4 am on the morning of June 4, 2008. As she tells the story, several minutes after her arrival, the two went to sleep and woke up in the early afternoon. By her own account Ms. Arias woke up first and took a shower. After Mr. Alexander woke up the couple had sex and they also took nude photographs of each other. After this encounter the two hung out and eventually went into Mr. Alexander's office sometime before 5pm to look at a CD containing pictures of their travels. The way Ms. Arias tells it, the CD would not work and Mr. Alexander displayed his anger by throwing the CD across his office. The two then had sex again after which time Mr. Alexander went up to take a shower. As the story goes on, Mr. Alexander consents to Ms. Arias taking "tasteful" pictures of him in the shower. At some point in time during this photo shoot Ms. Arias drops the camera and Mr. Alexander jumps out of the shower and attacks Ms. Arias by throwing her to the ground. Ms. Arias eventually breaks free from Mr. Alexander runs into his closet and grabs a gun, Mr. Alexander's gun as she tells it. Ms. Arias points this gun at Mr. Alexander who tries to tackle her "like a linebacker" and during this interaction the gun goes off and Mr. Alexander gets shot in the face. Further struggle ensues and Ms. Arias picks up the knife and nothing is recalled by Ms. Arias until she is driving near the Grand Canyon. Without disclosing confidential information, that was her story and she was sticking to it. Did the physical evidence change because the story changed? No. Regardless of the story the physical evidence at the crime scene demonstrated the physical struggle, it did not definitely portray the motive of the killer other than the fact that it seemed that Ms. Arias was determined not to stop until she had killed Mr. Alexander.

What I was left with after all this evidence was reviewed was that I had a case that involved two young people who were in an intense relationship. For lack of a better word, they were "addicted" to each other. This addiction could have been based on sexual chemistry, it could have been based on the unhealthy love the two seemed to have for each other or it could have been based on the psychological traumas they experienced as children and were still dealing with. Why exactly they were addicted I did not know but it certainly seemed to me that these two were definitely addicted to each other and apart from Ms. Arias returning to Yreka, it seemed that neither of them took meaningful steps to end this addiction.

As for my client, I had a client, with no prior criminal history who killed her former lover. She had stabbed him 27 times, shot him, slit his throat and was claiming self-defense. Did I believe her? No, I did not. However, as I have discussed in greater detail elsewhere in this book, what I believed was not important in a court of law. With few exceptions the client gets to tell their own story. However, I have to believe that if you bought this book you are at least a bit curious as to what I think happened on June 4, 2008.

CHAPTER 47

WHAT DID I BELIEVE HAPPENED ON JUNE 4, 2008?

So what do I believe happened on June 4, 2008? I certainly have a theory on that. However, as this book is about the days before trial, what I offer you in this chapter represents my thinking and/or theory I had before trial began. This is the theory I had before I saw two trials worth of evidence play out before me. Before I describe my thinking back then, I want to be clear. The theory I had then and the theory I have now are vastly different. In fact, there are only a few aspects of my thinking about what happened that day that has remained consistent from the first day that I received the file until the present day. The most prominent being that what happened to Mr. Alexander on June 4, 2008, was horrific. It was a fate that he did not deserve and as I discussed in Chapter 4, this was a true tragedy. The other being that his killing was fueled by a strong passionate rage.

As to the theory of events I had before trial began, though I do not currently believe this theory to be correct at the same time it might very well be spot on as I did not simply pull it out of thin air. Instead, the question of what happened on June 4, 2008 and why it happened were questions that I contemplated a great deal for a number of years. It was the preeminent question in my head from August of 2009, to the day the trial began. In fact, it was one of the first questions that came to mind from the first day I was assigned the case.

In my mind answering these questions meant I had to begin with what was clear and undisputable. First on that list was the clear reality that Mr. Alexander was shot in the face, stabbed 27 times and had his throat slit. What was also clear was the fact that while this was occurring one heck of a struggle took place between Mr. Alexander and his killer. Finally, no further clarity was needed to conclude that Ms. Arias was the person who had killed Mr. Alexander as both the evidence and her admission left little doubt about this reality.

What was not clear was why this killing took place. The crime scene itself did not speak to the motivation behind this killing. The preeminent question of the case became; what motivated Ms. Arias to kill Mr. Alexander? This was a question that I would often ponder despite the fact that Ms. Arias provided an answer when she claimed to have acted in self-defense.

I did not see my role in this case as to simply accept what Ms. Arias said as being the truth. Given Ms. Arias' history of lying that would have been foolish. Instead the question of why, the questions related to Ms. Arias' motivations were questions that I would consistently ponder and questions that I would re-examine when new evidence was discovered. Why did I do this? Because I had to be able to combat any theory the State might offer and/or look for the best way to present the case to the jury.

The more I pondered this question the more I came to realize that no piece of evidence, regardless of when it came into my possession, would ever provide absolute clarity on the issue of; why Ms. Arias killed Mr. Alexander on June 4, 2008? I came to the conclusion that only Ms. Arias truly knows and the rest of us are simply left to theorize. However, given the amount of pondering I did before trial began, I would submit to you that I had some pretty well developed thoughts back in late 2012.

As the theory I believed to be true before trial began in January of 2013, I think that properly explaining it to you requires that I step back a bit and remind you that at the point in time when I was assigned the case, the story was that two masked intruders broke in and killed Mr. Alexander and that Ms. Arias was not killed because the gun being pointed in her direction jammed and would not fire. This was of course the same story Ms. Arias told

Detective Flores on July 10, 2008 and that she retold on CBS's "48 Hours." As time went on this story became known as the "ninja story." Like nearly everyone I didn't believe the "ninja story" when I first heard it. Like most people I really wanted to know what happened in Mr. Alexander's master bedroom and the nearby bathroom.

As an observer your interest in what happened on June 4, 2008, is a matter of curiosity. For me it was an aspect of my job. You see, before I go to trial in a death penalty case I like to have a pretty good idea of what actually happened and why it happened. Typically, this is not a problem. In a typical case either the evidence or the client advises you of what happened. Not in this case. For the curious, I like to have a good working theory regarding what happened because one never knows exactly what is going to happen during trial. Witnesses often say unexpected things and distractions are plentiful. I find it helpful to have a theory of events in my head to serve as a filter through which I process unexpected information as this helps me stay focused on the things that are the most important.

I realize many of my skeptics think I have no clue what happened that day. I have read that some who support Jodi Arias believe that the "ninja story" was true and I talked her out of it (which I guess further illustrates the point of Ms. Arias having abilities similar to a cult leader). I also read theories that Ms. Arias really did act in self-defense and I just couldn't prove that because I am too inept of a lawyer to do so. On the flip side it seems that many who support Mr. Alexander believe that I am an idiot on several levels. However, as it relates to what happened on June 4, 2008, these people seem to believe that I am an idiot because they think I believe Ms. Arias' self-defense story even though I have never publicly said I did. These supporters of Mr. Alexander seem to think that I supported either her story and/or what she did that day simply because I was her lawyer.

Obviously, I can't win with either side. Regardless of what I say, somebody thinks I am an idiot. So be it. I am not too concerned with what people think of me. Instead of trying to win with one side or the other, what I can do is continue to question why there are sides to begin with. You see in my mind the events of June 4, 2008, were tragic and that there is no other sane way to view these events. Thus, there is nothing for the sane to fight about. This is not a sporting event with teams or sides, it is a tragedy. Having said this, I suspect that even saying something like this in and of itself, might only add to the reasons why people that chose sides see me as an idiot. If so, so be it. I cannot account for the rabid insanity that surrounds this case. The good news for me in this regard is that I have nothing to lose because I am an idiot either way. The great thing about having nothing to lose makes me unafraid to offer you an unrestrained look into the theory I had back in 2012, about what happened on June 4, 2008. So what does this idiot think happened?

To begin with, in my mind, one cannot truly discern what happened on June 4, 2008, by simply looking at that day in a vacuum. Instead, my mindset was such that I believed that the days that proceeded June 4, 2008, contain many events and/or facts that provide insight into what actually happened that day. Ultimately, as my thinking went in 2012, that meant in order to seek out answers we needed to go back in time to April of 2008. Why April of 2008? If you will recall, that is the point in time that Ms. Arias moved away from Mesa and back to Yreka. We have to assume that Ms. Arias did not want to kill Mr. Alexander before this point in time because she didn't do it. Remember, they had a fight the day she left and she was alone in his home with him. If she wanted to kill him she could have made efforts then and drove off in her U-Haul as if nothing happened.

So my thinking in 2012, went that if Ms. Arias had the motivation to kill Mr. Alexander it would have to have been obtained after she moved away from Mesa and sometime before she actually killed him. So my analysis centered around what could have happened during that time period that would have motivated Ms. Arias to kill Mr. Alexander. As you might guess, figuring out the motivation for the killing would go a long way to explaining what actually happened. In this regard I thought there were three "suspects."

The first "suspect," "Suspect #1" would be the conversation that Ms. Arias and Mr. Alexander had on or about May 10, 2008. The conversation that was recorded by Ms. Arias, the conversation that was later played in court and became known as the "phone sex tape." As it related to this "suspect" it did not seem to me to be the sort of interaction that would motivate Ms. Arias to kill Mr. Alexander. So in essence this "suspect" was dismissed.

However, the second "suspect," "Suspect #2" could not be so easily dismissed. The second "suspect" being the online conversation that Ms. Arias and Mr. Alexander had on May 26, 2008. If you recall, the bulk of this conversation was a fight and during this fight, which I also discuss in Chapter 15, Mr. Alexander, was obviously very angry with Ms. Arias. During this conversation Mr. Alexander calls Ms. Arias a "slut", a "whore", a "3-hole wonder." Mr. Alexander also calls Ms. Arias soulless, evil and generally berates her character. If you will recall, during this conversation Ms. Arias responded to these attacks in a passive and/or apologetic manner but that did not absolve this "suspect" as being the motivating force. In fact, there was certainly more evidence that pointed to this "suspect." One prominent piece of evidence that pointed towards this "suspect" was the fact that on May 28, 2008, a gun was stolen from the home Ms. Arias was living in, the home of her grandparents, Caroline and Sunny. The timing of this theft made it seem as if the May 26, 2008, conversation may very well have motivated Ms. Arias to begin planning to kill Mr. Alexander and that the first step in this plan would be to obtain a gun. However, in my mind full analysis didn't mean just connecting the dots in terms of time. Full analysis required that I look at the circumstances surrounding the gun theft.

The police report, related to the gun theft, detailed the fact that Ms. Arias was off on a drive with her sister, Angela when this break-in occurred. As the story goes on, when the police arrived Ms. Arias and her sister were called back to the home. Once at the home the relevant police reports document the fact that Ms. Arias spoke to the police and reported a few items missing. Of note was the fact that Ms. Arias' laptop was hidden and/or sitting in her clothing hamper. Many other things of value were also not taken and the house, relatively speaking was not in too much disarray.

This "suspect" was looking pretty guilty already. However, there was more evidence of guilt related to this "suspect." Remember if you will that only a few days after this gun was stolen Ms. Arias starts driving south from Yreka and she eventually arrives somewhere near Pasadena, California on June 3, 2008. Recall further that it was at this location that Ms. Arias goes "off the grid" just before she starts driving to Mesa. To clarify when I say "off the grid" I mean that Ms. Arias' cell phone was off and she makes no purchase with a credit card. Thus her movements are by in large not traceable through electronic means. Also don't forget that this happens between 9pm and 10pm on the night of June 3, 2008 and that Ms. Arias' presence cannot be accounted for by objective evidence until nude photographs of her lying on Mr. Alexander's bed are taken on the afternoon of June 4, 2008.

Undoubtedly, these facts make it seem as if this "suspect" is guilty and that the online chat that occurred on May 26, 2008, is what motivated Ms. Arias to kill Mr. Alexander. However, not so fast, there was one more "suspect."

I thought it was also possible that something happened after Ms. Arias got into Mr. Alexander's home that motivated her to kill Mr. Alexander. This was the third "suspect." "Suspect #3" centered around the idea that some sort of interaction, some sort of fight caused Ms. Arias to go into a rage around 5:20 on the evening of June 4, 2008. Why was this "suspect" a possibility in my mind? Not because Ms. Arias said that she acted in self-defense but because, in sum, Ms. Arias had been in Mr. Alexander's home for several hours before she killed him and when she did, the killing itself was clearly fueled by anger.

Based on the facts above, I am sure you can tell that neither of these "suspects" could conclusively be eliminated as suspects nor could either be proven "guilty" without actual physical evidence. Thus, the question I had to grapple with before the first trial in 2013, was which "suspect" was it? Was Ms. Arias so angered by the names Mr. Alexander called her on May 26, 2008, that she plotted to steal a gun from her grandparent's home and then drive from Yreka, California to Mesa, Arizona with the sole purpose of killing Mr. Alexander? (Suspect #2) Or; did she show up to the home with no plans to kill Mr. Alexander and later decide to kill him due to something that occurred while they were alone in his home? (Suspect #3)

Certainly, I realize most of you will disagree with me but at the time I believed that it was the final "suspect," "Suspect #3" who was the guilty party.

I believed that Ms. Arias' motivation to kill Mr. Alexander did not arise until after she arrived at his home. Why did I think this way back before 2013?

I begin with the reality that if Ms. Arias left her grandparent's home in Yreka with the intent to kill Mr. Alexander the motivating factor would have to be "Suspect #2" the substance of the online chat. Which means that Ms. Arias, who didn't even respond with anger to the verbal grenades that Mr. Alexander launched at her on that day, was so angered by what he said that after the conversation was over she decided that she would kill Travis Alexander. Furthermore, her anger about what Mr. Alexander said to her during this conversation would have to be so strong and powerful that it fueled her homicidal wrath for approximately 10 days. Furthermore, if this "suspect" was guilty we would also have to accept the premise that the homicidal wrath that fueled Ms. Arias' trip to Mesa was somehow tapped for several hours while she and Mr. Alexander had their sexual rendezvous. As an initial matter, this theory did not make sense to me because this theory gave rise to many questions for which clear answers were not apparent.

Why would Ms. Arias be so angry over what was said during this conversation that she became determined to kill Mr. Alexander? What could Mr. Alexander have said in this conversation that would have made her so angry that she would have created this plot to kill him? Why wouldn't she simply think "screw him" and go on with her life? If she really wanted to attack him why wouldn't she just record another phone sex session and post it online or send a copy of the recording to his Bishop? That certainly would have caused a great deal of stress to Mr. Alexander. Why kill him over these words? This certainly was not the first time Mr. Alexander had called Ms. Arias vile names or otherwise attacked her verbally. Thus, it did not make sense to me how this conversation alone could have created the motive, a motive that would have been sufficient to fuel Ms. Arias for so many days to the point in time at which this brutal killing occurred.

The idea that Ms. Arias stole the gun she used to shoot Mr. Alexander from her grandparent's home also did not make a lot of sense to me at the time. In my mind, vintage 2012, she could have simply taken the gun without staging a break-in. Given what I knew of Ms. Arias' grandfather, I doubt that he would have otherwise noticed that his gun was missing. It also did not make sense to me for Ms. Arias to stage a break-in as once the break-in was discovered the police would inevitably be called. Once involved, it would then follow that the police, via their report, would create a record of the type of weapon that was stolen. Adding to the nonsensical nature of the idea that Ms. Arias had taken the gun from her grandparent's home is the fact that, as subsequent police reports document, Ms. Arias' father had illegal firearms in his home. Of note is the fact that these guns were illegal because they were not registered with the State of California. Thus, it logically follows that it was highly likely that evidence related to these guns did not exist in law enforcement databases. For this reason, they were guns that were likely untraceable. They were the kind of guns that someone looking to commit a murder would want to have. Thus, it seemed to me that if Ms. Arias wanted a gun with which to kill someone she could have obtained one from her dad with or without his knowledge. Think about it, even if she stole the gun or otherwise took it from her father without his knowledge and her dad later discovered it was missing, he couldn't report the theft. It was illegal for him to have the item in the first place. Thus, before trial began, it didn't make sense to me that Ms. Arias stole the gun from her grandparent's home.

The next moment of note that speaks to the issue of whether or not premeditation arose in Yreka back in May or at a later time is Ms. Arias' choice to rent a car at the Redding Airport. Did Ms. Arias rent the car that she drove to Mesa at the Redding Airport to avoid detection? I did not believe so. It did not make sense to me for several reasons. At the top of the list of my reasons would be the fact that when anyone rents a car they have to give their driver's license and credit card to a rental agency. There was simply no way for Ms. Arias to rent a car covertly. Ms. Arias also spent time at her brother's house and her brother's neighbor drove her to the airport so that she could pick up this rental car. In so doing, she created witnesses and a paper trail leading me to the conclusion that this car rental was not a covert mission for which an advantage could be gained by renting it in Redding as opposed to Yreka. I believe Ms. Arias when she says that Redding was simply a bigger town with better prices.

However, as my thinking went, the more important questions as it related to the issue of premeditation and Ms. Arias' choice to rent a car in Redding were the precursory questions; why would Ms. Arias rent a car to begin with? Why wouldn't she just drive her own car to Mesa? One possible theory would be that she didn't want someone to recognize her car when she was driving around in Mesa. However, I would suggest to you that not that many people in Mesa really knew what type of car she drove. Instead, in my mind the real reason that Ms. Arias rented a car was for one reason and one reason alone. So she could get where she wanted to go safely. The way my thinking went Ms. Arias, who had little to no routine maintenance performed on her car, simply doubted that her car would make it to Southern California and Utah. It was for these reasons that I did not believe that Ms. Arias was renting a car in Redding to help her facilitate a murder; her actions were far from covert and in that regard it didn't make sense to me that she was planning to kill Mr. Alexander at this time.

The next stop of significance on Ms. Arias' road trip from Yreka, California, the road trip that would eventually lead her to Mesa, Arizona is Monterey, California. Several things of note happened in the Monterey area but as it relates to my theory of what happened only two things that I can share with you really matter. The first noteworthy act is that Ms. Arias visits her two former boyfriends, Matt and Darryl. It did not make sense to me that she would do this if she were truly on her way to Mesa to kill Mr. Alexander. Why create witnesses? Why create a witness from whom you borrowed a gas can that you did not need to begin with? The second noteworthy act is that she created an electronic trail of herself by conducting several banking trans-actions in Monterey. Furthermore, many of these transactions demonstrate the fact that she had plenty of cash available to her if she wanted to go into Arizona covertly. Ms. Arias could have easily purchased things in Arizona with cash, including gas and there would have been no record of the transac-tion. Instead of taking this tactic, the transactions she engaged in while in Monterey demonstrate that she actually deposited cash into her accounts. To me, leaving such a trail and cash in the bank did not make sense to me if one is planning a murder.

The next point in time on which significance was placed at trial was the purchase of the gas can at Walmart in Salinas, California. Did this factor into my thinking? Did I see it as an issue of significance? It might sound silly but I did not place too much significance on the purchase of the gas can back in 2012. Certainly, I realized that it could be (and was) argued that she bought this can as a way to prevent her from needing to but any gas while in Arizona, as a way to remain covert. However, as Ms. Arias had plenty of cash to buy gas and/or the can itself, it actually negated premeditation in my mind because (though it made no real sense to buy it at all), as my thinking went; why would you buy a gas can if you already had two cans and were going on a covert mission? Not only that, she kept the receipt. If the plan was to kill Mr. Alexander in Mesa wouldn't she throw away the receipt?

The next significant point in time on Ms. Arias' journey was when she was in Pasadena, California. The first significant act that occurred in Pasadena was that Ms. Arias purchased several gallons of gas at a convenience store. Some purchases were paid for with cash, others with a credit card. The fact that some of these purchases were made with credit cards made it very hard for me to believe that this was Ms. Arias' final fueling stop before heading to Mesa with the intent to kill Mr. Alexander. If she had paid cash there would have been no trace of her buying gas or how much gas she purchased. The second significant thing that happened near Pasadena is that somewhere very close to the city of Pasadena is where Ms. Arias goes "off the grid." That is to say that just before she starts driving to Mesa, Ms. Arias' cell phone is off and she makes no purchases with a credit card. In this regard, she is "off the grid" because her movements by in large are not traceable via electronic means. Of note is the fact that Ms. Arias goes "off the grid" between 9pm and 10pm on the night of June 3, 2008.

The next stop in Ms. Arias' journey is Mr. Alexander's home. Certainly as to what happened once Ms. Arias got to Mr. Alexander's house, all of us who theorize as to what happened must, at least in part, rely on what Ms. Arias said occurred once she arrived. However, much of my thinking, as it relates to these events, is based on facts that stand alone. In formulating my theory, I chose to rely on facts that do not depend exclusively on Ms. Arias' word but may ultimately be consistent with the portions of her story that make sense. Ms. Arias tells Detective Flores that she got to Mr. Alexander's house about 4am on the morning of June 4, 2008. Given the time she went "off the grid" near Pasadena and given how long it takes to drive from Pasadena to Mesa this made sense to me (and some computer forensics introduced at trial further supports this claim). As we are forced to rely on Ms. Arias' word, recall that during questioning she tells Detective Flores that she and Mr. Alexander slept until early that afternoon and that after they woke up they had sex. The pictures found on Mr. Alexander's camera objectively demonstrate that this encounter took place in the early afternoon as Ms. Arias claims. Additional pictures found on Mr. Alexander's camera also tell us that around 5:20 that evening Ms. Arias, the only other person in the home was taking pictures of Mr. Alexander in the shower and that within a matter of minutes his severely wounded or dead body was being drug across the bathroom floor. These are the facts, the stubborn things that they are, and as you might guess, in my thinking at the time, the idea that Ms. Arias would drive from Yreka, California to Mesa, Arizona with designs on killing Mr. Alexander, finally arrive at his home and not kill him right away, made no sense to me. If Ms. Arias had the gun with her, she simply could have shot him. Had she had the desire to do so, Ms. Arias could have killed him then and there. She could have then gotten back in her car and drove away and it would have been highly likely that no living human being would have ever known she was there. Such actions would make further sense when one considers that Ryan Burns was expecting Ms. Arias in Utah only a few hours after she arrived at Mr. Alexander's home. It also did not make sense to me that she would have sex with Mr. Alexander and let him take nude pictures of her at the soon-to-be crime scene if her plan was to kill Mr. Alexander that day. It was for these reasons that I believed that Ms. Arias' motivation to kill Mr. Alexander arose after she arrived at his home aka "Suspect #3."

Now you might think I am crazy or that I am an idiot for ever thinking this way about what occurred. You might think that I thought this way because of some affection I had for Ms. Arias, far from it. This was my objective analysis at the time. You might also think I am crazy or an idiot because I am ignoring all the signs of premeditation related to Ms. Arias' trip. In this regard, let me concede to you as I have to myself, that I could be wrong. The truth of the matter could be that Ms. Arias pulled into the driveway of Mr. Alexander's home with the idea that she was going to walk in and kill him. At the same time then, those who believe that killing Mr. Alexander was Ms. Arias' plan when she pulled up to his house, would have to concede that if that was her plan she did not carry it out when she had the chance. That Ms. Arias did not initiate her plan at the point in time in which she was most likely to get away with it.

To me this meant that even if "Suspect # 2" is what motivated her trip to Mesa, when she got to his home, she changed her mind. If she arrived at Mr. Alexander's home with the intention of killing him, her premeditation to do so ended when she did not do it when they were alone together in his office. This, in my mind supports my theory of the fact that something happened in Mr. Alexander's home that day. That when they were together on that day something set Ms. Arias off, which would ultimately turn us back to "Suspect #3." Of course, the fact that I believed that "Suspect #3" was the guilty party does not completely explain specifically what I think happened.

At the time, I believed that Ms. Arias did arrive at Mr. Alexander's home at 4am, not because Ms. Arias said so but because the timeline was consistent with when she went "off the grid." I believed, based on the computer records that Mr. Alexander did wait up for Ms. Arias to arrive. I believed that Mr. Alexander did want to have sex with Ms. Arias when she arrived. Why? Because Mr. Alexander always seemed interested in having sex with Ms. Arias and it had been several weeks since the two had had sex. It just made sense to me that he would be anxiously awaiting her arrival hoping to have sex soon thereafter. In my mind, they did not have sex until they woke up early that afternoon. It is my belief that it was during this afternoon sex session that the nude photos of the two were taken. I also believed, without any physical evidence to support it, that they had a second sex session just before Mr. Alexander got into the shower. Why do I believe this? Because given the sexual appetite Mr. Alexander showed towards Ms. Arias it made sense to me that he would want to have sex again before she left. Certainly, the ultimate question is what happened after Mr. Alexander was in the shower. I believed that Ms. Arias went to say goodbye to Mr. Alexander and I believed that when she did so he made it obvious to her that he wanted her out of the house before anyone saw her. I believed that Mr. Alexander made it obvious to her that they were done having sex, so they were done hanging out. I believed Ms. Arias felt used by Mr. Alexander. I believed that she felt as if she blew her chances with Ryan Burns over this tryst and she had simply had enough. I believed she felt like this toxic relationship would haunt her for life if she did not put a stop to it. In my mind, she decided then and there, during a fit of rage, to put an end to this relationship.

How did she kill Mr. Alexander? My thinking at the time was that once she decided to kill him she grabbed a gun. Could it have been the gun from her grandparent's home? Yes. Could this gun have been in Mr. Alexander's home? Yes. Could it have been a gun she obtained elsewhere? Yes. Did it matter to me which gun it truly was? No, because regardless of where the gun came from or who it belonged to, she did not grab this gun with ill intent until this point in time. Either way it seemed clear from the forensic data that after she grabbed this gun, that Ms. Arias pointed it at Mr. Alexander. That in response to having this gun pointed at him Mr. Alexander leapt towards Ms. Arias in an effort to knock it out of her hand. It further seemed to me when he did this that Ms. Arias fired the gun and shot Mr. Alexander in the face. In my mind this was the first injury that Mr. Alexander suffered. After this occurred, it was my belief that Ms. Arias was surprised that Mr. Alexander was still alive. I believe that at this point in time, the gun, whomever it belonged to, did jam and that it was for this reason that Ms. Arias went to grab the knife. While Ms. Arias was seeking the knife I believed that Mr. Alexander made his way to his feet. That once on his feet he leaned against the bathroom counter and looked in the mirror to assess what had happened. I believed that it was at this point in time that Ms. Arias began stabbing Mr. Alexander in the back which gave rise to the struggle that ensued in the bathroom. This would thus explain the defensive wounds on Mr. Alexander's hands and much of the blood splatter that could be seen throughout the bathroom. I further believed that at some point in time during this struggle in the bathroom that Ms. Arias stabbed Mr. Alexander in the chest. I believed that, due to the amount of blood in the hallway, after suffering this deep stab wound to the chest that Mr. Alexander tried to make it down the hallway. I believed he ultimately fell at the end of the hall where Ms. Arias slit Mr. Alexander's throat. After which time Mr. Alexander was dead and she drug his body back down the hall.

Is my thinking fool proof? No. In fact, I have another theory I will share in my final book that I believe is as close to fool proof as it gets. However, I think when you put aside whatever emotion you may have about the case and consider what I have said this theory makes a lot of sense.

CHAPTER 48

WHAT I BELIEVED THE STATE WOULD ARGUE

Obviously, I knew that the State was going to claim that Ms. Arias committed the crime of First Degree Murder. However, if you recall from Chapter 41, there was really two ways for them to do this, either via the theory that this was a premeditated murder or under the felony murder rule. Thus, one question I had to contemplate was what, if any, attention the State was going to give to this felony murder theory in terms of how they presented their evidence to the jury. I assumed that they would not give much attention to this theory at all in that it was very confusing and rather circular in its reasoning. I assumed instead that the focus of the evidence presented by the State would relate to the theory that Ms. Arias planned to kill Mr. Alexander and carried out her plan on June 4, 2008.

The bigger question in my mind was what motive would the State attribute to Ms. Arias. How would the State answer the ultimate question of; why Ms. Arias killed Mr. Alexander? Did you notice that the ultimate question was not; "how would the State prove that Ms. Arias did not act in self-defense?" Perhaps now that I have pointed this out to you those who did not already notice might now be asking the same question as those who did notice originally; why was I more concerned about the attribution of motive to Ms. Arias than I was her self-defense claim? The answer goes back to some of the things I discussed in Chapter 2, wherein I point out that my main goal was to save Ms. Arias' life and the finding of guilt is really a secondary consideration. Certainly, I will go into my strategy more in Chapter 50 but in addition to the general rule I discussed in Chapter 2, I never harbored any illusions that Ms. Arias would not be convicted of First Degree Murder. I never assumed that a jury would accept Ms. Arias' claims of self-defense. Instead, I assumed we would get to the point in the proceedings that why Ms. Arias killed Mr. Alexander would become the preeminent issue. In this regard, the "why" of the State's argument was always very important to me. The way I saw things, whichever side better defined "why" this crime occurred would ultimately prevail on the issue of life versus death. However, as I began to contemplate the State's theory of "why," I had a hard time reconciling the possible motives that they might attribute to Ms. Arias with their theory of the case.

As it pertains to trying to understand the State's arguments I assumed that the State was going to argue that Ms. Arias took her grandfather's gun so she could kill Mr. Alexander with it. As for the rental car I assumed that the State was going to make a big deal out of the fact that Ms. Arias rented the car in Redding as opposed to Yreka and that her desire for a white car evidenced a desire to be more covert. I had no idea how they were going to account for the fact that a car cannot be rented on a covert basis, but this fact did not seem to matter to the State, to them the rental car was a big deal.

As it related to her time in Monterrey, my suspicion was that the State would not comment much on it. Why? Because apart from Ms. Arias borrowing a gas can from Mr. Brewer, nothing that Ms. Arias did in Monterey, particularly the banking transactions, was consistent with the idea that she was on a covert mission to kill Mr. Alexander.

As for when Ms. Arias arrived at Mr. Alexander's home I had some insight into what the State was going to argue based on the theory that the State had asserted in prior proceedings. You see, in order to prove to the court that Ms. Arias should be eligible for the death penalty the State had to prove at least one aggravating factor to a Judge. Putting the legal technicalities of these hearings aside, proving these factors requires the State to give a description to the court of how the killing took place and sometimes why the killing occurred in an effort to convince a judge that the required legal standard had been met. When this hearing occurred I was not Ms. Arias' lawyer so I was not in a position to watch the State present their theory. I was limited to reading the transcript of what had occurred. From reading the transcripts it seemed to me that the State was going to argue that Ms. Arias arrived in Mr. Alexander's home with the intention of killing him. That Ms. Arias hung out at his home for several hours and had sex with him in an effort to make him tired and vulnerable. With the goal being that when Mr. Alexander was tired and vulnerable, that it would be easier for her to kill him. As I read on in the transcripts it was the State's argument at this hearing that Ms. Arias saw the opportune moment to strike when Mr. Alexander was in the shower. The State's theory of what happened next was told to the court through the testimony of Detective Flores. In describing these events, Detective Flores advised the court that he had talked to Dr. Horn recently and that based on what Dr. Horn had told him Ms. Arias had shot Mr. Alexander first. Detective Flores went on to testify that this wound only stunned Mr. Alexander and that after suffering this wound he was able to stagger to his bathroom counter where he aspirated blood onto his sink. As the story being told by Detective Flores goes on, Ms. Arias then begins inflicting the knife wounds upon Mr. Alexander, some twenty-seven of them. The fatal wounds being either the deep stab to Mr. Alexander's chest or the slashing of his throat, either alternative most certainly created a truly horrific demise. By way of further detail it was asserted that these fatal wounds occurred last because of the defensive wounds that were found on Mr. Alexander's hands.

Finally, before moving past what occurred at this hearing, note should be made of the fact that, at no time did the State assert why Ms. Arias did this, "why" was still a question that the State had not been able to fit into the factual scenario that they adhered to so rigidly.

Did I assume that the version of events that I described above would be the version that the State would stick with at trial? Yes. Why? Because as it related to the events before Ms. Arias arrived at Mr. Alexander's home, in order to weave a tale of premeditation, the State had to assert the idea that Ms. Arias had some sort of plan that was in place when she pulled up to Mr.

Alexander's home.   As it related to the other portion of the story that the State would tell, the part that occurred after Mr. Alexander was in his shower, minutes before his death, I assumed that this story would be the State's story going forward because Detective Flores was under oath when he relayed this version of events and because Detective Flores also retold this version of events to CBS when he was interviewed on "48 Hours." However, most of all, I thought that this would be the story because it fit the evidence.

So in sum, the theory I was expecting at trial was that Ms. Arias stole the gun from her grandparents and went on a covert mission to kill Travis Alexander. This covert mission was to include driving to Redding, California to rent a car and driving that car to Mesa with the intent of killing Mr. Alexander. Furthermore, I believed that the State was going to argue that the reason Ms. Arias did not kill Mr. Alexander when she first got to his home was because she wanted to look for the right opportunity, a moment in time when Mr. Alexander was vulnerable and could be killed more easily.

When I contemplated this theory it really didn't take too much time for me to think of all the holes in this theory. To be clear, I took no issue with the order of the wounds, just what preceded the killing. In this regard, my issues began with the reasons why Ms. Arias rented the car in Redding, California instead of Yreka. Renting a car is not a covert operation wherever it is done and this rental car facility was at an airport with surveillance cameras. I still believed that the most covert way of operating was for her to drive her own car. I took further issue with the covert nature of this operation given that Ms. Arias visited with two former boyfriends and performed some banking transactions in Monterey, California.   Finally, the idea that Ms. Arias had to wait 13 hours before the right moment arrived, the moment when Mr. Alexander was weak and vulnerable, made no sense to me either because if we believe she stole the gun back in Yreka and that she did so to shoot Mr. Alexander with it, why would Ms. Arias need to wait until her intended target was weakened? Made no sense to me, no sense at all but I was not the one who was deciding what made sense.

However, if we put my quibbles with the State's theory of events aside we still are left with the question I raised earlier. The question I believed that would make the difference between Ms. Arias being sentenced to life or sentenced to death. Why did she do all of this? Based on the State's theory of events at some point in time Ms. Arias decided that she wanted to kill Mr. Alexander. I never heard the State make any sort of argument that even implied that she had such an inclination before she moved back to Yreka, so I will start there. If we were to accept the State's version of events, Ms. Arias, after moving home decided that she needed to kill Mr. Alexander. Why did she decide this? Because after moving back home she became so enraged with jealousy about the relationship that Mr. Alexander was having with Mimi Hall? That did not make sense to me as that relationship existed well before she moved back. How would the State explain that to the jury?

If the State's theory was to be that Ms. Arias was so angry at Mr. Alexander due to the names he called her during the online chat the two had on May 26, 2008 and that this anger motivated her to take all the steps that they attribute to her. How would the State account for the fact that when she gets to Mr. Alexander's home she does not immediately kill him?

In fact, I could not see how any theory, asserted by anyone, under which Ms. Arias arrived at Mr. Alexander's home with the intent to kill him accounted for why she did not kill Mr. Alexander directly after they were alone together in his office or at the very least in the early afternoon before the nude photos were taken. I saw this as a huge problem for the State on two levels. One, because it necessarily shortened the time of any premeditation that may have existed with Ms. Arias' mind to that day and that day alone. Secondly, when such a temporal restraint is placed onto Ms. Arias' motivation, the motivation for the murder becomes directly related to what transpired on that fateful day between the two of them.

It was in these realities that I saw the opportunity to save Ms. Arias' life. Of course, this brings up the obvious reality that if I was actually going to save her life, I needed a plan.

SECTION 10

HOW WAS I GOING TO SAVE MS. ARIAS' LIFE?

Chapter 2 of this book was the first time that I described to you that my ultimate job was to save my client's life. Since describing this goal for you I have made mention of this goal several other times and by now I suspect you get the point. Fear not, the goal of this section is not to remind you of that goal yet again. Instead, my goal in this section is to give you an understanding of why and how I planned to save my client's life. Specifically, in Chapter 49, given what I have already said about how I felt about Ms. Arias, I describe for you why I was still interested in accomplishing this goal. In Chapter 50, I describe my plan to save her life and in the final chapter of this book, Chapter 51, I share the last few moments of peace that I tried to capture, before the storm of trial began.

CHAPTER 49

WHY DID I FIGHT FOR MS. ARIAS' LIFE?

In Chapter 1 of this book I mention my general opposition to the death penalty and how that led me to joining the capital unit at the Office of the Public Defender. In Chapter 2 of this book I expound a bit on my feelings on the death penalty a little further so as to give you some insight as to why I oppose the death penalty. I also suspect that throughout this book there are little phrases from which insight into my beliefs can be garnered. In this Chapter, I want to address the issue of why I did not think the death penalty was appropriate for Ms. Arias. That is not to say that these more generic reasons did not play a role in my belief. Instead what I am saying is that when it came to Ms. Arias there was something more specific than this basic philosophy. I truly believed that Ms. Arias did not deserve to be killed for her crime. Thus, I was thus willing to do what it took, within the bounds of my ethical duties, those ethical duties I had as a lawyer, to prevent that from happening. Would you like to know why I felt this way?

I will certainly answer that question for you but before describing for you the reasons why I did not believe the death penalty was appropriate for Ms. Arias, I feel compelled to address two other issues first because I suspect these issues are now in the forefront of so many minds.

The first and most important issue in this regard relates to Mr. Alexander and those who cared about him. I do not want anyone to think that by asserting my opinion that the death penalty was not an appropriate sanction for Ms. Arias that I am somehow minimizing the killing of Mr. Alexander, his personal loss of life, or the suffering that his death caused his family and loved ones. As I have said repeatedly, the killing of Mr. Alexander was a horrible tragedy and those who cared about him, particularly his family have my sympathy for their loss.

Secondly, I realize that for many of you the idea that Ms. Arias should not have been sentenced to die for her crime is inconceivable. I realize that there are many of you who are so passionate in your belief that Ms. Arias should have been sentenced to death that you think that anyone who feels to the contrary must be either insane or that they must be in love with Ms. Arias (perhaps both). However, I hate to break it to you but I suspect that there are many of us out there in this world who do not like Ms. Arias, who do not support what she did on June 4, 2008, that still believe that she should not have been sentenced to death for her crime. Certainly, many of these people share my general opposition to the death penalty. However, I suspect that there are still many others that might not share my firm opposition to the death penalty that also believed Ms. Arias should not be sentenced to death. Each of these people likely has their own unique reasons for their stance, I am only aware of mine.

Why did I feel that Ms. Arias did not deserve a sentence of death beyond my generic anti-death penalty stance? Two reasons, first, simply put, in my mind her conduct did not meet the criteria for what a death penalty case should be. Secondly, I saw inequity in the penalty that Ms. Arias was facing and the penalty being sought out against others who had committed similar if not more horrific acts.

Certainly, I suspect that I shocked many of you when I said that Ms. Arias' conduct did not meet the criteria for what a death penalty case should be. Again, as I stated earlier, I do not say this to minimize the tragedy surrounding this case. Instead I say this because under the laws of our nation a death penalty case is not simply what we might call a typical murder. Instead, a death penalty case is, per these same laws, supposed to be an atypical murder, the worst of the worst. The laws of our nation are such that if every murder is a death penalty eligible offense that the imposition of a death sentence becomes cruel and unusual punishment. Granted, this is a massive oversimplification of the law but I hope it illustrates the reality that from a legal perspective for a murder to be death penalty eligible it must be beyond the norm, even when the category is murder. All of this naturally leads to the question of what constitutes an atypical murder so as to justify a sentence of death under the law. A few examples of such murders are those in which there were several victims and when the victim is a child. Undoubtedly, there are many more examples of murders that can be deemed atypical but my point here is not to get into a lengthy discussion about aggravating factors and the breadth of their scope. Instead, my point is to merely illustrate that, the way I saw things, Ms. Arias' killing of Mr. Alexander did not fit within the parameters of the type of homicide that should be charged as a death penalty case. However horrific it was, it was not an atypical murder. Again, many of you might find it hard to believe that anyone could view the Arias case this way. However, like it or not, this is the way our legal system is set up as it relates to the death penalty and some of us believe in the Constitution. Some of us also believe that if we as a nation are going to allow for the death penalty, such a penalty is supposed to be reserved for the worst of the worst and at the risk of repeating myself, to me Ms. Arias' crime and her personal history did not make her the worst of the worst.

As to my second reason that I did not believe that Ms. Arias should be sentenced to death, the issue of disparity, I am sure I could provide dozens of cases for you that illustrate this point but such a list might bore you. So in my effort to illustrate my point as briefly as possible, I will limit myself to two cases that were taking place in Maricopa County while Ms. Arias' case was pending. In one of these cases, the defendant, who was a man, stabbed his wife to death. In fact he stabbed her about 27 times and drove her body to the police station. A pretty awful crime I am sure we can all agree. The man brutally killed his wife, drove her body to the police station and turned himself in as if he was checking in for an appointment of some sort. You might think that he would be charged with first-degree murder, a death penalty eligible offense. Given the charges Ms. Arias faced, that would make sense right? Regardless of what sense it might make, this man did not face a charge of first-degree murder, only second-degree murder and he pled guilty to that charge. In what I believe is one of the most egregious examples of this disparity about the time we were wrapping up the penalty phase retrial another case was about to hit the Maricopa County Superior Court system. The defendant in that case was Jerice Hunter and Ms. Hunter stood accused of killing her 5 year-old daughter Jhessye Shockley. The circumstances that surrounded the case involved assertions that Ms. Hunter had beaten young Jhessye, forced her to live in a closet with little food and that after Jhessye was dead, her body was dumped in a landfill. Before being charged with murder, Ms. Hunter claimed that her daughter had been kidnapped and/or was missing. A huge public search took place. There were marches and all sorts of carrying on related to the missing young girl. Most of which, near as I can tell, were inspired by Ms. Hunter, the woman who apparently killed her daughter. I ask you to think about this case for a minute. Ms. Hunter tortures and kills her own daughter. She then lies to the world about it and causes a huge public outcry. Surely, such actions would motivate the State to seek the death penalty against Ms. Hunter right? Wrong. While Ms. Hunter faced the charge of first-degree murder, the State did not seek to impose the death penalty upon her. Why? I do not know for sure. However, to me, as it related to Ms. Arias, regardless of the reason for it, this disparity was mindboggling.

Related to the idea of the disparity between these horrific cases in which the death penalty was not being sought and Ms. Arias' case in which the death penalty was going to be pursued, I had to ask myself one simple question; why? Those who research the death penalty on a grand scale would say that I would only need to review the social science research on the issue to find my answer. That research would tell me that Ms. Arias was facing the death penalty and Ms. Hunter was not because of the fact that Ms. Arias killed a white male and Ms. Hunter killed a black girl. This same research would also tell me the man who killed his wife by stabbing her 27 times, did not face death because he killed a woman. Yes, it is true, death penalty researchers and the statistics they have compiled point to the clear reality that who the defendant kills is the most prominent correlating factor that determines whether prosecutors seek the death penalty. Think about it, it is not who the defendant is as a person or their history but who they killed. Those most likely to face a death sentence are those who kill white males. So yes, I could not discount the fact that the inherent racism of the death penalty provided an explanation for this disparity. However, my opinion was that this had little if anything to do with race and more to do with the notoriety that surrounded the case.

In this regard, I was of the opinion that the media attention that had already been paid to this case motivated the State to seek the death penalty against Ms. Arias, because, as I said earlier, it truly was not warranted. However, while I could not be certain of the motivations, I was of the opinion that certain prosecutors like the limelight and/or have big egos. Likewise, I was aware that if death was not sought against Ms. Arias that the attention given to the case would not be as great. Furthermore, once death was sought, the failure to obtain such a sentence would be a huge public failure. Such a failure would be a huge public embarrassment for the prosecutor and could result in a decrease in the value of the prosecutor's potential book deal. I was of the opinion that once death was sought against Ms. Arias, unfair and improper tactics might very well be used against Ms. Arias so as to avoid such an embarrassment.

In this, I saw injustice. As someone who believes in the Constitution and as someone who believes that as a criminal defense attorney my job is to enforce the laws that protect us all. I was not going to let Ms. Arias receive an unjust sentence of death, period. I was not going to let her be sent to death row because a prosecutor, any prosecutor, wanted fame or adulation. I was not going to allow a prosecutor to send a client, any client of mine, to death row when they did not deserve to be there. In this regard, it did not matter to me that the way I had to do this would not reflect well on me. It did not matter to me that I did not like Ms. Arias. It did not matter that I did not believe everything Ms. Arias was saying only that she did not deserve to be on death row. This belief would serve as my rock, my foundation, when the world, including Ms. Arias herself was against me.

CHAPTER 50

WHAT WAS MY PLAN?

By the fall of 2012, I had collected and digested all the evidence in the case. I had a theory as to what happened on June 4, 2008 and why it happened. I also felt as if I had a fairly good idea as to what the State was going to argue and I was well aware that it was a virtual certainty that Ms. Arias would be convicted of First Degree Murder. However, perhaps more than anything, I had the firm belief, the belief that I described in Chapter 49, that it would be unjust if my client were to wind up on death row. My goal was to somehow save Ms. Arias' life. All I needed was a plan of how to do so.

In one sense this may seem simple enough in that my client was a female and she had no prior felony convictions. Certainly, under normal circumstances, I would have to concede that Ms. Arias' gender and her lack of criminal history weighed heavily in favor of her not receiving a sentence of death. However, these were not normal circumstances. My female client with no criminal history also was intent on claiming that the man she killed was abusive and a pedophile. This made my job extremely difficult to say the least. Why? Because I knew that if, or more accurately when, Ms. Arias was convicted of First-Degree Murder, her accusations against Mr. Alexander would certainly turn off or enrage the jury. Likewise I knew that if her jury was enraged by her accusations they would be much more inclined to sentence my client to death. So, what was I going to do in such a situation? How was I going to save the life of my self-destructive client? How was I going to save the life of a woman whose goal seemed to have nothing to do with her future or her life and everything to do with vilifying Mr. Alexander?

Before answering that question I want to be very clear on one point, if I had complete control and was in a position where I could have "designed" the defense in this case, it would have been much different. If I had my way, putting aside some of the death penalty related complexities I will discuss later in this Chapter, Ms. Arias would not have told the stories she told about Mr. Alexander. In fact, she really would have told no story at all. If I had my way, Ms. Arias would have sat silent during trial, she would have never taken the stand and thus would not have been in a position to make any accusations against Mr. Alexander. I simply would have argued that the facts demonstrated the killing was not done with significant or any premeditation and that Ms. Arias was actually guilty of either second degree murder or manslaughter. In sum, the argument would have been related to the theory that I advanced in Chapter 47. My argument would have been based on the idea that even if she had arrived at Mr. Alexander's home with the intent on killing him that this intent went away when she saw him and that her intent to kill did not come to life again until moments before she actually killed him, hence the argument for second degree murder or manslaughter. Would this have worked? I do not know but beyond that fact that it was all I had to work with, I suspect that the jury would have been more open to this argument if Ms. Arias did not make the accusations she made against Mr. Alexander. Had she been convicted of First Degree Murder my argument at sentencing would have related to Ms. Arias' lack of criminal history and the dynamics of the relationship she shared with Mr. Alexander. I certainly believed that employing such tactics would have saved her life. Obviously, we will never know if I was right or not because Ms. Arias had her own agenda. I had to play by those rules; yes, I had to play by her rules and I had to figure out how to save her life despite the story she was going to tell.

In explaining why I had to play by her rules I want to take it out of the context of Ms. Arias because people get so angry about her accusations that they get blinded to the realities of the situation that I was in as a lawyer.

You see a lawyer cannot stop a criminal defendant from testifying. The 6th Amendment to the United States Constitution in essence dictates that a client can get up there and testify to anything they want and that their lawyer cannot stop them. That is not to say that a lawyer can suborn perjury, in fact, just the opposite is true. If and when a lawyer knows a client is perjuring themselves they have to move to withdraw from the case. Those requests are typically denied. However, when this happens a defendant usually testifies in the form of a narrative and the attorney resumes representation after the client's testimony is complete. However, the one important caveat to this is that in order to have a basis to withdraw, the attorney must know that the client is perjuring himself or herself. To be clear, the attorney cannot merely suspect that their client might be lying. Doubt about the truthfulness of the testimony is also not enough. Instead what is required is that the attorney must actually know via objective evidence that the client is perjuring himself or herself.

By way of example let me set up a hypothetical wherein Mr. Brown, an attorney, represents Frank. Frank stands accused of armed robbery, of holding up a liquor store. When they get to trial, Frank wants to take the stand and say that at the time of the robbery he was out of town visiting his mom at the nursing home. However, during the course of his investigation Mr. Brown uncovered a cell phone video given to him by one of Frank's friends, Mac. Mac's cell phone video shows Frank outside the liquor store wearing the same clothes described by the store manager who was held up at gunpoint. The video on Mac's cell phone is date and time stamped it is easily discernable that this video was recorded 5 minutes before the robbery. There is now clear objective evidence proving that Frank was not out of town visiting his mother at the time of the robbery but was instead at the liquor store. Thus, when Frank wants to take the stand and say he was with his mother at the time of the robbery Mr. Brown would actually know that he was lying because he had the cell phone video and could thus move to withdraw. Conversely, if Mr. Brown did not have Mac's cell phone video and just felt as if Frank was lying, because Frank had a history of lying he could not withdraw. Under those circumstances Mr. Brown would simply be required to help Frank tell his story because he had no proof that it was not true. Certainly, this is a rather simple sort of situation in a non-capital case but I hope it illustrates the point related to an attorney knowing a client is lying and when that attorney can bring up the issue.

Admittedly, things can get much more complex in a capital case when there is no actual proof that a client intends to offer perjured testimony. However, if you take what we learned from the previous example I believe that I can make some sense of it for you. Again, keeping away from Ms. Arias' situation so that your understanding is not affected by any rage you may have against her, let's go back to our hypothetical lawyer Mr. Brown and his client Frank. The difference in this hypothetical will be that this time Frank is charged with First Degree Murder and to make matters worse for Frank the State is seeking to impose the death penalty against him. For the sake of this example, let us also say that the person that Frank killed was his Uncle John and that John was a very popular person in town. In fact let us say that many people loved John and outrage surrounded his murder. When Mr. Brown meets with Frank, Frank tells him "Yes, I killed my Uncle John. He molested me when I was a child and I never told anyone. When I saw him talking to a young boy at his store I went into a rage and moments after the young boy and his mother left the store, I was still in a rage so I grabbed the gun he kept near the cash register and shot him and I would do it again because I wanted to make sure he never touched another little boy like he had touched me." As a capital defense attorney in this situation, Mr. Brown would not be free to ignore these claims regardless of what he thought of them. The fact that Mr. Brown personally may not believe these claims is entirely irrelevant. In fact, in this situation, he has the obligation to search out evidence related to Frank's accusation. Now let us say that Mr. Brown finds no evidence whatsoever to support Frank's claims. Let us further say that, as time goes on, Mr. Brown's disbelief only grows. That over time he himself does not believe what Frank says about having been molested by his Uncle John when he was a child. Does the fact that Mr. Brown does not believe his client and did not find any evidence to support Frank's claim mean that he can keep Frank off the stand or move to withdraw because he does not want to suborn perjury? No, because Mr. Brown has no actual proof that Frank is actually lying. A lawyer in Mr. Brown's situation has to aid his client in telling his story. This is particularly true in the context of a capital case because if Mr. Brown chose not to investigate his client's claims and/or chose not to present evidence of these claims to the jury during any potential sentencing phase at the very least the reversal of any death sentence would be virtually automatic. I say this because the law on this issue is that clear. A client facing death has an absolute right to present mitigating circumstances to the jury and at the same time the jury is obligated to consider them. To that end a lawyer cannot interfere with the presentation of this evidence because of whatever personal opinion they have about the truthfulness of the testimony.

Returning back to Ms. Arias' case and my situation, what I believed about the accusations that Ms. Arias wanted to level against Mr. Alexander was completely irrelevant as it related to the job I had to perform. Even if I thought these accusations amounted to nothing more than lies designed to assault Mr. Alexander's good name, I had no choice but to pursue any evidence related to them. I was duty bound to see if my team could find any support for her claims and allow her to testify to them. Why? As I tried to illustrate during my hypotheticals about Mr. Brown and Frank, I could not disprove them with actual evidence that proved these claims to be false. Now I realize many of you think that these accusations are lies or perhaps it is more accurate to say that you "know" they are lies but the reality is there is no proof that these accusations were actually untruthful. Instead, let's face the facts, your so called knowledge is just your opinion. I certainly had no objective tangible evidence that her claims were untruthful. In fact, I had some evidence supporting her claims, evidence that had I ignored would provide fertile ground from which a retrial could have been granted if Ms. Arias received a sentence of death.

I had not one but two experts tell me that Ms. Arias had symptoms related to PTSD. Additionally, I had not one but two domestic violence experts telling me that Ms. Arias was a victim of domestic violence during her relationship with Mr. Alexander. Beyond that, there were the emails from the Hughes to Mr. Alexander regarding how he abused women. There were the comments the Hughes made to Detective Flores about how they could see Mr. Alexander being physical with Ms. Arias. In addition to all of this there was the sex tape. Now those who want to call me all sorts of names for supposedly calling Mr. Alexander a pedophile, something I have never done, may not like facing a reminder of this particular fact. However, like it or not do not forget that Mr. Alexander did reference a twelve year-old girl having her first orgasm and corking the pot of a twelve year-old girl during this conversation with Ms. Arias ("facts are stubborn things").

So the bottom line for me was; how do I save my client's life, knowing that I have to, in essence, assist her in making these assertions against Mr. Alexander? How do I save her life when her assertions will turn the whole jury against her? In most cases a lawyer shows his acumen by getting in there and fighting the allegations and believing in his client's story, by being a strong advocate for their client. Client's like to see this because they believe that you are fighting for them and other lawyers respect those who fight in this manner as well. It tends to be what we do. Could I have done this for Ms. Arias in the first trial? Yes, what was later dubbed as Nurmi 2.0, or something to that effect is the way I tended to lawyer on a regular basis. If my primary concern was my business or making myself look good for the critics, I would have lawyered in this manner. However, as a person who opposes the death penalty and as a lawyer who was mindful of my ethical duty to put saving her life above all else, I could not do that. I could not lawyer in my normal "2.0" mode. Why? Because if I went "all in" on Ms. Arias' claims that she defended herself from her pedophile of a boyfriend, with little support for her claims, I strongly suspected that the jury would undoubtedly sentence my client to death because not only would the jury hate her, they would hate me and tune me out at the mitigation phase.

At the same time, I was well aware that even standing near Ms. Arias could cause her jury and the world to hate me. Thus, what I had to do was come up with a strategy that would result in a life sentence for my client even if the jury and the entire world would wind up hating us both.

Certainly, doing all of this while Ms. Arias was making her assertions was a tall order. Fortunately, for Ms. Arias I had a plan. A plan that I thought might make me look like a bad lawyer on worldwide television, but a plan that might just spare Ms. Arias' life. Ultimately, as we now know this plan worked but the "weird" part is I have not yet received a thank you card from Ms. Arias or her family. In this regard, I guess I should also point out that I have not received an apology from any of my critics in the media. Thankfully, for my own sake, I am not holding my breath in anticipation of either event.

As for the plan and how I devised it, my first move was to digest what I knew apart from the evidence in the case. In this regard, the most prominent issue was that Ms. Arias was a liar who likely would not be believed even if she did in fact tell the truth on occasion. I knew that apart from the objective testing that even the opinions of the experts testifying for Ms. Arias relied at least in part on what she told them. Thus, I suspected that these opinions would not be well received. I also knew Ms. Arias well enough to know that she was going to take the stand and gleefully make these accusations about Mr. Alexander. I thus had two options, the first, dive right into the fray merge whatever strategy I arrived at with Ms. Arias' claims and hope for the best. This was certainly my inclination as it was typically how I went about things, but I did not believe that following my inclinations would lead to a life sentence. The alternative was to do something unorthodox that might just save Ms. Arias' life.

The alternative was to run as far away from her story as I could while still presenting the viable aspects of her story to the jury. What did this mean in terms of most of the witnesses? It meant letting them present what Ms. Arias had told them and the conclusions that they made from testing her or whatever means they used and letting the jury absorb the idea that there was at least some merit to Ms. Arias' assertions that she had suffered from symptoms of trauma and that she was a victim of domestic violence without fully embracing her claims that Mr. Alexander had a sexual interest in children. The plan was to let Jennifer handle these witnesses as she thought these claims were the key to the case when I thought otherwise. Thus, by letting Jennifer do this Ms. Arias' story would be embraced to some degree and I would be left free to work on saving Ms. Arias' life.

That is why I chose to direct Ms. Arias' testimony. I wanted to make sure that it was done right, meaning consistent with my plan to run away from her story as much as possible at the same time she was telling it. My plan to let Ms. Arias articulate her defense while at the same time slipping in some facts about the relationship that Ms. Arias shared with Mr. Alexander that were undeniable. I suspected that because Ms. Arias valued her reputation so deeply, this would be a slow and painful process. However, I also suspected that this process would ultimately result in me getting my points across to at least one juror. At the same time in my mind I thought that this process, however painful, would provide the jury the opportunity to either make some sort of connection with Ms. Arias or provide them with the opportunity to see she is not right in the head. It was my thought that the opportunity to either connect or assess Ms. Arias combined with the clear reality of these undeniable truths would be enough to cause at least one juror to spare Ms. Arias' life. Implicit in my strategy was the idea that it is harder to kill someone with whom one is familiar with. So part of my goal was to make the jury familiar with her and thus less likely to kill her. Certainly, I knew that being familiar with her could lead to contempt for her to say the least but that was simply the risk I had to take because at the same time, I also knew that some jurors might feel sorry for her or sense what I already knew that something was off with Ms. Arias even if that something was hard to define.

Another aspect of my plan is that I assumed Mr. Martinez would cross examine Ms. Arias very aggressively. That he could not help himself regardless of how it would impact the sentence Ms. Arias received. To that end, an added aspect of my strategy was that Mr. Martinez, through his antics might himself very well cause the jury to feel sympathy towards Ms. Arias. That he himself might provide the jury with the sympathetic view of Ms. Arias that they needed to give her a life sentence.

Undoubtedly, my plan was risky. Furthermore, it was not going to be good for my personal reputation as I ultimately had to keep what I was doing to myself. I certainly could not advise the media what I was up to. However, I thought it was the only way that Ms. Arias was going to "get out of this alive." What we all know now is that as it turned out this gamble paid off for her. I was right and by implementing this strategy, she did "get out alive." Sadly for me, I was also right that this would come at great personal cost to the good reputation I had built over the years. Ultimately that was okay with me because it is not the lawyer's job to put their reputation above their client's life. I will talk more about implementing this strategy in my next book but for now, at the very least you have an idea what I was up to during trial and those eighteen days of Ms. Arias' testimony.

Having read all this I realize that my explanation may give rise to a fair amount of questions, many of which I will fail to anticipate. However, if you will allow me to be so bold and speculate about the questions you might have, I suspect that one question that many of you will have is; what were the inevitable truths that I felt as if I needed to get out of Ms. Arias in order to employ my strategy while she was trying to advance her agenda?

The short answer to that question is sex. It was an undeniable reality that Travis Alexander and Ms. Arias had an intense sexual relationship. Some might call it kinky, some might call it perverse some might call it normal but I do not see how anyone could quibble with the idea that it was intense. Sex seemed to be the focal point of the relationship and I did not see how legitimate issue could be taken with the fact that these two were having all kinds of sex behind closed doors. Why was this important? Because it demonstrated that unless Mr. Alexander truly loved Ms. Arias, he was using her for sex. That unless, Mr. Alexander loved Ms. Arias, she truly was his "booty call." Even Sky Hughes referred to Ms. Arias in this manner. It was obvious. In my mind, it was an undeniable reality that whether Mr. Alexander loved Ms. Arias or hated her that he was never going to commit to her. However, as evidenced by his actions, he was more than happy to have sex with her.

Why was it important to show this undeniable reality in court? Because, even if Ms. Arias failed to make a connection with her jury it would be much harder for the members of her jury to kill a woman who had no prior criminal history who could be characterized as a woman who fell in love with a man who was using her for sex than it would be for those same people to kill a woman who was being characterized as an obsessed former girlfriend that could not let her victim go.

So there you have it, going into trial that was my plan in a nutshell. In saying this I realize that those who support Jodi will be upset because the plan did not involve proving she was "innocent," something that could not have ever been done. I also realize that those who support Mr. Alexander believe that this involved "dragging him through the mud." However, face it, no matter what kind of horrible slut you want to make Ms. Arias out to be, Mr. Alexander was still having sex with her. It was the undeniable reality of this case, like it or not and it was at the heart of my strategy, a strategy that worked and a strategy for which I will offer no apologies.

CHAPTER 51

NEW YEAR'S DAY

New Year's Day was always a big deal to me growing up. Those of you old enough to remember may recall that back in the 1970's almost every college bowl game took place on New Year's Day. At the very least it was the day that all of the good ones seemed to be played. Those old enough to remember the 1970's will likely also recall that back then there were only three major networks, which meant all these good games went all day long, back to back. All you had to do was turn the dial. As a kid who loved football it was an awesome day. As a kid who loved his grandfather who himself loved football it was extra- awesome because we watched these games together, all day. Simply put, New Year's Day was one of the best days of the year for me as a child.

Sadly, as it relates to college football things are very different now. There are now several college bowl games. Instead of taking place on one day, the games are spread out and take place from mid- December to mid-January. For this reason, not all of the good ones take place on New Year's Day. There are now dozens of sports channels, hockey has moved into the picture etcetera. However, despite these changes, which I think hurt the New Year's Day experience, as an adult, I still love New Year's Day. As an adult, I still spend as much time in front of my television watching as much football as I can and every New Year's Day I still reflect back to the days gone by when I would be watching these games with my grandfather.

Why am I telling you this? So that I can give you a sense of what it was like for me as I braced myself for trial. You see on New Year's Day of 2013, I wanted nothing more than to embrace one of my favorite days of the year. I wanted to embrace the day without concern for the next day. However, because I was "Trapped with Ms. Arias," I could not do that. Instead as I sat in my recliner watching the games trying to block out thoughts of the days that would follow, I could not help but think about the impending storm that would hit my life the next day. I knew that this storm would last for months and have devastating consequences. It was a storm I did not want to be a part of, but I had no choice. The best I could do for myself was to allow Jennifer to do the opening so that I could cling to these last few moments of peace that always came to me while watching football on New Year's Day.

As you might guess I did a lot of thinking that day. I thought about many things that do not come to mind presently or that are too personal to share, but I do certainly remember thinking on that New Year's Day that at least next year I could enjoy my New Year's Day (2014) experience without having to be concerned about Ms. Arias' case or her self-destructive antics. Well I guess I was wrong about that one, very wrong, but in fairness to me, I do not think anyone could have guessed that things would go the way they did. Heck, if I had known that things would work out the way they did after January 2, 2013, I might have driven to the airport instead of the courthouse. I might have instead flown to a country that did not extradite runaway lawyers back to the United States. Instead, on January 2, 2013, I drove toward the courthouse, parked my car and took one last deep breath.

Coming in 2016
Trapped with Ms. Arias Part II
"From Trial to Mistrial"

After I took that last breath in my car, I walked into the courthouse. It was January 2, 2013, an otherwise beautiful winter's day in Arizona. Typically, when an attorney walks into court not much of anything is going on outside the courthouse doors. At most, you might find a few people talking in the hallway. However, for the reasons you have just read, Ms. Arias' case was far from typical and rather than facing the typical scene outside the courthouse door, the scene outside of the Arias trial was quite different. There were several people, many reporters and others who would best be described as groupies who just wanted to be part of the show, and what a show it turned out to be. A show that was live streamed to the world, a show that would capture the attention of millions. As you might guess, to me, The State of Arizona v. Jodi Arias, was more than a show, it was a trial, a serious trial where a person's life was at stake. I had a different perspective than most because I lived it. In my next book, I will be providing you with insight into what it was like for me to live through this trial, this show that captured the attention of millions. I will share my thoughts with you and let you in on the things you did not see on television. Part Two of Trapped with Ms. Arias "From Trial to Mistrial" will be coming soon. Look for it in 2016.

Made in the USA
Lexington, KY
31 March 2016